RETHINKING ZION

How the Print Media Placed Fundamentalism in the South

Mary Beth Swetnam Mathews

The University of Tennessee Press • Knoxville

PN
4888
.F86
M38
2006

Mathews, Mary Beth Swetnam.
  Rethinking Zion : how the print media placed fundamentalism in the South /
Mary Beth Swetnam Mathews.—1st ed.
      p. cm.
ISBN 1-57233-493-2 (hardcover)

1. Fundamentalism—Southern States—Press coverage—United States.
2. Fundamentalism—Southern States—History—20th century.
I. Title.

PN4888.F86M38 2006

070.442775082—dc22   2006004518

RETHINKING
ZION

For Lydia and Jim

CONTENTS

ACKNOWLEDGMENTS

This book began as a question someone asked in a graduate class on religion and American culture: "Why do we think of the South as fundamentalist?" After struggling, hopefully successfully, with that question for almost a decade now, I have a long list of people to thank for sustaining me through my work.

At the top of the list is my dissertation advisor, Heather Warren, who ably guided this research from its earliest stages. She was immeasurably helpful in shaping the question into a dissertation and then into a book. Her wisdom, sharp eye, and insistence that I look into subjects I at first thought were unrelated made this effort more rewarding.

Also working hard to guide this project through its dissertation stage at the University of Virginia were Father Gerald P. Fogarty, Bill Wilson, Ed Ayers, and Grace Hale. They gave me the benefit of their collective knowledge, and I thank them for it.

Outside readers, including the two anonymous readers for the University of Tennessee Press, provided helpful comments and suggestions. Paul Harvey kindly read the manuscript and improved it with his observations. Beth Barton Schweiger provided encouragement early on in the process, Don Mathews suggested the use of a particularly valuable source, and Charles Lippy took time out from a conference at Princeton to give publication assistance.

Other readers also helped shepherd me through some tough times and some rough prose. They include Karen White, Chris and Martita Fleming, Mike and Becky Koning, Ben Jesup, and Pam Koger-Jesup. Thank you for spending your free time with this book.

Thanks also to David Holmes, who first sparked my interest in American religious history, and to the students of Mary Washington College's Religious Conservatives seminar. Their enthusiasm and discussions aided me in my analysis of fundamentalism.

Finally, I turn to my family. My mother and stepfather, Fran and Floyd Lindsey, gave much encouragement throughout the process, and more than once the memory of my late father, George Swetnam, Jr., kept me from giving up. But the largest share of the family support came from my husband, Jim, and my daughter, Lydia. They gave up time with me so that I could work on this project, and they helped me forget about it when I needed a break. I owe them a debt of gratitude, and I dedicate this book to them.

Mary Beth Swetnam Mathews
Arlington, Virginia
July 2005

INTRODUCTION

The editor of the *Montgomery (Alabama) Advertiser* was adamant in his eulogy of fundamentalism in the South. In pronouncing the death of all things bad in the region, Grover C. Hall wrote:

> The Klan is a mere temporary convenience to shady politicians, rascally adventurers, and third-rate preachers, and is already cracking. Fundamentalism is not a permanent problem with us; in fact, it is by no means as serious a problem right now as it may appear on the surface. We are not half so religious, anyway, as reported.[1]

For Hall, and indeed for many other writers, editors, and readers, North and South, fundamentalism by 1928 did appear to be defunct. A movement that had been tied to perceptions of ignorance, intolerance, poverty, and even violence appeared to be gone, if not forgotten. But even if Americans were ready to turn their backs on the religious conservatives known as fundamentalists, they had created a permanent connection between fundamentalism and the South long before the Scopes Trial began in Tennessee in 1925. Observers of the South and of fundamentalism in general had forged in the American mind an indelible link between the two, one that persists to this day.

Americans, in both the popular media and the scholarly press, have embraced the notion that the South provides, and always has provided, a hospitable home to Christian fundamentalism. This notion arose decades before Jimmy Carter's famous evangelicalism and before the heyday of southern televangelists like Jimmy Swaggart, Jerry Falwell, Pat Robertson, and Jim Bakker. It came even before Billy Graham's rise to national prominence. Despite fundamentalism's origins in the Northeast and Midwest, observers of religion in the South quickly attached the moniker of "fundamentalist" to the region even before the Scopes Trial brought widespread attention and ridicule to both the South and conservative Christians who opposed the teaching of evolution in public schools.[2] The labeling of the South as fundamentalist occurred without an analysis of the theological points of fundamentalism or an understanding of what comprised "southern" religion and without a determination of whether such a category as southern religion existed. In fact, southern religion, a geographic term, became a theological term, one with certain connotations. This notion of southern propensity for fundamentalism sprang from cultural observations and prejudices, both real and unfounded, about the region and its perceived monolithic faith. This book documents the process by which the South received its fundamentalist characterization, and it chronicles the forces at work in creating the image of the South as the Bible Belt. It is not a book about religion in the South per se, but one about perceptions of religion in the South, perceptions of northern and southern observers.

Writers of the time as well as later observers have conflated the meaning of *evangelicalism* and *fundamentalism*. Although these terms are often used interchangeably, they are distinct religious movements. Evangelicalism can best be understood as a belief in the need for a "personal relationship" with God (although that term is more associated with the twentieth century, earlier evangelicals would have said that a believer needs to know God personally), which produces a conversion experience in the believer. This conversion is usually, although not always, an emotional event. After the conversion, the new believer should lead a pious life, eschewing temptations such as drinking and gambling. The new convert should also demonstrate an interest in spreading the gospel to other people.[3] The most universal characteristic of evangelicals is the role they see for the Bible. For them, the Bible is the sole and "final authority" for life and culture.[4]

Fundamentalism began with a group of socially conservative evangelicals who banded together in the early twentieth century in reaction to liberal Christians' call for religion to adapt itself to culture. These theologically liberal Christians held that changes in American society demanded changes in the dominant religion—Protestantism. Liberals (or modernists, as they often called themselves) tended to ignore doctrines like the Virgin Birth and Original Sin in favor of more broad statements about the universality of religious faith and the Fatherhood of God. These changes in belief angered fundamentalists. The fundamentalists were also reacting to the same changes in American society that the liberal Christians saw as indicative of the need for religious change. But for the fundamentalists, these social changes were signs that religion needed to hold fast to its conservative moorings in a storm of unprecedented proportions and fury. According to the fundamentalists, the United States was a fallen country in need of immediate atonement, although many believed that American culture could not be saved. The country needed to turn away from liberal Christianity. In general, fundamentalists believed and still believe in biblical inerrancy (that the Bible is accurate in matters of faith, morals, history, and science), dispensational premillennialism, the reality of sin, and the divinity of Jesus (rather than Jesus as an example of human goodness).[5] During the 1920s, fundamentalism was marked by a militant, antimodern reaction to rapid social changes in the United States, a militancy that both contemporary observers and later historians have noted, and which helped link them to the South.[6] Since that time, however, most fundamentalists have moderated their stance regarding modern life; they believe that religious belief should inform modern life. In other words, many fundamentalists would say that it is acceptable to go to a Christian movie or buy a Christian music recording—religion dictating culture, not vice versa.[7]

The emergence of the Holiness movement in the late nineteenth and early twentieth centuries has also served to confuse observers. The Holiness movement, which emphasized correct living and a "sanctification" experience for believers, emerged in the South and on the West Coast during this period. The often more emotional and charismatic worship style may have led outside observers to label it as fundamentalist or evangelical. Indeed, scholars today disagree over how to categorize it.[8] The best indicator that a writer had seen a Holiness or even a Pentecostal service was the use of the term "Holy Rollers" to describe the very emotional and physical behaviors at Holiness gatherings.[9] While the context of the religious service was not always important for contemporary observers, their comments helped shape the notion that the South was home to ultrareligious people.

Although satirist H. L. Mencken coined the term *Bible Belt* to describe the South, he plays a very minor role in this book. His scathing diatribes about the region, including the famous "The Sahara of the Bozart," are extreme caricatures of a more pervasive view of the region, one that developed before Mencken had sharpened his pencil and done battle with the former Confederacy.[10] The image of the Bible Belt arose in large part from changes occurring in both magazine and newspaper publishing at the end of the nineteenth and the beginning of the twentieth century. The increasing industrialization of the nation's economy, combined with changes in how products were sold, made magazines available to larger audiences and for lower prices. As readership changed, content changed as well. Editors targeted the middle class increasingly. Moreover, daily newspapers also underwent changes, as circulation increased along with profits. The turn of the twentieth century was the heyday of "yellow journalism," and muckrakers abounded. Like magazine content, newspaper editorial content became shorter and simpler, as editors aimed at the lowest common denominator of their audience. On the other side of the equation, readers tended to impose their own uniform biases and interpretations across a wide range of news topics.[11]

The linkage between the South and fundamentalism in general arose from assumptions that writers both outside and within the region made about the class and racial aspects of the South. For journalists outside the South, white southerners appeared to be ignorant, uneducated people who were poorer than their northern cousins and lacked access to the educational and occupational opportunities that the rest of the country enjoyed. One journalist, writing for the *New Republic*, damned the South with faint praise as he covered the Scopes Trial. "Badly off as she is in matters of education, roads, and religion," he wrote, "Tennessee is on the whole several degrees better than the worst in the South."[12] For such writers, the South was a rural backwater that harbored no real intellectual life.

In terms of race, nonsouthern journalists tended to define the term *southerners* solely as white southerners. Both southern and nonsouthern writers ignored the presence of black southerners and their influence on the culture and daily activity of the region. Outside writers had fallen prey to the white South's contention that the two races were, to paraphrase the famous Atlanta speech of Booker T. Washington, as separate as fingers in a glove. When addressing the South, writers, regardless of region, saw their audience as white. The few times black voices appear in this book are, from my investigation, the few times that black voices managed to make themselves heard in the white discussion. The exception to this intentional ignorance of racial interaction came with coverage of lynch mobs, which by their very nature, the writers implied, showed that the South was unintellectual.

Indeed, many authors and editors saw the South as intolerant of divergent opinions—religious or secular—and thus, anti-intellectual. Harvard history professor Albert Bushnell Hart, writing in 1905 about the "Southern Problem," charged that "Southern society . . . shows extraordinary solidarity of sentiment; in religion, in education, in literature, in politics, in morals there is a recognized standard from which divergence marks a man or woman as a suspicious character."[13] Writers with southern roots often bought into the theory that the South was different and that southern religious practice was unintellectual or even anti-intellectual. In their efforts to distance themselves from the perceived cultural deficiency of their home region, or in an attempt to join the condemnation of it, these insiders frequently wrote even more harshly than their nonsouthern counterparts.[14] For example, in an article entitled "Free Speech in the South," an anonymous southern woman began, "It does not exist," and then quoted an acquaintance who said, "'What impresses me most in Southerners is their determined resistance to the inroads of civilization.'"[15]

As if the southern economy and educational system were not proof of the white South's cultural inferiority, journalists also turned to graphic depictions of lynching and racial unrest in the region to make their case that the South had fallen behind the nation in terms of civilization. Detailed accounts of the ritual killings of black men under the auspices of "Judge Lynch" were common in the national media, and editorial writers called upon white southerners to join the modern world and forgo mob violence. Many accounts referred to the South as "medieval," a term that would later make an appearance in descriptions of the South's resistance to the theory of evolution. In covering the region's all too real violence against blacks, outside observers credited a variety of factors with the region's attraction to lynching, including, as a sociology professor from Hamilton College phrased it, "impulsive and emotional revivalism." *World's Work* writer Robert L. Duffus in 1923 held that the fundamentalist movement had helped to spread the Ku Klux Klan's message of hate.[16] Mob violence was equated with ignorance and lower-class culture. Therefore, the home of lynching must itself have been poor and lower class. But whether it was class or race that caused the violence, nonsouthern publications saw the South as different, poor, and stupid. This divide between North and South on lynching was not so much a disagreement on the role of African Americans in society; it was, rather, a condemnation of the real violence with which the white South meted out what it called "justice."

This disparagement of the South occurred simultaneously with commentaries that romanticized or even sentimentalized the South. Other historians have already documented the extent to which the North and the South used the subjugation of race as a means of achieving cultural reunion following the Civil War, as well as the way that both regions embraced notions of the South as "junior partner" in a masculine/feminine relationship that allowed the North to romanticize the role of white planters and allowed the South more discretion in how it dealt with African Americans.[17] But at the same time that the North was mending relations with the South, there were conversations that sought to distance the South from a perceived standard of "Americanness"—a standard that emphasized education, tolerance, and progress. For participants in this debate, the South was not moving toward reconciliation with American ideals; it was moving away from them.

While other authors have noticed the development of a set of derogatory images of the South, this book is the first to study in depth the explicit connection between the negative images and the notion of religious difference in the South. The disparaging of the South began in the 1890s and continued through to the 1920s.[18] These negative notions of white southern society dovetailed well with the general media's ideas about fundamentalism. By the summer of 1925, when the forces of modernism and fundamentalism gathered in Dayton, Tennessee, many northern and midwestern journalists had concluded that fundamentalism was a backward religious movement that championed the Bible against scientific inquiry. Unable to see legitimate scientific theories at work in the antievolutionists' worldview, the proponents of modernism successfully tagged them as unreasonable zealots who would not respond to careful arguments.[19] Such a characterization sounds similar to the idea that prevailed about southerners of the day: that they were temperamental and unable to understand reason and logic. Writers had already matched fundamentalism with the South before the Scopes Trial, and the arguments over monkeys and God at Dayton only served to cement the two caricatures more firmly together in the American mind.

The image of the "fundamentalist South" in the American mind came from accounts in both nonfictional and fictional sources. Magazines such as the *Century, Time, Harper's Weekly,* and the *Atlantic Monthly* often ran stories that disparaged the South and its religious faith. Daily newspapers also provided firsthand accounts of lynchings and religious revivals in the South and colorful figures who preached from below the Mason-Dixon Line. The regional bias of these accounts reflects the nature of magazine publishing at the turn of the twentieth century. Boston and New York City were home to a majority of the magazines and journals published then.

Moreover, fictional accounts of the South written by white southerners reached an even wider audience than some large newspapers. Often novels by white southerners portrayed the South in a way that northerners could recognize and identify with, despite the intentions of their authors. For example, Corra Harris's account of a Methodist circuit-rider's wife was serialized in the *Saturday Evening Post* and received widespread attention. Harris portrayed the circuit rider as a man of deep devotion but no real appetite for theological scholarship. She intentionally advocated conservative values and resisted society's changes in the second decade of the twentieth century, but the net effect of her fiction was to reinforce the popular notion that the South was religiously simple and therefore different in a decidedly inferior way.[20] Harris was in good company in her efforts to portray the South as the home of old-fashioned traditions. According to at least one historian, white southerners used Confederate memories to deal with the rapid industrial and social changes of the Gilded Age.[21]

The picture that Harris and other writers created, whether intentionally or not, neglected the theological points of fundamentalism. Rather than concentrating on whether churches in the South as a whole embraced certain dogmas, such as the Virgin Birth (whether Jesus was born of the Virgin Mary), substitutionary atonement (the theory that Jesus died as a substitute for humanity, thus enduring the punishment all people deserved), or dispensational premillennialism (that time is divided into certain divine dispensations and that after a time marked by suffering, Christ will return to earth before a thousand-year period preceding the end of time and the final judgment), the creators of the notion of the Bible Belt South relied upon the sociological assumption that fundamentalism was a backward faith that enjoyed support only among the rural bumpkins. The ignorance of theological points, however, was not entirely universal. *Time,* for example, provided a discussion of the points of debate between the fundamentalists and the modernists, and other periodicals did, at first, pay attention to the arguments and counterarguments.[22] The process by which journals ended up ignoring or disparaging fundamentalism's tenets will be explored in chapter 5.

Religion in the South was, the sources both primary and secondary agree, more decidedly conservative than Protestant theology in the rest of the country.[23] White southerners were quite comfortable with "that old-time religion," and they were frequent attendees at revivals and prayer meetings led by evangelicals who kept to the standards of traditional Protestant religion—an emphasis on how tainted human nature was, a need for the divine intervention and salvation, and a belief in miracles and biblical inerrancy. But this emphasis on more traditional and conservative Protestant thought does not mean that the South was already fundamentalist, nor does it mean that theological debates were absent in the region.[24] Denominational newspapers of the period debated the merits of heresy trials occurring in northern denominations, and there were attempts at "Social Gospel–style" reforms in the region.[25]

Rather than examine the intricacies of the religious debate, American commentators employed a cultural definition of fundamentalism that they then applied to southern religious expression. Indeed, many editors saw religious faith as incompatible with intellectual prowess altogether. These same journalists also assumed that the fundamentalist reaction to modern life was indicative of a lack of intellectual activity in general. If fundamentalists were antimodern, they must also be lower class and uneducated. Since writers had already made these generalizations about the South, it was not difficult to extend the syllogism to the fundamentalists. If southerners were antimodern, poor, violent, and uneducated, and fundamentalists were antimodern, poor, violent in their discourse, and uneducated, then southerners must, therefore, be fundamentalists.

The notion was formed both from real observations about the South and from ideas of culture that prevailed among the reading public. The South did have less in terms of economic production and educational facilities, and more in terms of lynch mobs and racial violence. Writers, however, augmented and amplified such generalizations to create an inaccurate and biased image of the South. As creators, the media highlighted and elaborated southern distinctiveness. As respondents, the media gave the people what they wanted. To do otherwise would risk a decline in readership. Journalists and some novelists worked within and at the head of a growing movement that embraced a definition of culture that looked at the South with disdain.

This movement grew out of a dispute over the proper relationship between religion and culture. A series of momentous changes had occurred in the United States in the late nineteenth and early twentieth centuries—changes that unsettled many Americans and led them to question the values and institutions they knew. The rapid increase in immigration, the movement of Americans away from rural and into urban areas, and the U.S. involvement in World War I all led to a basic questioning of the foundations of American culture.[26]

It is no coincidence that the discussion about the apparent regional character of fundamentalism took place at the same time as the social and economic changes of this period and at the same time that the fundamentalist reaction to liberal Christianity occurred. The political, economic, and social upheaval influenced the debate over what it meant to be an American. Intellectuals argued that there was a "right" race—Anglo-Saxon. That perception "swept under the rug the Native American Indians, Irish, blacks, and Jews," as well as "the Asians, Slavs, and Italians."[27] The proponents of this narrow vision of Americanism included in their definition a "right" religion—Protestantism. Roman Catholics were considered not fully Christianized and in need of salvation from their pope. But the definition of what Protestantism should encompass also drew disagreements.[28]

Participants in this debate over Protestantism for the most part divided themselves into two camps—those who believed that religion should dictate to culture and those who believed that religion should accommodate culture.[29] The former camp held that Christian doctrine should inform decisions about all facets of American life: family, community, and nation. For these doctrinally orthodox people, there was no other standard by which to measure the actions of an individual or a community. God stood in judgment of society and culture. No other criteria were necessary, and the tenets of Protestant Christianity, as fundamentalists and their allies understood them, were not subject to the whims of culture. The Bible and its teachings, they believed, remained constant throughout human history. At the outset of the debate, the doctrinally orthodox, many of whom would become fundamentalists, were particularly militant in their debate against their opponents, a militancy that is not lost on historians and was not lost on their contemporary observers.[30]

On the opposite side of the debate were those intellectuals who believed that religion was a more fluid and adaptable human institution. These intellectuals were influenced by two schools of thought. Some drew their inspiration from French thinkers Auguste Comte and Emile Durkheim. Both Comte and Durkheim saw society as the most important component in a culture. Comte placed great emphasis on social change through his Religion of Humanity, which made humanity, not God, the object of worship. Led by a "priesthood" of intellectual and educational elites, Comte's vision called for greater social progress through scientific observation and political action.[31] Durkheim, like Comte, believed in "scientific analysis of social phenomena," but he was less enthusiastic about the ability of society to progress.[32] Durkheim, however, contributed to modern thought the notion that religion was a human creation and therefore the symbols and beliefs of religion were fungible. In Durkheim's words, "sacred things are simply collective ideals that have fixed themselves on material objects."[33] Since the notion of sacredness was a human invention, religion's "true purpose [was] not intellectual but social."[34] If religion were merely social, then society, followers of Comte and Durkheim would argue, should be able to change religion's norms and expectations rather than allowing religion to dictate these terms.

Another influence on the culturally orthodox thinkers was the emergence of liberal Protestant thought (the very movement fundamentalists opposed) and its cousin, the Social Gospel. Men like Washington Gladden, Walter Rauschenbusch, and Richard T. Ely held that Christianity needed to adapt to the changing America they saw around them. In their view, the church needed to reach out to inhabitants of slums, the poor, and the recently immigrated in order to ameliorate social ills and bring about the Kingdom of God on earth. Their gospel, their "good news," was a social one, and they believed that Christ had charged them with this Social Gospel to improve the material conditions of humanity. Like the Social Gospelers, liberal Christians held that Christianity was in need of change in order to continue its plausibility in a rapidly modernizing world. These liberals, or modernists as they called themselves, held that changes in biblical scholarship and changes in society demanded a reevaluation of Protestant Christianity. They believed that secular education, political debate, and technological advances could all influence the formation of culture and should inform religion. One historian has argued persuasively that this reliance on experts and the creation of an "'educational elite'" were major irritants that spurred the start of the fundamentalist movement.[35] The doctrinally orthodox rejected the notion of elites leading and instead wished to place authority in the Bible as they read it.

The majority of journalists covering the South belonged to the culturally orthodox group of thinkers—people who believed that Americans formed their culture with an eye to the teachings of religion but not that religion should dictate culture. Notions of hierarchy of thought and civilization dominated their prose as they sought to prove that the South was less civilized and progressive than the North and that liberal Christianity was more advanced than traditional Christianity. In these journalists' view, the South was not fully Americanized because it embraced the wrong sort of Protestant faith, a faith that was less adaptive than their own. Ideas about the adaptive nature of religion colored their perceptions of the South.

These notions appeared in magazines and newspapers of the era. Editors read and adopted liberal Protestant, Social Gospel, and positivist philosophical ideas and used their publications as a way of advancing social change. For example, "utopian" ideas permeated American magazines during the late nineteenth and early twentieth centuries.[36] University of Chicago sociologists, influenced by Auguste Comte, published studies of the South that urged reform of both education and religion in the region.[37] Editors like the *New Republic's* Herbert Croly allowed positivist philosophy and a firm belief in human progress to influence their magazines' content.[38] The overwhelming message of the press of the era was that the South needed to adapt its culture and religion to a standard that these writers believed was predominant in the North.

The indictment of the South by the culturally orthodox did not occur overnight but took several decades to develop, from approximately the end of the 1880s to the late 1920s. Several key events helped to precipitate this outlook. First, the persistence of lynchings across the South, especially those called "spectacle lynchings," demonstrated a vicious and abhorrent face of American racism that reflected the national disdain for African Americans with a particular horror.[39] Second, the passage of statewide prohibition laws in the early 1900s in southern states helped to secure the South's preeminence in the area of "moral crusades." Although the South was credited with leading a moral crusade, in matters such as lynching and child labor laws writers condemned the South as lacking moral fiber. Third, the U.S. involvement in World War I and the subsequent unrest in 1919 helped to unsettle writers about the social and political trends at work in both the nation and the South. Finally, the famous Scopes Trial and the emergence of colorful fundamentalist leaders like Texan J. Frank Norris served to locate fundamentalism below the Mason-Dixon Line.[40]

The geographic placement of fundamentalism was another chapter in the continuing story of regional identity in the United States. Regional identity was, and still is, a reciprocating phenomenon; each region of the country defines itself against another, and other regions participate in that process of definition. During the years before and after the Civil War, the North and South were engaged in a complicated process of definition and redefinition, with the regions ultimately tied to each other through their debates. The North bound itself to the South as an example that the South should emulate; the South tied itself to the North by arguing that it, not the North, had preserved the proper order. Fundamentalism quickly became another way to define the South against the North, a tie that both sides exploited.

To date, no scholar has written extensively on the interplay between North and South, the subsequent understanding of southern religion as fundamentalist, and the role of religion in the formation of regional identity. Most works on the nature and history of fundamentalism tend to ignore the South altogether.[41] Historians of southern religion before the twentieth century are unanimous in their contention that the South was always home to the more religiously conservative

in terms of theology.[42] But even if the South were inclined toward religious orthodoxy and away from religious liberalism, that inclination itself does not constitute
fundamentalism, especially as recent scholars have defined it. Nor does religious
homogeneity, which the South had in its overwhelming majority of Protestants,
mean increased religious piety.

Recent scholarship in the area of American religious history has yielded new
understandings of how religion and culture interacted both in the South and across
the country. In the last five years, several monographs have called into question
the assumptions that the South has a monolithic, culturally captive Protestant religion.[43] Rather, these recent studies have refreshed interest in the field of southern
religion by demonstrating that it was adaptable, engaged with cultures and races,
and by no means predestined to become dominated by Baptists and Methodists
and revivals and evangelism. The development of the varieties of southern religion occurred as theologies encountered cultures, and vice versa.

This book will tie together the various aspects of northern and southern media
coverage and their subsequent understanding and portrayal of religion. Rather than
accepting the stereotype of the fundamentalist South, the book explores and ex-
plains how that view came to dominate depictions of the region. The way in which
American print media influenced American culture will also play a role in the
study.[44] The mainstream press and authors of fiction provide a lens through which
the current historian can examine the culture of the day, but these same writers
also played a role in creating a notion of what American culture should and should
not include. The writers who embraced a separation between religion and culture
and who believed that religion should not dictate culture were more likely to perceive the South and fundamentalism along sociological lines. To these authors,
fundamentalism was a dangerous force that threatened their cultural assumptions.
Rather than understand the doctrine behind the movement, the "custodians of
culture" instead sought only to identify the sociological tendencies (or apparent
tendencies) of both white southerners and fundamentalists.[45] Meanwhile, fundamentalist writers and people who sympathized with them held that religion was im-
mutable and that American culture should be held to divine, not human, standards—something that had been argued since the eighteenth century as American
exceptionalism. That belief centered on the idea that America was God's chosen
country and as such had to abide by God's laws. Presented in these terms, the debate
is more easily understood and helps to illuminate the development of the stereotype of the South as fundamentalist.

The abundance of sources available to the historian of the late-nineteenth-
and early-twentieth-century dialogue about the South is daunting, but for the purposes of this study, I chose to limit my investigation to print sources for several

reasons. First, the print media were widely available to most Americans during the period. To determine what the popular perceptions about the South and about fundamentalism were, newspapers and magazines seemed to be the best choice. Second, although their accuracy is not absolute, estimations and self-reports of the circulation of these periodicals are available, providing an idea of how many readers might see a particular article about lynching, for example. I have included a brief appendix giving circulation figures as reported to N. W. Ayers and Sons Directory of Newspapers and Periodicals. Finally, the print media of the day occasionally included letters to the editors and follow-up articles on specific events, and these "second-chance" pieces provide a window on the exchange of ideas as they were promulgated by the journalists and reacted to by the readers.

I selected specific events to study and tried as much as possible to trace those events across a variety of sources. For example, the lynching of Jesse Washington received national attention, so I read magazine and newspaper articles commenting on it. I also used the Reader's Guide to Periodical Literature to look for specific topics that might escape an event search—general articles about education in the South or colorful coverage of Appalachian feuds. While this system did not result in a complete reading of every newspaper and magazine for a forty-year period, it did provide both a broad cross-section of coverage and a way to track the persistence of certain stereotypes and opinions.

In order to trace the development of those stereotypes, this book adopts a thematic approach to the popular literature from the late 1880s to the late 1920s. During this period, the South earned many different nicknames, most of them pejorative. The South became known as violent, teetotaling, uneducated, unscientific, and the home of colorful preachers. These labels do not necessarily correspond to chronological periods, so a thematic approach that traces changes in each area provides the best method for studying the period.[46] For example, although racism and racial violence against African Americans were present nationwide, depictions of lynch mobs evoked shock and disgust particularly with regard to the South. Likewise, temperance leaders from the South, such as the Reverend Sam P. Jones, drew praise for their efforts, but by the time of the Scopes Trial, Tennessee and the South were ridiculed for their early support of antialcohol efforts. These changes in perceptions of the white South's stands on race relations and alcohol coincide with shifts in the public's perception of the home of fundamentalism. Thus the thematic approach allows an investigation of change over time but does not limit the investigation to artificially defined periods.

The first chapter, "'We Don't Want Religion, We Want Blood': The Violent South," will examine the creation of the violent image of the South in American print media. As the southern tendency to lynch blacks skyrocketed in the 1880s, journalists in both the North and South decried this alarming trend. The chapter will trace media responses to lynchings in general, as well as focus on several "spectacle" lynchings that brought especially vehement condemnation from the press. As a part of their coverage of these deaths, the media often noted the region's ties to Baptist and Methodist denominations and questioned the ability of white southern religious leaders to inculcate proper Christian values in their congregants. This chapter will also examine the perception that the South was intolerant of divergent religious views and that white southern society and religion were "medieval" in nature.

The second chapter, "'The School Backward, the People Illiberal': The Uneducated South," explores the perception of the South as uneducated. Almost concurrently with the notion of southern intolerance arose the popular conception that the South suffered from serious educational deficits. These deficits were, for the most part, real, but the method by which the press covered them and tied them to the region led to a picture of an illiterate, inbred South. Influenced by liberal Christian, Social Gospel, and positivist philosophical ideas, many observers believed that education and religion were means of social uplift. The popular perception among critics was that white southern Christians parked their morality at the church door and that southerners in general saw religion as a means to eternal salvation rather than a vehicle for social change.[47] Thus the conservative religion of the South was seen as one of the educational and social impediments to the region's progress. While it was true that religious sentiment in the South was more focused on the otherworldly, observers once again exaggerated and caricatured this tendency almost beyond recognition. Moreover, the distorted notion failed to take into account a southern focus on individual rather than corporate morality. Individual morality was a means to an ends—salvation—but it was valuable to southerners in and of itself.

As a part of the coverage of educational problems in the South, newspapers and magazines were fond of reporting on conditions in Appalachia. In the mountains, according to the accounts, resided a remnant of the "pure" Anglo-Saxon strain of pioneers who had created the United States. But these mountaineers had been so long removed from the uplifting effects of civilization that they had withered intellectually and socially. The South, the outside judges held, was a land with no real intelligence.

The third chapter, "The Long Meter Doxology in the State House: The Teetotaling South," examines critics' perception of clergy in the South as needing reform. In contrast to the prevailing notion of the southern clergy's inability to stop lynchings, when it came to matters of personal behavior and laws governing it, white southern preachers took on superhuman powers in the eyes of the North. When the preachers turned their efforts to prohibition, the northern observers praised them at first. Coverage of statewide prohibition campaigns in the South, especially in Georgia and Alabama, led to a perception that the area was dry and that religious leaders called the political shots. To northern observers, southern preachers were at once bumbling leaders and theocrats. The former characterization affronted the American and Protestant notion of the preacher as a common person who could provide moral leadership and exhortation. The latter model was frightening, as theocracy was seen as anti-American and extremely dangerous.[48] After the advent of nationwide prohibition, coverage of southern dryness turned sour, and the South once again found itself ridiculed.

The fourth chapter, "'Salesmen of Hate': Fundamentalism Becomes Southern," will briefly outline the initial coverage fundamentalism in the North received and then examine the South's alleged love affair with this new variety of conservative Christianity. Although a few newspapers and magazines initially gave detailed coverage of fundamentalism, the denominational struggles over dogma and the controversy over Harry Emerson Fosdick, a liberal Baptist who held an appointment in a New York Presbyterian church, quickly led to a negative image of fundamentalists as Christian warriors who would pillage their own denominations in the name of their beliefs. Beginning in the early 1920s, even as fundamentalism was bursting onto the national scene, writers began to tie it to the South and to groups like the Ku Klux Klan. Once again, the South was called "medieval," this time for its religious opinions, and the Scopes Trial in Tennessee only served to reinforce further the connection between the South's outmoded, intolerant religious beliefs and the outmoded, intolerant worldview of the fundamentalists.

The fifth chapter, "'Gundamentalist': J. Frank Norris and the South's Fate," will address the murder trial of J. Frank Norris, a Baptist fundamentalist minister from Fort Worth, Texas, who furnished yet more grist for the media mill by shooting an unarmed man to death. It will also connect the themes at work in the coverage of the South with the 1928 presidential campaign of Al Smith, a wet, Catholic Democrat who failed to carry several southern states because of his religion and his stand on prohibition.

Finally, the conclusion will explore more fully the reasons locating the fundamentalist movement in another geographic area of the country helped northern intellectuals further refine their definitions of Americanism.

The South has long served as a mirror for the rest of the country, although the images at times appear distorted, as if reflected in a funhouse mirror.[49] Racism within the United States was not confined to Dixie, yet in that region racism took on some of its most terrible forms. Likewise, fundamentalism did not start in the South, but it quickly became associated with the former Confederacy, for better or for worse. Americans tend to view the doctrinally strict and cultural outsiders with suspicion.[50] White southerners lost the Civil War, and they lost most of their ability to control the debate over what constituted American culture. Black southerners, who won their freedom, nonetheless never had the ability to influence the debate either. As much as white southerners tried to hold to northern expectations, they could never meet them. For instance, southerners embraced patriotism and national pride, but their concurrent embrace of segregation and lynching placed them outside the American mainstream. Most white southerners professed the Protestant notion that a person had to be literate to understand the salvific power of the Bible, yet they could not and would not make the necessary economic investment in education. Moreover, the apparent location of a strictly orthodox group—the fundamentalists—within the South served to place both the doctrinally strict and their alleged hosts outside the definition of America. Ironically, in their efforts to create a national identity, northern intellectuals and writers created a regional one, tailored to their own perceptions of their region and written to exclude the South.

Why is the geographic location of fundamentalism important? Why does "southern religion" need further definition and qualification? The answer to both questions lies in the need for additional attention to the nuances of "southern religion" in the larger context of the nation. The American South did not have large numbers of non-Protestant residents, but the people who made it their home did have a wide variety of religious beliefs. They, like so many Protestants before them, split from each other into different denominations and congregations because they each interpreted the lessons they read in the Bible with a slightly different emphasis. They were convinced that there was a Truth to which they had to remain faithful. Their salvation depended on it, and they could not put such an important commodity in jeopardy. And while the observations about the South were largely true—that it was home to more violence, to less-educated people, to teetotaling crusaders—they have become so distorted in the American consciousness that it is time to tease out the truth from the fiction, or as the fundamentalists and modernists alike would have said, the wheat from the chaff.

CHAPTER 1

"We Don't Want Religion, We Want Blood": The Violent South

B y 1915, after the lynching of Leo Frank, the editor of the *Chicago Tribune* had had enough of stories of violence and lynching that his southern correspondents had relayed to him. The South, he railed, was "a region of illiteracy, blatant self-righteousness, cruelty, and violence." He continued:

> The South is backward. It shames the United States by its illiteracy and incompetence. Its hill-men and poor whites, its masses of feared and bullied blacks, its ignorant and violent politicians, its rotten industrial conditions, and its rotten social ideas exist in circumstances which disgrace the United States in the thought of Americans and the opinions of foreigners.[1]

This editorial outburst was not an isolated rampage by a northern editor. Instead, it was the culmination of years of recording and publishing the violence that appeared to be endemic to the region. And after so many stories of lynching, feuds, and massacres, this editor could contain his disgust no longer.

Violence in the South has a long and storied past. Certainly, the region was no stranger to duels, fistfights, beatings, and murders.[2] Southern chivalry and honor were already topics of discussion. The South seemed to cling to an older method of settling disputes and to the need to protect and maintain one's good family name, as some historians have already noted.[3] But toward the end of the nineteenth century, the number of lynchings rose steeply—peaking in "1892 when mobs executed an estimated 71 whites and 155 blacks" nationwide. Within the South, between 1880 and 1930, over 700 whites and over 3,000 blacks were lynched.[4] Scholars have employed various reasons to explain why the South lynched so many African Americans, but for the purposes of this study, the operative question will be, how did the press perceive and portray those lynchings and that violence?[5] During the late nineteenth and early twentieth centuries, the media covering the South saw the region as lawless, given to violence, and thoroughly contrary to American ideals of justice and deliberation.

To be sure, writers on both sides of the Mason-Dixon Line acknowledged that lynching occurred in virtually every region of the country. Southern writers were especially fond of pointing out that northern cities had their share of race riots and that western states often resorted to mob violence. But the vast majority of these murders took place in the former Confederacy, and contemporary writers knew this fact, amplifying it in their coverage of these grisly crimes. The South was home to national trends, but these trends, as a result of both southern actions and outside press coverage, became larger than life, like the funhouse hall of mirrors. Moreover, even though the number of lynchings decreased after 1900, "the cultural impact of the practice became more powerful. More people participated in, read about, [and] saw pictures of . . . lynchings."[6] There was also an increased interest in the feuding among white southerners living in the Appalachian Mountains. Both these phenomena demonstrated to the reading public that white southerners were unlike their fellow Americans.[7]

Lynchings and riots provided critical writers with examples of brutal violence by whites against blacks. These same writers and editors did not hesitate to publish the gory details of the lynch mobs' actions, which demonstrated how far southern civilization had lagged behind. With this fact established, the media were able to argue that the South was barbaric, that it lacked proper civilization, that religion did not play an important role in shaping a healthy public discourse, and that white southerners were more at home in the Dark Ages than in the Modern Age.

The single most effective manner in which nonsouthern editors and reporters were able to place the South outside cultural boundaries was by publishing graphic details of the lynching process. Daily newspapers and monthly magazines frequently included sensational accounts of how mobs in the South had tortured and killed black men and women. These articles appealed to the audience's prurient interests and at the same time painted a macabre picture of life and death in the South.

The lynching death of Henry Smith in Paris, Texas, in 1893, provided the first opportunity for journalists to publish shocking descriptions of the lynching process.[8] Smith was accused of raping and murdering a young child, Myrtle Vance. The lynch mob included the father, brother, and uncles of the murdered girl, and their participation in the killing of Smith was chronicled by many newspapers and magazines. A summary of the event, as related by the *St. Louis Daily Republic* and included in the Boston-based *Arena* magazine, described how Mr. Vance took part in the torture:

> Taking one [heated iron], Vance thrust it under first one and then the other side of his victim's feet, who, helpless, writhed, and the flesh seared and peeled from the bones. . . . By turns Smith screamed, prayed, begged, and cursed his torturer. When his face was reached, his tongue was silenced by fire, and henceforth he only moaned, or gave a cry that echoed over the prairie like the wail of a wild animal.[9]

In this account, both the mob and the victim lost their humanity. Smith became a creature that could only haunt the wilderness with his inhuman sounds. But the reader had to wonder how so many people could watch and not halt such an awful event.

Coverage of the Smith lynching in the *Washington Post* omitted the participation of Mr. Vance, but it did provide a short account of the torture and the opportunity afforded to the mob to witness Smith's agony. According to the *Post*, as the mob returned from Texarkana, where Smith had fled in vain, "at the open prairie, 300 yards from the Texas and Pacific depot, the scaffold awaited [Smith]. It was six feet square and ten feet high, well within the sight of all." Rather than give meticulous coverage of the torture, the reporter summarized that "for fifty minutes the maddened mob tortured him. Red hot irons were thrust from every side into his body. His shrieks added vigor to his persecutors. First the hot irons branded his feet, and inch by inch they crept up to his face."[10] These details, although less comprehensive than those included in the *Arena*, served to horrify the reader nonetheless.

The *New York Times* added coverage of what happened after the relatives of the murdered child had finished exacting their personal retribution:

> The men of the Vance family having wreaked vengeance, the crowd set the fire. The negro rolled and wriggled and tossed out of the mass only to be pushed back by the people nearest him. He tossed out again, and was roped and pulled back. Hundreds of people turned away, but the vast crowd looked on calmly.[11]

To the *Times* reporter, the apparent disgust of hundreds of onlookers was outweighed by the apparent approval of many hundreds more. The white residents of

Paris, Texas, were obviously unmoved by the agonies Smith suffered and were able to watch the outrageous treatment of a fellow human being. The *Times* portrayed them as curious or even approving of the horrors visited upon Smith.

Similarly, daily newspaper coverage of the lynching of Sam Hose in Georgia in 1899 provided in excruciating detail accounts of how the crowd burned Hose to death. The *New York Times* and the *Chicago Daily Tribune* gave similar accounts of how a lynch mob executed Sam Hose for the death of his employer, Alfred Cranford. Both papers included an account of how Hose's ears and then fingers were amputated and "passed among the members of the yelling and now thoroughly maddened crowd."[12] While the *Boston Globe* refrained from giving details "too horrible for description," it did inform its readers that "when the flames had done their work, the terrible onslaught of the souvenir hunters commenced. Not a vestige of the chair, tree, or skeleton was left."[13]

The awful characteristics of the crime of lynching were also accompanied by graphic accounts of the cases against the alleged murderers. Reports from the lynching and editorials after it included horrifying accounts of the crimes Hose was accused of having committed. An *Atlanta Constitution* editorial justifying the lynching of Hose received widespread attention outside Georgia, in part for its description of the crime. According to the *Constitution*, after Hose had killed Alfred Cranford with an ax, Hose allegedly tore Cranford's child "from the mother's breast, [and] flung it into the pool of blood oozing from its father's wound." Moreover, the newspaper charged, "the wife was seized, choked, thrown upon the floor, where her clothing soaked up the blood of her husband, and ravished!"[14] While the *Boston Globe* and the *San Francisco Chronicle* reported the contents of the *Constitution's* editorial, the *Chronicle* did not comment on the allegations of the Georgia editor. The *Globe* editorial, on the other hand, condemned the mob with almost equally inflammatory language:

> Whatever influence the lynching exerted upon its victim perished with his breath, but its influence upon all the thousands who participated as actual spectators or in sympathy survives. Is it for good or evil? Will the men who plunged their knives into this man or lighted the flames that enveloped him in death, be better men because of what they did? . . . Will the four train loads of Atlantans who hurried eagerly to the mob-ridden town, will all the Georgians who applauded or palliate this form of execution thereby make their community nobler?[15]

Even a denominational newspaper could not resist the temptation to use gruesome language as it condemned the practice of lynching. Following the Hose lynching, the *Southern Churchman*, a regional publication of the Episcopalian Church, wrote that "these people whose fiendish glee taunts their victim as his flesh crackles in the flames do not represent the South. They slander the South."[16] Yet the phrase "flesh crackles in the flames," while meant to stir up visions of the awful death of a black man, also evoked the popular notion of punishment in Hell and served to portray white southerners as demons. Although the *Southern Churchman* was aimed at a regional readership, it, like many other denominational newspapers, had an audience outside its immediate place of publication. Methodists, Presbyterians, Episcopalians, and Baptists all read newspapers across regional lines, as is apparent in their church notices and letters to the editors. Even a denominational newspaper could not resist the graphic details of these awful events.

Neither could concerned African Americans, who occasionally made their voices heard in the white media. One African American writer, Mary Church Terrell, honorary president of the National Association of Colored Women, was concerned that Americans needed to know the details of what was happening in the South and expressed her desire to refute white southerners' claims that lynched black men were not being tortured to death. In her 1904 article in the *North American Review*, Terrell cited the case of a double lynching in Doddsville, Mississippi, in which the man accused of murder and his wife, who fled with him, were tortured. She offered an account that told of a mob that employed a "large corkscrew" to "bore into the flesh of the man and the woman, in the arms, legs and body, [which was] then pulled out, the spirals tearing out big pieces of raw quivering flesh every time it was withdrawn."[17] Such intimate and horrible details were meant not to edify but to horrify readers and to marginalize the people who performed the torture. White southerners became a ghoulish people bent on sadism as they lurched through life hysterically.

Accounts of lynchings also included macabre descriptions of how members of the mobs often picked through the charred rubble in order to obtain "souvenirs" of the event. An editorial in the *World's Work*, edited by expatriate white southerner Walter Hines Page, chronicled what happened after a mob of white men lynched a black man for murder near Winchester, Tennessee, in late August 1901:

> After the fire died down there was a rush for souvenirs. The chains holding the charred body to the tree were cut off and the links divided out among those present. One man took out his knife and cut out two of the Negro's ribs, which he took with him. The ropes with which the Negro was bound were also cut into fragments, and divided among the men.[18]

In a similar vein, Herbert J. Seligmann, writing for the *Nation*, provided a chilling description of a lynching in Vicksburg, Mississippi, in May 1919. A black man, identified only as Clay, was accused of raping a white woman, and according to Seligmann, the *Vicksburg Evening Post* gave the following front-page testimony:

The Negro, with head twisted, dangled limply from the line. Seeing that Clay was merely suffering discomfort, men below began to jerk his legs. Others smeared kerosene upon the body, while others prepared a bonfire below, saturating material with gasoline. . . . The flesh on the body began to crinkle and blister. The face of the Negro became horribly distorted with pain. He assumed an attitude of prayer, raising his hands' palms together. . . . The legs of the corpse curled backward grewsomely. . . . The grizzly form was allowed to dangle for an hour and a half in the moonlight. . . . When the body fell to the gutter there was a great rush for bits of rope as souvenirs.[19]

The daily newspapers noticed this souvenir-hunting and included mentions of such activities. According to the *San Francisco Chronicle*, the mob that killed Sam Hose made a profit by selling his relics. "Before the body was cool it was cut into pieces," the *Chronicle* said, observing the entrepreneurial spirit of the New South, "the bones were crushed into small pieces as was also his liver. Those unable to obtain the ghastly relics direct paid their more fortunate possessors extravagant sums for them. Small pieces of bone went for 25 cents."[20] The *Washington Post* noted that "a piece of the liver crisply cooked sold for 10 cents." The *New York Times* account of the same lynching described how "the crowd fought for places about the smouldering tree, and with knives secured such pieces of his carcass as had not crumbled away. The chain was severed by hammers, the tree was chopped down, and the chips and such pieces of firewood as had not burned away were carried away as souvenirs."[21]

By publishing these details, and the details of how men and women were killed, the print media helped amplify the image of the white residents of the South as a vicious mob of hotheaded fiends who murdered men and women in terrible ways and then searched desperately for mementos by which to remember their gruesome actions. Clearly, the message underlying these accounts read, white southern society was abnormally different. That many of the accounts ran first in southern papers is no accident. Many southern editors counted themselves among the culturally orthodox who believed that the South's violent methods of punishing alleged criminals were wrong. But at the same time, they were a part of the machine driving the emotionalism of mob violence. By repeating inflammatory details about alleged crimes, whether as a response to the prevailing journalistic style or as a callous attempt to sell more copies, the editors were at once part of lynch mobs and critics of them. They expounded and deplored the mobs' actions simultaneously. The New South was not so new in many ways.

The repeated use of graphic accounts of torture and lynching of black men by white mobs allowed journalists to portray the South as a place where lawlessness reigned. The extralegal nature of mob violence made southern law enforcement seem powerless to act. Newspapers and magazines also noted when law enforcement officials gave their tacit approval to lynch mobs.

As it reported the case in which a group of white men bent on revenge for the disturbance of a "religious meeting in the neighborhood of Tiptonville" in Tennessee, the *Outlook*, a former Congregational journal edited by liberal Protestant thought's "champion popularizer," Lyman Abbott, and published in Boston, described how the mob captured three men, placed them in jail, and then got the local justice of the peace to set up a court in the middle of the night. The group selected twelve men as jury members and heard testimony from witnesses. Before state troops sent by the governor could arrive, "with shouts and with shooting of firearms the mob acted as executioner, and, dragging the negroes to a tree, hanged them there. This was something more than the usual exhibition of lawlessness."[22] An editorial in the *Nation* saw lynching as proceeding "with the steady march of lawlessness."[23] The 1904 lynching of two black men in Statesboro, Georgia, led the *Outlook* to proclaim that "cowardice is the companion of lawlessness, and courage the intimate of self-restraint."[24] The same event prompted the *Minneapolis Tribune* to argue that "this human degeneration is the inevitable fruit of indulgence in lawless violence."[25] And writing in 1918, when much of the world's attention was focused on events in Europe, the *World's Work* argued that every "lynching degrades the white men engaged in it, [and] lowers the morality and lawfulness of the community in which it occurs. . . ."[26] To the nonsouthern editor, reporter, and reader, it seemed that law and order had vanished across the South.[27]

Other events brought charges of lawlessness upon the South. Following the Atlanta race riots in 1906, commentators argued that the city of Atlanta had lost any semblance of law and order. The riots, which occurred in late September, were the result of a series of rumored attacks by black men on white women. The violence was actually perpetrated by whites on blacks, although white southerners did their best to make it seem as if blacks had instigated the mayhem. On September 22, 1906, several crowds of white men rampaged through the streets of Atlanta, attacking and killing black men wherever they found them. The *Washington Evening Star* reported, "Atlanta is in a reign of terror." As evidence, the paper noted that "the police reserves and fire department were called out and troops will be ordered on the streets to maintain order. The whole city is in a state of panic, and the authorities are not yet able to master the situation. . . ."[28] Readers in Chicago heard how "the police are powerless, and the city authorities are appealing frantically for troops."[29] By September 23, the day after the riots began, the *Boston Globe* reported that the city had returned to a relatively calm state, since Atlanta "was controlled by the police, aided by nearly a thousand of the state militia."[30] The mobs acted "in sheer savagery," the *New York Times* said.[31] The Atlanta riots in fact and in image helped make the South seem like a lawless place. Indeed, the *San Francisco Chronicle* reported that the mayhem seemed to be spreading across the South. According to the paper, there were fears that Memphis would follow Atlanta "in a lawless effort to suppress the race that seems to know no law save its own passions."[32] Both races, white and black, the paper believed, made the South a lawless region.

White-on-black violence was not the only activity that led to charges of lawlessness. The stories of feuding mountaineers emanating from the Appalachian Mountains helped reinforce the notion of lawlessness in the region. In 1885, the *Philadelphia Inquirer* reported the story of Pineville, Kentucky, where a man named Andrew J. Johnson "and ten or fifteen of his friends, were still in possession of Pineville, parading the streets with Winchester rifles." Johnson had reportedly killed a man and a child, and he and his mob held power over the local authorities. According to the *Inquirer*, "a reign of terror exists in the village."[33] Several years later, in 1893, the *New York Times* carried a story about a feud in Magoffin County, Kentucky. Apparently, a majority of the residents of the town of Salyersville were involved in the battle, and "there were eight or ten of the county's best-known citizens engaged on each side armed with repeating rifles and navy pistols."[34] In 1900, the *Nation* described recent violence in Kentucky over disputed elections, noting that "that is the Kentucky way of deciding important legal questions."[35] C. T. Revere, writing in *Outing* magazine, said that "during feud time, the combatants are regular walking arsenals," describing one man who had a total of "six revolvers in all" strapped to his body, as well as a rifle.[36] And in a 1902 piece about moonshiners in Tennessee, Leonidas Hubbard wrote in the *Atlantic Monthly* that "man killing in the mountains is common."[37] These stories and others showed how the citizens of Kentucky and Tennessee were inclined to take the law into their own hands, contributing to the picture of the South as a lawless frontier. The mention of the "best-known citizens" also implies that white southerners were less likely to emerge from their violent tendencies when they were exposed to the finer points of culture and social standing. If this is what the "best" people did, the accounts hinted, what could be expected of the less-educated and lower-class residents?

But the attention that these isolated feuds received paled in comparison to the coverage accorded to a brazen attack on a county court in Hillsville, Virginia, in 1912. As the judge was about to pass sentence upon a man newly convicted by a jury on a charge of obstruction of justice, a group of the defendant's relatives pulled out firearms and shot the judge, sheriff, and commonwealth's attorney to death. A young woman in the courtroom also received a fatal wound, as did one member of the jury. The attack, escape, and pursuit of the outlaws garnered nationwide attention for days. The *New York Times* gave a colorful synopsis of the shocking crime:

> Down to the quaint old red-brick Court House at Hillsville, the seat of Carroll County, where sentence was being pronounced upon one of their number, a troop of twenty mud-splashed mountaineers galloped in with rifles from the surrounding

hills early this morning, and in less time than it takes to tell it, the Judge upon the bench, the prosecutor before the bar, and the Sheriff at the door lay dead in the courtroom. Several of the jurors were shot, one probably mortally, and the prisoner was also wounded. The courtroom, which was crowded with country folks, was turned into a scene of panic and confusion.[38]

The *Boston Globe* noted that "the shooting paralyzed Hillsville with terror. There was not a man to give an order or organize a pursuit, people fled to places of safety, and mothers gathered up their children while the assassins rode out of town."[39] The same paper called the incident "unprecedented outlawry."[40] The *Washington Evening Star* was more optimistic in its assessment of the situation, noting that "a posse of citizens soon was in pursuit," but in an editorial, it called the crime an "extreme instance of gang violence on the part of a crude, lawless people."[41] The *New York Times* agreed, calling the "people of the Hillsville neighborhood . . . rude, unlettered, and traditionally lawless."[42] Whether they covered mob violence against blacks or whites, reporters from nonsouthern papers saw the South as a vigilante frontier, not a refined, aristocratic region. Indeed, even Virginia seemed to distance itself from its own residents. According to William Brown Meloney, writing in *Everybody's Magazine*, there was a common Virginia saying about Carroll County: "'Nothing good can come out of Carroll County.'"[43] The cavalier, Virginians said, was not kin to the cracker.[44]

In the midst of these violent outbreaks, the preachers of the South often received little credit for trying to stop the mayhem, nor did they often deserve any credit. Outside observers, and even some from the South, were quick to condemn men of the cloth for their lack of influence over their parishioners—which means that these writers believed that lynchers were indeed churchgoers. The occasional minister who condoned lynching was also the recipient of harsh words. For the most part, however, the popular media viewed the pulpit as ineffective in the effort to stop mob violence.

Occasionally accounts accused the clergy of tacit approval of lynching. In 1892, Frederick Douglass argued in the *North American Review* that lynch mobs in the South "simply obey the public sentiment of the South, the sentiment created by wealth and respectability, by the press and the pulpit."[45] Douglass clearly believed that white southern clergy were taking part in these murders by stirring up public opinion in favor of them. But he was not the only one to make this accusation. In 1894, the *Nation* chastised the Right Reverend Hugh Miller Thompson, Episcopal Bishop of Mississippi, for lauding lynch mobs as "people 'who save delay by simply resuming the natural sovereignty delegated by them to the courts, and hang the criminal.'"[46] In 1893, Atticus G. Haygood, bishop of the Methodist Episcopal Church, South, wrote an article for the *Forum* in which he defended the practice of lynching.[47] More than twenty years later, following the lynching of Leo Frank, several publications declared their horror at reports that a minister in Atlanta had preached a sermon in support of the lynching. Frank, a Jewish businessman from Brooklyn, was convicted of the rape and murder of one of his employees, Mary Phagan, and sentenced to life in prison. In 1915, a group of white men forcibly removed Frank from his jail cell (although there was little if any resistance from the jailers), and hung him from a tree. According to the *World's Work*, the "humiliating climax to the Frank lynching came in the shape of an Atlanta pastor's approval of the murder from the pulpit. A city in which a preacher can do that has at least some very rotten spots in its civilization."[48] The northern Methodist publication the *Christian Advocate*, published in New York, concluded that "the extent to which public sentiment is diseased is shown by the fact that a minister of Christ could applaud the lynching from an Atlanta pulpit!"[49] National Association of Colored Women honorary president Mary Terrell called her readers' attention to the fact that some ministers "actually condone the crime without incurring the displeasure of their congregations or invoking the censure of the church."[50] With allegations and examples like these, it was little wonder that, in 1924, pundit and curmudgeon H. L. Mencken attributed lynching and the rise of the Ku Klux Klan to ministers who "preached . . . the bitter, savage morality of the Old Testament. . . ." As chapter 5 will demonstrate, the head of the Ku Klux Klan in the 1920s was a former Methodist "exhorter," and reporters often mentioned that tie.[51]

It seemed to reporters that even the laity invoked divine approval of the lynchers' cause. In its coverage of the Leo Frank murder, the *Washington Post* quoted a Georgia woman as saying, "'I hate to hear of people being lynched. . . . But this—this is different. I think it is the justice of God.'"[52] In an even more morbid example, both the *Philadelphia Inquirer* and the *Atlanta Journal* reported that during the torture of Sam Hose a man praised God. According to the *Inquirer*, the "gray-haired old man yelled, 'Glory! Glory! This is God's vengeance!'" The *Journal* quoted the man as saying, "'Glory to God! . . . God bless every man who had a hand in this. Thank God for vengeance.'"[53] Mary Terrell, addressing Sam Hose's death, noted that it occurred on a Sunday, and that "special trains were made up to take the Christian people of Atlanta to the scene of the burning."[54] B. J. Ramage, writing about homicide in the South, put "ministers of the gospel" in his list of perpetrators.[55] Clearly, these periodicals implied, white ministers and their parishioners were involved to some degree in the mob violence so common in the South. The prevalence of these observations, combined with later perceptions of fundamentalism as intolerant and militant, would lead W. E. B. Du Bois to declare in 1925 that "Georgia's religion is . . . 'fundamental,'" as he tied Georgia Ku Klux Klan members to lynchings in the state. He concluded that "there is little hope in Georgia religion despite a light here and there."[56]

More common before World War I, however, was the view that lynch mobs had simply rejected the advice of the clergy. For example, the *Nation*, citing a lynching in Maysville, Kentucky, said mockingly in 1899 that "it is no wonder the clergy call for more Bible-reading" but predicted that would do little to stem the tide, adding that "Methodists and Baptists among us hold up their hands over the atrocities of the Inquisition in Spain," compared to which the "atrocities" of lynching were even worse.[57] Three years later, the *Nation* reported that a 1902 mob in Leesburg, Virginia, "consisted largely of men of standing and education, and . . . they acted with deliberation after refusing to heed earnest appeals from preachers and laymen to let the law take its course."[58] The *Methodist Advocate Journal*, a publication of the Methodist Episcopal Church, South, reprinted a letter from Booker T. Washington, who pointed out that several lynchings in Alabama in 1904 had taken place "in sight of a Christian church."[59] Ray Stannard Baker's article for *McClure's Magazine*, which was published in New York and famous for its "muckraking" exposés, provided a similar scenario. A mob had gathered to lynch two black men in Statesboro, Georgia, in 1904 for murdering a man by the last name of Hodges. According to Baker, "a brother of the murdered Hodges, a minister from Texas, rose splendidly to the occasion. With tears streaming down his face, he begged the mob to let the law take its course." But the minister's pleas went unheeded, and instead he heard the response from the crowd: "'We don't want religion, we want blood.'"[60]

Underlying these indictments of southern religion and society was an assumption that the overwhelming majority of white southerners were indeed church members. Some southerners reinforced this notion, including the noted pundit and essayist Walter Hines Page. Writing for the *Forum*, published in New York City, Page described a typical town where a lynching had occurred. The residents, he claimed, "all belong to the churches, with hardly an exception, but the keepers of the groggeries, and the most frequent little jars in the social life of the town are caused by the friction of the church-cliques or an argument about theology." Page ascribed great influence to the preachers of the South, saying that the "preacher is in certain ways a greater power in most Southern communities than in any other part of the country."[61] Unfortunately, it appeared that preachers, despite their desire to the contrary, could not summon their great power to halt the onslaught of lynchings. Page, a man born in the South, had a more forgiving view of his fellow white southerners even as he called them to task for their lack of moral leadership.

Other observers of the South were not so kind. Columbia sociologist Franklin H. Giddings, ignoring the large population of African Americans in the

South, deemed homogeneity the essence of white southern society and the cause of the southern propensity for lynching. According to Giddings,

> The rural community is relatively homogeneous. The "neighbors" for miles in every direction are nearly all of one blood. . . . For the most part they are of one religious confession or of two or three confessions not very unlike in creeds and practices. . . . An exciting event or suggestion that moves one will, almost certainly, move the others.[62]

The notion of the South as religiously uniform also entered the observations of Ray Stannard Baker's article on lynching. As he described the residents of Statesboro, Georgia, he claimed that "fully seventy percent of the inhabitants are church members—Baptists, Presbyterians, and Methodists—and the town has not had a saloon in twenty-five years and rarely has a case of drunkenness."[63] Northerners clearly believed that most white southerners were church members, but they were unsure what effect that church attendance had on the moral character of the parishioners.

This image of lackluster preaching and absence of moral leadership stands in stark contrast to the pictures painted of white southern clergy as they campaigned for prohibition measures and the image of white southern preachers once fundamentalism made its public appearance. The idea that the South was particularly religious and dry was already a popular notion by the early 1900s, but the preachers were seen as less powerful only in certain instances and not in others. Outside observers saw the white southern clergy as both powerless and theocratic at once. In the eyes of the North, the white ministers of the South were unable to effect significant social change, but they were able to command great power in matters of individual morality. The inability to change society frightened northern authors who believed firmly in the need for rational thought and social betterment, while the image of a theocratic class ran counter to the American ideal of the separation of church and state. Even though the Protestant majority in this country has managed to blur that distinction between church and state, as Roman Catholics and other religious minorities have been painfully aware, there was a limit to how powerful Protestants wanted their clergy to be. For them, the white southern clergy came too close to this line for comfort. The outside commentators sent mixed messages of their views on theocracy. On one hand, they were opposed to it, but on the other, they wanted the clergy to exercise its "great" power against lynching.

To be sure, white southern ministers occasionally received credit for trying to stop lynch mobs or for preaching sermons condemning mob justice. The *Nation*, which never missed a chance to criticize the South, reported in 1906 on some "refreshingly vigorous [anti-lynching] resolutions passed by the Etowah [Alabama] County Bar Association," which called on the "minister to instill a better spirit into the youth of the community."[64] Ten years later, the *Nation* relied on southern informants to apprise it of clerical efforts against lynching, noting that a Presbyterian minister in Waco led a group of clergy in the denunciation of a proposed lynching.[65] Occasionally other publications would give attention to religious efforts in the South to stop mob violence.[66]

For the most part, however, the press viewed the preachers as unable to play their proper role in guiding the moral development of southern society. After the murder of Sam Hose, the *San Francisco Chronicle* carried an impassioned editorial that questioned the lack of moral leadership in the South and even faulted northern denominations for their inaction:

> The churches protest the savagery of the Turk. Where are the pulpits that will thunder against the deviltry of white Americans? We call to mind no pulpit eloquence that made the Texarkana tragedies their theme. We do not remember that missionaries were sent to Texas after a negro had been roasted at the stake in a public market place, while white demons danced about the sizzling pyre. We do not believe that any white preacher, mindful of the political ire he might arouse, will venture to condemn the death orgy of Sunday afternoon. Yet there can be no cause of pagan redemption or of apostolic duty which is more importunate to honest minds than that of opening the Darkest South to the spirit of Christian civilization.[67]

And in 1897, a writer in the *Atlantic Monthly* decried the "baleful ignorance" in the southern "pulpit" as the reason that white southern clergy did not do more against mob violence.[68]

In this respect, nonsouthern opinions of the South closely followed the Social Gospel and liberal Protestant notions that the clergy and the church should lead the effort to improve social conditions and bring about the Kingdom of God on earth. As one historian has explained, the leaders of the Social Gospel were clergy who believed "wholeheartedly in progress. . . . they were so confident of human goodness as to be sure that men could be educated to choose the good and contribute directly to 'the building of the kingdom.'"[69] Such an argument pervaded the commentary on the South's continued propensity for mob violence. Indeed, in this instance, liberal Protestant thought argued that religion should dictate to culture—that the Christian religion held certain values that society must also hold fast to in order for civilization to continue. And if religion were to dictate culture in this case, the clergy needed to be leaders of the corporate reform of American society. A belief in the power of education to ameliorate social ills and a confidence that things could get better permeated the commentary of these optimistic writers whose opinions appeared in denominational and secular publications.

Writers called upon white southerners to exercise "Christian tolerance" in their relations with blacks.[70] A white southerner, John Carlisle Kilgo, who was a

Methodist minister and President of Trinity College (later Duke University), writing in the *South Atlantic Quarterly*, extolled the virtues of liberal Protestant theology as he called on the South to strengthen itself through uplift and education:

> Southern society will be stronger when it becomes less sensitive and excitable, and not only will the evil of lynchings be corrected, but every phase of social life will be improved. Partizanships [sic], social distinctions, religious antagonisms, in fact, all the evils that spring from this peculiar sensitiveness will pass away.[71]

Kilgo's forecast for the future of the South sounds like a sermon from Social Gospel leaders Walter Rauschenbusch or Washington Gladden. Kilgo called on the South to use Social Gospel methods to alleviate its current problems and to improve society.

Kilgo was not alone in his belief in the power of education. A reader of the *Nation* wrote to the editor to suggest that education would stop lynching. According to S. R. Taber of Lake Forest, Illinois, some teachers in the South were already seeing progress by using animals as "object-lessons in the teaching of justice and kindness to our brothers of the air and of the field."[72] Mr. Taber believed that a lesson in animal rights would help white southerners learn how to treat their fellow humans better. Following the death of Sam Hose, the editor of the *Methodist Protestant* (a northern Methodist paper published in Baltimore) argued that "patience, justice, religion, must rule the white man; education, moral training, and religious instruction must be given the colored race. . . ."[73] A "Southern Lawyer" writing for the *Sewanee Review* argued that "the whole system of public instruction ought to be reconstructed" in order to stop the cycle of crimes and lynching, placing the blame for lynching both on whites who lynched and blacks who allegedly committed crimes that led to lynchings.[74] And in 1916, the *Literary Digest* reported on an effort in North Carolina to get "the college men" to help stop lynching, as "they should be 'in the front ranks of those fighting for moral and social progress.'"[75] These writers believed that justice and kindness were in short supply in the South and that an infusion of such qualities would alleviate the racial tensions and ease, if not erase, the tendency toward violence.

The Social Gospel movement was not the only one to color perceptions about the South. A report in the *Survey* in 1916 included an allusion to Auguste Comte's Religion of Humanity. At the meeting of the Southern Sociological Congress in New Orleans, W. D. Weatherford, "field executive secretary of the Robert E. Lee Hall of the Blue Ridge Association and author of several books on Negro life," addressed the participants. According to the magazine, Weatherford called on the South to recognize the "sacredness" of personality. "'Personality,'" Weatherford reasoned, "'must become sacred in our eyes. . . . The law of sacredness of personality knows no class distinctions, it knows no aristocracy, and it knows no race differences.'"[76] The presence of such a strongly positivist statement in a national magazine is important for two reasons. First, it shows the willingness that the *Survey* had to publish a notion that humanity could be sacred. Second, it demonstrates that Comtean ideas had permeated all regions of the country, not just the intellectual circles in New York City and Boston. Alternative thoughts about how to organize civilization and society had a wide range, and they show that the North and the South had more common ground than the culturally orthodox generally believed.[77]

The prevalence of violent deaths, however, led many authors to argue that the region lacked civilization. Indeed, the apparent loss of civilization in a country that prided itself as a city on a hill, a shining example to the world, was frightening for most journalists. Mob rule had eliminated from the South the trappings of an advanced culture and had plunged the region instead into chaos and barbarism. The lawlessness of lynching parties was held up as an example of how the white South was in desperate need of uplift and progress, which could best be provided by northerners who would help restore civilized society to the South.

Calls for the South to improve its level of civilization regularly followed widely publicized lynchings. After the death of Sam Hose, the *Boston Globe* asserted that the lynching "brutalize[d] society as a whole," and mourned that "it is deplorable that we still have to wait, with what patience we can, for any American community to learn this simple and primary lesson of civilization."[78] The *Washington Post* called the lynching "a disgrace to our civilization," while the *Chicago Tribune* found it "almost inconceivable in these days of enlightenment that men professing to be civilized can be found practicing cruelties more revolting than those of the Apaches."[79] Writing for the *North American Review* in 1905, Cardinal Gibbons, Roman Catholic prelate and "the last archbishop . . . to exercise *de facto* primacy among fellow bishops," called the outbreak of lynchings in the South "a blot on our American civilization."[80] The editor of the *Newark Star* called a 1915 Georgia lynching of a "father, son, and two daughters" "the most appalling outrage upon civilization in the hideous annals of lynch law."[81]

Writers and editors for the *Nation* also used the terms "barbarism" and "barbaric" in describing the South. In 1893, the magazine referred to lynching in defense of women's honor as a "relic of barbarism of which the South must rid itself."[82] Six years later, in 1899, it called lynching "simply a descent into barbarism by people who pretend to be civilized," and in 1917, it asked rhetorically "how long . . . this disgraceful, barbaric practice" would be tolerated. There were many additional accusations of barbarism.[83]

Other lynchings, especially that of Leo Frank, brought a great outcry about the lack of southern civilization. Following that event, Arthur Page, editor of the *World's Work* and son of Walter Hines Page, boldly stated that "the State of Georgia needs a heavy inoculation of civilization. The chief virus in that inoculation is education and the broadening of viewpoint that comes with it."[84] Congregational minister Lyman Abbott wrote in *Outlook* that "Georgia, as a State, has abandoned civilized government. In exigencies, Georgia has proved that she will have recourse, not to civilization, but to the mob."[85] In Abbott's mind, Georgia had lagged behind the rest of the country and provided an example of what Christianity needed to remedy.

Events other than lynchings made outside observers question the quality of civilization in the South. The Atlanta race riots of 1906 had a similar effect, with the *Chicago Daily Tribune* stating that "the Atlanta outbreak almost inclines one to doubt the value of civilization."[86] An editorial writer for the *Churchman*, the denominational newspaper of the northern branch of the Episcopal Church, believed the riots signaled that "a peril to our civilization is imminent."[87] The *Philadelphia Inquirer* called into question the rationality of southerners, saying they had acted in "an unreasoning, mad frenzy."[88]

The murders in Hillsville, Virginia, led the *Washington Evening Star* to report that "that particular part of Virginia has never been brought into close contact with the refinements of civilization."[89] According to the *Boston Globe*, the fault for the Hillsville massacre lay with the Commonwealth of Virginia. The editorial held,

> No civilized community, small or large, can afford to let any considerable number of its inhabitants remain unassimilated, and the State must represent to them not only law, order and equal justice, but also helpfulness, kindness and sympathy. Especially it must educate them and change their point of view.[90]

These confidences in education, broadened horizons, and uplift reflect the reporters' bias toward liberal Protestant theology and its accompanying assumptions about human society and the improvement of civilization.[91]

The questions about the "civilization" of white southerners were raised at the same time that white Americans in general were calling into question the "civilization" of millions of Eastern European Jews and Catholics who were flocking to the United States in search of a better life. A best-selling book during this period, Josiah Strong's *Our Country*, held that Anglo-Saxon Americans needed to assimilate these new immigrants, replacing their old and apparently undemocratic religions with "pure *spiritual* Christianity"—that is, Protestantism.[92] The expression of doubts about white southerners' civilization, which had, presumably, been influenced by this same "pure spiritual Christianity," indicates that nonsouthern commentators were formulating their own ideas about the identity of Americans. To them, ideal Americans were Protestant, white, and preferably Anglo-Saxon in origin and valued literacy, the careful meting out of justice, and intellectual rather than emotional response to problems. Southerners as they were perceived at the time did not fit this of an "American."

As writers struggled for ways to place the violence into a historical context, many turned to the analogy of the South being trapped in the Dark Ages or Middle Ages (using the terms synonymously, they tended to blur the distinction between these two periods). One writer even likened white southerners to cave men who killed with clubs and in groups.[93] The terms "medieval" and "feudal" would make an appearance again as writers began to perceive the South as the home of fundamentalism, and the likening of lynch mobs to the Inquisition of the late medieval period also had echoes in the accounts of the Scopes Trial. The variety of analogies the writers employed conveys both a sense that they saw no distinction between barbarity in previous periods and a sense that historical periods that came before can be blurred together as long as the present age embodies civilized ideals. The lack of distinction between historical epochs demonstrates that for these writers the barbarity they witnessed was proof of a lack of civilization. Any prior period that demonstrated barbarity could be classified as uncivilized, and the differences among those periods were irrelevant.

According to one editorial in the *Nation*, members of lynch mobs were like the audiences at Roman fights, in that "what they want to see is a haunted man in terror of his life, or a human body torn to pieces without fear of consequences."[94] Following a lynching in Kentucky in 1899, the *Nation* asked, "[W]hat were the atrocities of the Inquisition in Spain, and what are the atrocities of arbitrary power *anywhere*, compared to the atrocities of lynching mobs among us?"[95] The *Nation* was hardly alone. The Sam Hose murder left the editor of the *Washington Evening Star* wondering whether the current epidemic of awful violence would lead to something worse:

> The stories told of the Inquisition, of African cannibals, of the Roman emperors, of the fanatical Aztecs, of all the savage and barbaric peoples who have left records for blood-lust to stain the pages of history, warrant the expectation that even this abomination may be soon exceeded by another, more sickening in its methods, more revolting in the spectacle of the pleasure of presumably civilized men and women in the torture of a fellow-being.[96]

B. O. Flowers, founder and editor of the Boston-based liberal *Arena*, compared white southerners' abuse of power to other examples in history: "Witness Nero and Rome under the Caesars. Witness the Spanish Inquisition; the struggle with Spain in the Netherlands, and the French Revolution."[97] The Jesse Washington lynching in Waco in 1916 prompted the *New Republic* to liken the affair to "a sort of a social orgy of cruelty, a communal auto-da-fé," while the *Nation* worried that "there is not evidence that these cruelties of the Middle Ages will soon cease."[98] But three years later, the *World's Work* was still calculating lynching statistics and commenting that the practice seemed to "belong to some age much darker than we like to consider our own."[99]

Southern writers were often the most brutal in their assessment of the lack of civilization in their region and their belief that the South had entered a period like the Dark Ages. The appearance of such indictments of the South by southerners raises the question of whether the authors spoke for a majority of white southerners or northern editors published their views because they believed their readers wanted to read such articles. Regardless of the motivation of the editors and the opinions of white southerners, commentaries critical of the South written by white southerners were commonplace before World War I. For instance, Chief Justice of the Georgia Supreme Court L. E. Bleckley argued in the *Forum* that "lynching is barbaric, anarchic, and wrong *per se*." He went on to categorize evil and state that lynching "belongs to the darker and deeper of the two classes of criminal conduct into which human wickedness has been divided; it is not merely *malum prohibitum*; it is *malum in se*."[100] Bleckley contended that lynching was not just wrong—it was evil. Southern Methodist bishop Atticus G. Haygood, in an article in which he defended lynching, denounced the practice of burning someone alive. For Haygood, such an activity was "so much of the Dark Ages surviving in modern and civilized life."[101]

Haygood was not the only clergyman in the South to compare contemporary conditions with the Dark Ages. The Reverend Quincy Ewing, an Episcopal minister in Greenville, Mississippi, compared the recent disenfranchisement of blacks in that state with a spirit "that was dominant in Europe in the Dark Ages—that ruled France more than five hundred years ago." Ewing, whose comments were published in the *World's Work*, likened the state to "Verdun [in Medieval France] where the Jews, mad with agony, huddled together in a tower of refuge, hurled down their children to the howling mob, hoping thus, vainly, to satiate their greed for Jewish blood."[102]

Some writers compared the hysteria of lynch mobs to that of the Salem witch hunts. A southern reader of the *Nation* in 1916 argued that "much of our lynching evil is simple mass-nervousness, like the somewhat similar witch-burnings of the past."[103] And sociologist George Elliott Howard of the University of Nebraska, writing in the *American Journal of Sociology*, said that the thirteen Georgia lynchings in the first seven months of 1916 "may be due, like the witchcraft craze at Salem, to special local suggestion," a form of "belated mania."[104]

Denominational newspapers also carried condemnations of lynching and violence from southern writers. The *Baptist and Reflector*, a Southern Baptist publication, called the Sam Hose and other lynchings "a severe reflection upon our boasted American civilization and suggest the inquiry if we are really a Christian nation."[105] According to the Baptist *Biblical Recorder* (published in North Carolina), "Southern civilization is threatened wherever lynching has an advocacy or an extenuation." Worried about the recent Atlanta riots, the *Biblical Recorder* asked what good could come from the South when "a blood-lust and a savagery . . . can riot almost without restraint in the very center of the leading, most be-churched city of the South?"[106] The riots also greatly disturbed the editor of the *Southern Churchman*, who asked, "[H]ow can a civilized, Christian community relapse so suddenly and so completely into a reign of lawlessness?"[107]

Indeed, both northern and southern observers often refused to believe that anyone who was at all educated could perpetrate such crimes. Instead, they saw lynch mobs as made up of lower-class citizens of the South—poor whites who lacked proper moral direction. White southern writers who attempted to explain the causes of lynching to their nonsouthern audience were the most likely to attribute the problem to the lower classes. Northern editors tended to accept this explanation, but the lynching of Leo Frank, with its obvious coordination with law enforcement officials, would call the assumption into question.

Writing for white southerners who saw lynch mob participants as lower class, white southern pastor William Hayne Levell provided an account of a lynching in Carrollton, Mississippi, for the *Outlook* in 1901. The Reverend Levell, who was a Presbyterian from Houston, Texas, explained that lower-class citizens approved of lynching in virtually any circumstance, but "the greater part of the educated, conservative, thoughtful, and in ordinary situations, more influential citizens" only approved of lynching in the case of the rape of a white woman.[108] The *Birmingham (Alabama) Age-Herald*, quoted in the *Nation*, argued that "'lynching bees . . . have become the pastime of the rougher element of a community. They seize upon each and every occasion for that purpose. Excitement is what they want—pastime and recreation.'"[109] Emory College professor Andrew Sledd echoed these sentiments in a 1902 article in the *Atlantic Monthly*. According to Sledd, "lynchings are the work of our lower and lowest classes." He continued:

> What these classes are is hardly comprehensible to one who has not lived among them and dealt with them. Wholly ignorant, absolutely without culture, apparently without even the capacity to appreciate the nicer feelings or higher sense, yet conceited on account of the white skin which they continually dishonor, they make up, when aroused, as wild and brutal a mob as ever disgraced the face of the earth. For them, lynching is not "justice," however rude; it is a wild and diabolical carnival of blood.[110]

Lynch mobs were not only the manifestation of lower class white violence. According to white southern writers, lower-class whites were also to blame for the Atlanta race riots. Lawyer Hooper Alexander, writing in the *Outlook*, held that the riot "was wholly wanting in responsible leadership, was lawlessness pure and simple, with no redeeming motive, and sprang from an unmitigated race hatred." Interestingly, Alexander defended lynch mobs, arguing that most were led by men "of at least comparative prominence in their several communities. . . ."[111] A north-ern correspondent for *Harper's Weekly*, published in New York, echoed Alexander's class sentiments about the Atlanta riots and reported that the mob "was composed principally of the very worst classes, with a large percentage of irresponsible boys."[112] It still appeared to outside observers that the majority of lynchers were poor whites and not the South's educated elite.

The death of Leo Frank in 1915 called attention to the complicity of law enforce-ment officials in his death and in lynching in general. The lack of resistance by jail-ers led to the inevitable conclusion that more than just poor whites were involved in mob murders. What other accounts had hinted at could now be ignored no longer—the "better class" of whites was involved in lynchings. After Frank's mur-der, the *Literary Digest*, a New York–based publication, reported on editorial reac-tions from across the country, noting that "we find lynching defended, or at least partially justified, by both newspapers and citizens of repute."[113] The *Independent* asked, "[H]ow can Georgia wipe out the stain?" and answered the question, "only by finding out, as can easily be done, who were the 'best citizens' guilty of this dastardly crime, and then sending them to prison for long terms."[114] After the lynching of Jesse Washington in Waco, Texas, in 1916, the *New Republic* rejected the notion that "Southern lynchings are usually ascribed to the class of 'cracker' farmers, illiterate whites of old 'American' stock." Instead, it noted that "the pictures of the Waco hor-ror showed a typical straw-hatted summer crowd gazing gleefully at the hideous crisp of what was once a negro youth."[115] And the *Independent* carried an article about a county judge and constable who threatened to lynch a representative of the National Association for the Advancement of Colored People when he visited Austin, Texas in 1919.[116]

By the outbreak of the First World War, the South had already proven, in the eyes of nonsouthern journalists, that it was unarguably alien. White southerners lacked a fair system of justice, advocated mob rule and death by torture, and killed each other with seeming impunity. Their religious leaders, according to both outside and inside accounts, were either ineffectual men or wielders of absolute power who abetted such a way of life. And the lower classes were no longer the only ones to blame for the reign of violence that seemed to grip the region. The best and the brightest of the South had blood on their hands. These images appeared in virtually every facet of American print journalism at the end of the nineteenth and the begin-ning of the twentieth centuries. A literate person could hardly miss the accounts of cruel and awful events in the South, and new publishing styles such as large head-lines and shortened editorials helped editors streamline and deliver their message with a new clarity. The South was different from the rest of the country, they informed their readers. It was violent and intolerant. It was brutal and uncivilized. Its lawlessness could only spread like a disease across the nation.[117]

The ineffectiveness of civilizing forces of American culture, including religion, in the South was largely explained through the observation that the region lacked the educational resources that the rest of the nation took for granted. If southerners would only embrace education, the reasoning went, they would be less likely to maim, feud, and torture. There was a very real educational achievement gap between the South and the rest of the country, but once again, the image of the region that emerged from the print media was that of a distorted, funhouse mirror that accentuated both the illiteracy of the region and the power of reason to achieve peace and prosperity. The next chapter will discuss this educational gap and its perceived effects more fully.

CHAPTER 2

"The School Backward, the People Illiberal": The Uneducated South

I n 1923, W. E. B. Du Bois, writing in the *New Republic*, called for a third political party in the South, one that would help to reenfranchise blacks and ameliorate social problems. In indicting the Democratic Party in the South, Du Bois wrote:

> The Southern states . . . have failed to consider great national issues . . . [and] have lamentably failed in their local legislation. . . . Murder in the South outruns the record of all civilization; education, while making noticeable and commendable progress, still lags so far behind the nation that the South is still the seat of the greatest ignorance even among white Americans. . . .[1]

Du Bois's comments were representative of the national image of the South and its educational system. While many commentators found signs of improvement, the South continued to post appalling educational statistics, and, to the dismay of many outside observers, conducted its society in a way that they believed ran counter to the civilizing effects of education, thus providing further evidence that the South was uneducated and therefore uncivilized.

The reality that the South faced great educational difficulties that far exceeded the challenges in the North and the notion that these deficiencies created the majority of the region's problems were nearly universal in the late nineteenth and early twentieth centuries. Through the use of statistics, graphic descriptions, and allusions to lost potential, northern writers created an image of the South as benighted, ignorant, and lost. The South desperately needed schooling, schools, and books in order to be reintegrated into the national fabric. The northern indictors had a variety of reasons for pointing to education as the remedy to the South's problems, but they all seemed to agree that education was the answer. Southern commentators and academics were nearly unanimous in their belief that the South needed educational improvement to solve its problems. In part, these writers' acceptance of the liberal Protestant emphasis on schools as the method of bringing civilization to a people meant that they could not and did not dispute the northern charges against their region. Instead, they served as coprosecutors.

Critics held that education would uplift the masses of white southerners and southern society in general. Social problems like lynching and mob violence would wither away in the light of a strong system of education.[2] With the vanishing of social problems would come a flowering of southern literature and art. The improvement of society would make the South more like the rest of the country, the northern writers reasoned, and thus restore the American character to a region that the *Nation* described in 1905 as "a land devastated, drenched in blood, robbed of the flower of its youth, crushed by poverty, dependence, and ignorance. . . ."[3]

Many observers, both contemporary and historical, have noted the gap between the South and the rest of the country in terms of education. The South, which had never had a strong tradition of universal schooling before the Civil War, reluctantly came to accept the practice for a variety of reasons. As one historian of education in the South has explained, "the rise of universal education in the 'New South' is best viewed as several educational movements by different and conflicting classes for different social purposes."[4] Freed slaves, populists, and northern reformers all had different reasons for supporting better access to education in the South, and their varying reasons had conflicting results. Race relations in the South made white southerners fearful of almost any effort to educate blacks, and northern educational reform efforts resulted in a white southern backlash, as "politicians, businessmen, school superintendents, editors, and university men portrayed the whole reform movement as Northern meddling."[5]

The southern debate over education and its role in the South received much attention in the national media. Once again, however, blacks were largely absent from the discussion. Northern writers, heavily influenced by the New England ideal of universal schooling, the Protestant need for a literate populace, and the progressive movement in American education (which held that education improved society), berated the South for its seemingly stubborn opposition to the schooling of its poorest residents, both black and white.[6] In magazines and journals, they cited a series of statistics to demonstrate that the South was uneducated. Blanket statements about southern educational deficiencies often accompanied these statistics, and northern editors frequently included descriptions of the challenging conditions that students in the South faced. The deficiencies, the writers believed, were signs that the southern educational system was failing to mold society in the way it should. As John Dewey, American philosopher and advocate of the progressive movement in education, explained, "'education is the fundamental method of social progress and reform.'"[7] If the school were lacking, it could not properly shape society.

Northern writers also used the residents of Appalachia as evidence of what happened to an Anglo-Saxon people who were isolated from education and progress in general. The mountaineers were ethnically identical to the New England elites, these writers argued, but a lack of the civilizing influence of education had arrested their development and prevented them from achieving their true potential. The geography of the mountains, combined with a distinctively southern lack of educational opportunities, had stunted the intellectual growth of the mountaineers.

In the midst of this discussion about the South's lack of educational prowess and the stultifying effects of mountain living, northern writers also managed to indict white southern preachers once again. This time, the observers argued, these preachers were failing to realize their role as educators. If only the ministers would take a greater part in educating the population, the argument went, southern morals and hygiene would improve. The image that emerged long before the 1925 Scopes Trial in Tennessee was that of an uneducated South, arrested in its intellectual development and desperate in its need for assistance and civilization. White southern educator Edgar W. Knight described the South in 1922 as a region in which "the school [was] backward, the people illiberal."[8]

Foremost in the critics' method of depicting southern education as lacking was the use of statistics that made the South appear to be hopelessly ignorant. These statistics were cited in a variety of publications by a variety of authors (both northern and often southern, who had bought into the notion that education was the remedy for the South's ills) for at least two decades beginning at the very end of the nineteenth century. Influenced by the progressive movement in education, writers relied on these statistics as scientific proof of an inherent problem south of the Mason-Dixon Line. They employed the new social sciences and their attendant data to discredit the educational system of the South.[9]

Writing from New York, Walter Hines Page, expatriate white southerner and editor of the *World's Work*, led the charge. In a 1902 editorial entitled "The Real Southern Question Again," Page began with the cautionary statement that in the South

(1) Adult white illiteracy is as great as it was before the Civil War; *and*
(2) The total public school expenditure in these States is five cents a day
      per pupil for only eighty-seven days a year.

Page continued to cite additional statistics to prove that education was deficient in the South, including the allegation that "one half of the Negro children and one white child in five never gets a chance to learn to read."[10]

Liberal commentator Lyman Abbott used his *Outlook* magazine to publicize information that demonstrated problems afoot, this time information gleaned from the Co-operative Education Commission of Virginia. According to Abbott, "only one-half of the children of school age are enrolled [in a public school], and only one-third in daily attendance for an average period of five and a half months of the year."[11] Writing for the New York–based *North American Review* in 1909, David Y. Thomas (a native Kentuckian, educated at Columbia, and working at the University of Arkansas) gave a dizzying list of numbers to illustrate that southern education suffered because the federal cotton tax was not returned to the states from which it was collected. According to Thomas, salaries paid to teachers in the South were especially low: the monthly "salaries ranged from $25.96 for males and $23.20 for females in South Carolina to $55.24 and $43.27 in Texas." This relatively coherent statistic was followed by a more confusing list:

> The per capita wealth of Georgia was $488; the smallest in any of the States under consideration was $403 in Mississippi; the largest, $841 in Texas. The school revenue of Georgia for each child was $2.74, or $1.83 for each $1,000 of wealth. The lowest was $1.92 in Alabama, or $1.29 for each $1,000 of wealth; the highest, $5.37 in Texas, or $2.13 for each $1,000 of wealth. In the distribution of the cotton tax, Alabama would be entitled to $10,338,072; Texas to $5,505,401.[12]

Even if his numbers overwhelmed the reader, Thomas conveyed the general gist of his argument well—the South was poor, and its schools needed help. His intentions may have been noble—to secure more money for financially strapped southern schools—but in his quest, Thomas helped to build the image of the impoverished South that neglected education.

The United States government also added its own statistics. By "measuring" the extent of southern educational deficiencies, the government helped to lend the notion of "scientific" analysis to the problem. In 1914, the *U.S. Bureau of Education Bulletin* reported that South Carolina, Georgia, Florida, Alabama, Mississippi, and Texas had no compulsory attendance laws and that between 1900 and 1910 there had been no decrease in the number of white male illiterates in Alabama and Mississippi, while South Carolina and Louisiana had increases in white male illiterates.[13] A report in the *Bulletin* of 1915 noted that in the southern Appalachian Mountains, "of the native white people 10 years of age or over in 1910, 15.9 per cent in the 98 'mountain counties' were illiterate," while the states that were home to the southern Appalachians maintained an overall adult illiteracy rate of "9.3 per cent."[14]

This march of statistics continued steadily over time and in a variety of publications. In 1914, Walter A. Dyer, writing in the *World's Work*, claimed that the 1910 census "showed that in North Carolina alone there were 122,189 grown white people who could neither read nor write."[15] In 1917, Littell McClung, special correspondent from Montgomery, Alabama, wrote in the *Outlook* that "Alabama, as she herself fully admits, is down close to the bottom of the list of States made up according to literacy tests." He continued that "ten per cent of the children were, according to recent statistics, illiterate." Additionally, McClung noted that "the total number of illiterates in the State was 360,000."[16] And in 1921, *School and Society*, a journal published in New York City by the Society for the Advancement of Education, carried an article entitled "Backward North Carolina," which cited a "press bulletin" from the University of North Carolina claiming that North Carolina teacher salaries were the lowest in the nation. The editors then put the statistics into a more accessible yet inflammatory context. According to their calculation, teachers in North Carolina were "paid less than its costs to feed prisoners in the county jails."[17] In 1922, the *Nation* declared that Mississippi's "educational appropriation" of "$7.49 per 'educable child'" was "the second lowest in the country."[18] The steady drumbeat of statistics continued, especially after the Scopes Trial, which lent new ammunition to the forces of educational reform. For example, one editorial in a 1925 issue of the *World's Work* noted that Tennessee was forty-forth of forty-eight states in a ranking of public school systems.[19]

The common assumption of these writers was that their use of statistics had demonstrated in a scientific way the educational gap between North and South.[20] Their constant use of statistics portrayed white southerners as people who cared little for education. Articles frequently referred to southerners as ignorant or uneducated.[21] Editors and writers also employed blanket statements about the impoverished educational (and sometimes living) conditions that southerners faced to prove their point that the South needed a good dose of education. Often the most damning of these statements came from white southerners themselves; tired of the South's social ills, they squarely placed the blame on the region's educational system. Here, like the critics who cited statistics, white southern commentators gave full credit to the progressive notion that the roots of the South's problems were almost always educational in nature. In an 1890 article in the Boston-based *New England Magazine*, the Reverend A. D. Mayo gave a depressing picture of the conditions southerners faced in trying to get to school, if they so desired. Mayo depicted the South as a region that was entirely rural:

> The South, in winter, outside the towns, lies under a fearful embargo of mud, which shuts up the people to such a home life as can be enjoyed under the circumstances. The average country school does not last a full four months, is placed at inconvenient distances, often kept in an unfit schoolhouse—a peril to the health of the children of the poorer people.[22]

According to Andrew Sledd, Professor of Latin at Emory College in Atlanta, "the South [was] the most ignorant section of the Union." Sledd went on to explain that this dismal state of affairs was the result of "a *defective public sentiment*, supported on either hand by ignorance and indifference."[23] Not surprisingly, Sledd's comments were not welcome in the South. Following his 1902 article in the *Atlantic Monthly* condemning the practice of lynching, Sledd was the victim of vitriolic attacks by his fellow white southerners. He eventually left his post at Emory for Yale University.[24] But despite Sledd's departure, dismal reports continued to appear in northern periodicals. In 1903, the *Outlook* stated that the "wasted wealth and crushed spirits of a people proud and brave" had led to North Carolina's being "the very citadel of illiteracy and educational insufficiency."[25]

Other writers gave different reasons for the South's failure to embrace education as the North did. A 1905 editorial in the *Nation* attributed the problem to a number of causes, including "poverty," "apathy," and the presence of blacks, "whom bigoted members of the superior race would keep in ignorance, on the theory that schools are too expensive a luxury for black folk."[26] Hindsight shows that racial tension in the South did in fact create a two-tiered system of education that served neither race well. But southern black educational leaders would find only limited sympathy in the North. Writing in the same year that the *Nation* blamed race for the South's lack of education, Agnes Valentine Kelley of Meadville, Pennsylvania, wrote in the Boston-based *Arena*, which concentrated on social reform, that the cause was simply poverty. She held that "no people in the confines of our republic are more eager or anxious for education to-day than the white citizens of the rural districts of Louisiana, Alabama, and adjoining states."[27] In the white South's own *Sewanee Review*, published by the University of the South in Sewanee, Tennessee, and devoted largely to literature, Frank T. Carlton of Toledo, Ohio, attributed the educational difficulties to the lack of industrialization in the South. "The South is in a very backward condition in regard to general public education," Carlton wrote, arguing that mill owners and other industrialists needed to focus on bolstering "common schools."[28]

One writer, who declined to sign her article for the New York weekly magazine the *Independent*, laid the blame at the feet of class warfare. This writer, who claimed to be "connected with one of the leading Southern educational institutions," asserted that "class prejudice . . . is so strong that the Southerner possessed of ancestry can hardly conceive the desirability of an educated working class." She also blamed the otherworldliness of southern religion, arguing that the rich white "wants his poor white brother to go to heaven . . . because the average Southerner is both religious and kind-hearted, but the idea of making the 'poor white' a factor in the betterment of this present world has not yet strongly appealed to him."[29] The link that critics of the South had made between "southern" piety and social movements will be explored more fully later in this chapter, but it was tied to a liberal Protestant belief that education in the South had failed to attain a modern, more mature conception of religion—one in which the believer sought to bring about the Kingdom of God on earth rather than postpone such improvements in favor of seeking salvation. A variety of causes contributed to the problems of southern schools, ranging from disease to poverty to the rural nature of the South, but writers were in agreement that there was something peculiar about the South that led to a substandard school system.[30]

Nowhere were the educational problems and crushing poverty more apparent to outside observers than in Appalachia. At the turn of the twentieth century, Appalachia was seen as a separate region, and writers and journalists were happy to supply it with a constructed history and cultural distinctiveness that did not exist before the romance with the mountains began.[31]

If the South itself was backward, its poorest white residents, the inhabitants of Appalachia, were symbols to northern liberals of the results of educational and social isolation. The mountains and their dwellers became a morality play for the rest of the country—a region that seemed to act out what could happen to the noble Anglo-Saxon race if it neglected to keep up with educational advances and chose instead to live in a premodern society. Appalachian "otherness," poverty, and ignorance became watchwords in the liberal Protestant effort to spread compulsory education laws and their civilizing influence across the South.

During the late nineteenth and early twentieth centuries, editors and authors helped construct the notions about Appalachia that exist today. They did so largely by writing about the poverty of the region, its lack of schools, and its native Anglo-Saxon population. In these writers' view, the first two characteristics of Appalachia—poverty and lack of educational opportunities—contributed to the intellectual deficiencies they saw in the white population. These deficiencies prevented the supposedly superior Anglo-Saxon race from achieving its full potential.

Accounts of Appalachian poverty abounded in newspapers and magazines, as we will see. One colporteur, W. C. Bayless, recounted his experience in the Tennessee mountains of meeting a woman who had no money to purchase a Bible. "'Every time any one comes along with Bibles,'" he reported her as saying, "'it seems I am out of money.'" According to Bayless, he was so "moved by the sad situation and the deep poverty of the family [he] gave her a Bible."[32] Bayless's description of the economic hardships of Appalachia was softer than other contemporary accounts. In an article for *Everybody's Magazine*, published in New York with a large circulation, John L. Mathews described how young Appalachian boys who wanted an education faced an immense trek, "tromping down from the mountains," to secure it. He related the story of one boy who made the trip on foot because he was "hungering for knowledge":

> Hungering for knowledge! Aye, and as that boy hungered for it so do thousands of others like him hunger in these forest-clad mountains of the South which stretch across Virginia and the Carolinas and deep into Georgia and Alabama. Their isolated cabins on the mountainsides are near no schools. Libraries, even single books, all the things requisite for the attainment of knowledge, are far from them.[33]

Mathews was not the only writer to notice how far mountaineers had to travel to learn. Martha Berry, writing about her school for children in the mountains of Georgia, explained that

> throughout the southern states a large portion of the people among the hills and surrounding country have no opportunity whatsoever, except the small country school which is supplied for a few months with a teacher who is supposed to meet the needs of all who come, no matter what their ages or classes might be. One of the problems to be met in the South is the establishing of practical industrial schools for the class of white people who are too poor to educate their children.[34]

According to Norman Frost, who published a report in the 1915 *U.S. Bureau of Education Bulletin*, education in southern Appalachia suffered from more than just a shortage of schools. He cited textbook shortages and argued that the texts in use were "ill-adapted to use in mountain schools." Frost was particularly concerned that "in one school in a place where wagons could not go [for lack of adequate roads] children were found reading a story of the personal reminiscences of a streetcar horse in New York City."[35] Apparently Frost had little confidence in the ability of the students to use their imagination in this cultural and economic wasteland he described. Elizabeth Wysor Klingberg, writing for the *South Atlantic Quarterly* in 1915, told the story of an Appalachian woman whose two youngest of a dozen children had "no Christian names" because the mother could not think of any more names for her offspring. Klingberg added that she was able to help the mother "by means of a list of names in securing their rights for these two forlorn youngsters." Once the children had names, they were permitted to enroll in the local school.[36] Yet another article described the residents of Appalachia as too slow-witted to solve their own infrastructure problems. The *Literary Digest* in 1923 summarized an article in the *Pictorial Review* in which a visitor to Tennessee was "appalled" that the children in a school "sat on hard, backless benches, their little legs dangling, with their feet six inches or more from the floor." According to the account, the visitor warned the "'prominent citizen'" who was acting as tour guide that such conditions would give the children "spinal curvature." The visitor asked, "'Why don't you shorten the legs of these benches?' The answer was: 'We have no money.' 'Money,' said the visitor, 'it's not a matter of money. Have you got a saw and five minutes of time?' They hadn't thought of that."[37] The *Digest*'s coverage of Appalachia reached 1.5 million readers, according to one historian, and because it was seen as an impartial publication, it was particularly popular for use in schools. Over a million readers, some of whom were just growing up, read how southern mountain whites were too ignorant to solve some of their most basic problems.[38]

The lack of educational opportunities in the Appalachians was not the only aspect of the region that writers noticed and interpreted. The University of Chicago's Sociology Department regularly sent graduate students to the region to discover, catalog, and interpret additional ways in which the region differed from the rest of the country. Their findings were often published in the *American Journal of Sociology* (*AJS*), an academic periodical published by the University of Chicago itself. In 1898, George Vincent called the area, "A Retarded Frontier," and provided readers of the *AJS* with photographs of a log cabin, a "home-made cotton gin," women "weaving on a hand-loom," and a "'moonshine' still."[39] In a two-part series, S. S. MacClintock analyzed the residents of the Kentucky mountains and their alleged propensity for feuding. MacClintock detailed the inadequate diet of mountain dwellers, the shortage of passable roads, and the "eternal gossiping and bickering" of Appalachian residents.[40] Much like others who wrote about white southerners' propensity for lynching, MacClintock saw an environmental factor at work, one that had its roots in the lack of educational opportunities available to rural southerners. While the *AJS* was not a widely read publication, the sociological analysis of the mountain residents appeared concurrently with the accounts of the region by journalists who covered the South in general and Appalachia in particular.[41]

The new discipline of sociology played a key role in portraying Appalachia as in dire need of help. The University of Chicago's Department of Sociology was dominated during the early twentieth century by "meliorists," scholars who agreed with Auguste Comte that the study of sociology "was a preparation for action."[42] According to one historian of the school, its leaders believed that "it was their duty to minister to society, not from the pulpit but from the investigating commission and the administrative board."[43] By publishing their pronouncements on Appalachia, the University of Chicago sociology faculty intended to influence public debate about and social policy toward the region.

A number of observers described Appalachia as a region that time had forgotten. Their analysis of the area rested upon the assumption that the cultural mores and way of living that existed there belonged to a different, premodern time. In a letter to the editor of the *Outlook* in 1910, the Right Reverend Junius M. Horner, Episcopal bishop of Asheville, North Carolina, depicted the region as arrested in time:

> The isolation in commerce, in education, and in the religion of the Highlanders of the Southern Appalachian Mountains is scarcely known or appreciated by the people who have been in the whirl of the educational and commercial life of the last two generations. . . . These people are living the life of nearly a hundred years ago. Many of them have never ridden on or seen a railway train. Nearly a quarter of a million people in the mountains of North Carolina alone are to-day without religious affiliations of any kind, untouched and uncared for by any religious denomination; fifty thousand children in these same mountains do not attend any school, and a hundred thousand have school advantages only four months in the year.[44]

The *New York Times* called the region home to "the crude conditions and ideals of the seventeenth century."[45] According to Berea (Kentucky) College president William Goodell Frost, in an article in the Boston-based *Atlantic Monthly*, mountaineers were

> an anachronism, and it will require a scientific spirit and some historical sense to enable us to appreciate their situation and their character. . . . They unconsciously stepped aside from the great avenues of commerce and of thought. This is the excuse for their Rip Van Winkle sleep. They have been beleaguered by nature.[46]

Although he was president of Berea, Frost was born in LeRoy, New York, and had graduated from Oberlin College.[47] In 1922, the *Literary Digest* published an article in which it quoted the Reverend Robert S. Wightman's concern that the people of Appalachia needed to "emerge from the eighteenth century and live abreast of the twentieth."[48] Which century Appalachia was dwelling in—seventeenth or eighteenth—was not of specific concern for these writers; they only knew that the region needed to join the twentieth century. While their cohorts had written about the white South's barbarity and lack of civilization, which they believed belonged to a different age, reporters of Appalachia also tied the arrested development of the region to a dearth of educators and a lack of interest in the civilizing effects of education.

This notion that Appalachia was a land that time forgot had interesting implications because the majority of its residents were white, with English and Scottish surnames. According to the commentators, these mountain people were cousins to the fine Anglo-Saxons who had originally settled the United States. They possessed, in the scientific racism of the time, the same superior intellectual abilities as did Anglo-Saxons living in other areas of the United States, but their apparent ignorance was explained away as the result of isolation.[49] If the adherents of scientific racism had acknowledged any other cause of their apparent ignorance, it would have cast doubt on the very superiority of Anglo-Saxons they believed they had correctly documented, and might have refuted their own racial theories.

Writers spent much time portraying the residents of Appalachia as fine "stock," while at the same time condemning the way of life of the region. After describing the residents as a "type very much worth conserving" and "Anglo-Celt as modified by life in the New World," sociologist Edward A. Ross told readers of the *New Republic* that "cousins mate with cousins and the offspring of such unions within the same clan intermarry until you get pedigrees so entangled that the heredity sharps at Woods Hole cannot chart them."[50] Lillian Walker Williams told readers of the *New England Magazine* that the residents of Kentucky could be "traced back to rural England, by distinct English traits, legends and even songs."[51] Writing in the *World's Work* almost fifteen years earlier, Thomas R. Dawley Jr. noted the region's "isolation," which he said led to "inbreeding" that added to "ignorance and degeneracy."[52] According to an article published in the *New York Evening Mail* and quoted in the *South Atlantic Quarterly*, the men who committed the mass murder in Hillsville, Virginia, in 1912 were "'the most zealous and earnest conservatives in the world.'" The *Evening Mail* went on to say that these "'Virginia and Kentuckian and Tennessean outlaws . . . regulate their lives by immemorial customs.'"[53] The same *South Atlantic Quarterly* reported that the *Baltimore Sun* proposed the "remedies" of "education and extermination."[54] Walter Dyer, in a 1914 article in the *World's Work*, claimed that the mountaineers came "from fine old stock; there is scarcely a foreign name in the entire census of them." Unlike Ross, he added that they were "intensely religious, and, as a whole, moral."[55] Writing in the *New England Magazine*, Frank Waldo referred to them as "our contemporary ancestors."[56] The Right Reverend Junius Horner, in his previously cited letter to the editor of the *Outlook*, called Appalachians "the descendents of the best Anglo-Saxon stock that came to this country in the early days." According to Horner, "they have wonderful capacity, and with opportunity to develop rapidly." He also contrasted his subjects with the great numbers of immigrants from Eastern Europe who were currently flooding into the Northeast. For Horner, the healthy birth rate in the southern Appalachians helped to counterbalance the "fifty per cent increase in many of our large cities . . . made up of a low type of immigrants from the slums of Europe."[57]

Even the *Ladies' Home Journal* joined the chorus of voices singing a strange praise of the Appalachian people. In 1915, it called the people of the region "the most typical representatives of the primitive American stock—the Anglo-Saxons who for one hundred and fifty years have preserved the purity of the colonial blood and the simplicity of colonial ideals."[58] Appalachia stood for these men and women as a bulwark of racial purity against the tides of "inferior" immigrants, who, as one scholar has noted, were blamed for "the breakdown of the family, the corruption of democracy, and the degeneration of the Anglo-Saxon race."[59] Observers saw in Appalachian residents a "racial instinct which has always stirred the Anglo-Saxon and the Scotch-Irishman, that demand which has driven these races upward toward higher civilization, is strong in these people and eager for expression."[60] American civilization would be further protected against the non-Protestant immigrants if only Appalachia were removed from its isolation and cultivated properly.[61]

The observers of Appalachia also saw a danger to civilization within the region—intermarriage. Hartley Davis and Clifford Smyth wrote in *Munsey's Magazine* that "consanguineous marriages, with their biological consequences, have been common" and that these intermarriages led to more feuds and violence.[62] Sociologist Ross had noted the practice of cousins marrying with disdain and ridicule.[63] According to Thomas R. Dawley Jr., "Our Southern Mountaineers" suffered from "inbreeding," which made them ignorant and impoverished.[64] Despite their fine "stock," the residents of Appalachia represented a step backward in culture for the commentators of the day, so there needed to be a way to explain how the arrested development arose. Laying the blame on inbreeding helped to solve the problem.

Amid all of this outside commentary about Appalachia, the fiction of John Fox Jr. reified the popular image of the region as backward, isolated, and uneducated yet racially pure and full of potential for the civilizing effects of education. Fox, a native of Kentucky, wrote a series of short stories and novels in which he depicted life in his homeland as bucolic, innocent, and full of promise. Fox saw at work in Appalachia "the diverse forces of religion, law, and education—all agents of progress." To these elements, Fox "adds the Anglo-Saxon theorizing, which places all of this in the grand march of history."[65]

Although Fox's novel *The Trail of the Lonesome Pine* (1908) may be better known today, his earlier novel *The Little Shepherd of Kingdom Come* (1903) had a wider readership and provides an excellent window on Fox's notions of Appalachia and its residents.[66] The book tells the story of a young boy, Chad Buford, who lives as an orphan in the mountains of antebellum Kentucky. Fox portrays Chad as a handsome fellow who possesses an amazing ability to hunt, fish, fight, ride, and learn. Chad can quote scripture by heart, fend for himself, and charm everyone who meets him. While Fox does not make Chad entirely a Christ-like figure, notwith-standing the title of the book, he does endow the boy with qualities that any Christian of the day would recognize as centered in the popular interpretation of Jesus' teachings—humility, courage, honesty, and loyalty. Fox follows Chad's adventures as he is taken in by two different families: first the Turner family of Kingdom Come in the mountains and then the family of Major Calvin Buford of Lexington. Major Buford recognizes Chad as a distant relative and provides for his upbringing and education. After great debate and against the wishes of the major, Chad decides to join the Union army (not the Confederacy's), where he fights valiantly for the preservation of the country.

The Little Shepherd of Kingdom Come had widespread appeal with the reading public. It received favorable reviews and "caught the heyday of the historical fiction fad that dominated tastes of American readers around the turn of the century."[67] It stayed on the best-seller lists for 1903, sold over 1 million copies, and was later adapted as both a stage play and a silent film.[68]

In his narrative, Fox embeds his ideas about Appalachia and the American values he believes it embodies. To be sure, those values are often hidden under the veneer of wilderness living, but Fox clings to them nonetheless. When Chad lives amid the mountain people of Kingdom Come, he proves his worth by herding sheep, performing chores, and fighting with children from a rival family, the Dillons. While superficially Chad appears to be a product wholly of his mountain roots—uneducated, combative, and occasionally rude—he blossoms into a fine citizen under the tutelage of Major Buford. The glimpses of potential that others saw in him in the mountains (for example, his quick study and newly found ability to read endear him to the schoolmaster) become full-fledged character traits when Chad leaves the mountains and undergoes the process of civilization through education. For Fox, like northern journalists and sociologists, the mountains of the southern states were home to a people who possessed great potential but who desperately needed the assistance of the outside world to succeed.[69]

Undergirding all of these statistics, descriptions, accounts, and fictional representations was an assumption on the part of critics that education was necessary to civilize and improve the South. Influenced both by the Social Gospel and the progressive movement in education, these writers believed that society could be improved and human nature could be perfected through the careful work of education. Once a person had received proper schooling, ran the argument, he or she would be morally sound, productive, and in a better position to help correct the variety of flaws that the South had.

As usual, the *Nation* in 1905 put the situation into plain language. It argued that the way to "rouse the listless thousands" in the South was to convince them that "the school is the way of salvation."[70] In a 1907 *South Atlantic Quarterly* article, Richmond College history professor (and Virginia Anti-Saloon League leader and Baptist minister) S. C. Mitchell compared reason to grace in its ability to perfect. According to Mitchell, "the primal duty of the college is to vitalize reason and stimulate it to do its perfect work." Like the critics of lynching, Mitchell believed the rational Age of Enlightenment needed to come to the South, which still held fast to "feudal ideals."[71] In a similar vein, Fronde Kennedy of Trinity College (later Duke University), wrote in 1920 that the lack of education in the South was dangerous and that "all over the South leaders awoke to a sense of danger."[72] And John H. Ashworth of Johns Hopkins University reported in the *South Atlantic Quarterly* in 1913 that the *Baltimore Sun* had recommended "'two remedies . . . education and extermination.'"[73] The South, these writers believed, desperately needed the saving power of education.

Edgar W. Knight, professor of education at the University of North Carolina, Chapel Hill, wrote often about the need for education as a means of social reform in the South. According to Knight, "education is now as it has ever been the first urgent need of the South." He qualified, however, what type of education was necessary:

> The need, however, is not for education in its narrow, traditional, or purely academic sense, but for that kind of instruction and training which will awaken popular interest and enthusiasm for public well-being, enlighten public opinion, and direct and lead the energies of men and women to human service and to the preservation of free government.[74]

Knight believed the right type of education in schools would alleviate all of society's ills. Writing for *School and Society* in 1922, he dismissed the sectarian efforts to bring religious schools to the southern Appalachians. He scoffed that

> the ills of isolation—ignorance and superstition, physical defects and disease, insanitary conditions, low standards of living, primitive means of making a living, poor schools, inert churches—cannot be cured by a visionary missionary zeal which often degenerates into denominational competition and the effort to recruit sectarian ranks.[75]

In Knight's view, the only way to bring the South into step with the rest of the country was through public education that emphasized civic virtues and the responsible role of citizens in society. The Reverend A. D. Mayo, writing in 1890 in the *New England Magazine*, had put it even more succinctly thirty years earlier. What the South needed, among other things, was a "free library in every neighborhood . . . [and] a movement to 'add faith to knowledge' in the church. . . ."[76]

The Reverend Mayo's prescription for the churches raises the topic of the role that white southern churches played in the education of society. Once again, the white southern clergy found itself on the receiving end of attacks, attacks that ranged from complaints about the sanitary conditions in churches to the education level of the preachers themselves to the need for clerical emphasis on education in sermons. Much as in the debate over the role of ministers in preventing southern violence, the clergy were seen at once as impotent and too powerful. They could block educational reforms, and they were uneducated themselves. Their role in white southern society was hard to judge, but they had their enemies in the northern press.

For example, in chronicling the condition of southern education after the Civil War, liberal Protestant Lyman Abbott and the *Outlook* took the white southern ministers to task for opposing education in the South. According to Abbott, "ecclesiastical opposition, on the grounds that the state can furnish only secular education and education should be religious," frustrated efforts to expand public education in the South.[77] Abbott, the consummate liberal, saw his white southern counterparts as being hopelessly conservative in their notions about education. He may have had in mind revivalist Sam Jones, who in 1898, in declaring his candidacy for the gubernatorial election in Georgia, announced his opposition to "Georgia's free school system."[78] Abbott's view that the South was not liberal in terms of religion and education was transmitted to his readers, who would later make the comparison of the South's religious heritage to that of fundamentalism.

Likewise, Frederick Morgan Davenport, professor of sociology at Hamilton College, informed readers of the *Outlook* in 1905 that "whites in the feud belt are not suffering from an absence of religion, but from the wrong kind." He continued that "their preachers are great 'soul savers,' but they lack the practical wisdom to build up their emotionalized converts into anything that approaches a higher life."[79] Echoing this concern, the *Literary Digest* printed an article from the *New York Times* by Berea College professor John F. Smith, who believed that many ministers in Appalachia were "painfully weak and inefficient."[80] Writing about the ecumenical movement in the *World's Work*, Tyler Dennett used the occasion to tell about how "ignorance and superstition prevail to an appalling extent among many isolated dwellers in the mountain regions of our southern states."[81]

Transplanted northerner William Goodell Frost, president of Berea College in Kentucky, shared this concern over the clergy's role in education. In 1901, Frost wrote in the *Missionary Review of the World* that because "preachers were scarce," white southerners, and especially residents of Appalachia, "began to 'put up with' men who had little or no education." For Frost, "this was the fatal fall, for Protestantism without intelligence is impossible."[82] In 1900, Frost had noted that in the Appalachians, "we thus have the startling anomaly of illiterate Protestants."[83] In true Protestant fashion, Frost embraced the notion that education was important to individual salvation, because the saving grace of the Bible was best apprehended when one read the Bible for oneself. Without the ability to read, Frost held, the Protestant lacked a means of understanding salvation.

Liberal Protestants in the South joined Abbott's and Frost's call for clerical support for education. John Carlisle Kilgo, president of Trinity College and a Methodist minister, bemoaned the lack of assistance from the pulpit in the attempt to further education in the South. Kilgo believed that religion had a large role to play in shaping education.[84] In a 1903 article in the *South Atlantic Quarterly*, he called on preachers to bear "a large share of the responsibilities for the educational conditions in America, and especially in the South where preachers have exercised a large influence." According to Kilgo, while the North had men the likes of "Jonathan Edwards, [William] Channing, [Horace] Bushnell, [Henry Ward] Beecher, [Phillips] Brooks, and [Edward Everett] Hale," the South had no such religious leaders. Instead, he lamented, white southern expectations for the ministry were "kept at a very low point."[85] Kilgo, Frost, Davenport, Smith, and Abbott saw the preachers of the South as constraining the efforts for educational improvement, efforts they believed were necessary for the advancement of civilization and the eradication of social problems besetting the region.

Other observers, often white southerners, held a similar view of the need for the Protestant churches of the South to take a stronger role in providing educational opportunities for their congregations. The Reverend B. M. Beckham, of Danville, Virginia, delivered a paper to the Sixteenth Conference for Education in the South (held in Richmond, Virginia) in 1913 in which he called for rural pastors to promote knowledge of current events, a favorite cause for liberal Protestants. Beckham opined:

> There is no reason why our rural pastors should not keep fully abreast of the times in all that pertains to the well-being of their community, and give their people the full benefit of their knowledge. Newspapers, magazines, and books are constantly pouring from the press on community subjects and the country preacher should take advantage of these to keep abreast of the times.[86]

At the same conference, Ennion G. Williams, M.D., health commissioner of Virginia, presented a paper entitled "The Rural Church and Public Health," in which he provided a graphic description of conditions inside rural southern churches and argued that these conditions thwarted the efforts of public health education. According to Commissioner Williams,

> Many of our rural churches fall far short of [the model]. Cleaned only when filth becomes unbearable, ventilated by chance or accident, generally without any out-

houses and supplying water from a rusty bucket and a dirty tin dipper, the church oftentimes is a focus of infection. If it is to stand as the evangel of good health, it must be sanitary. If it is to preach the gospel of fresh air, it must be well ventilated.

Williams contended that "the permanence of our fight for better health must rest, in part at least, upon an awakened public conscience which will view disease as second only to sin, cleanliness as next to godliness."[87] Conference participants must have left Richmond with the idea that southern ministers wallowed in filth, ignored current events, and preached only on otherworldly topics. The last of those assumptions was probably the most upsetting to advocates of the Social Gospel, the Age of Enlightenment, and the Religion of Humanity, all of whom would have preferred that the churches focus on current events and social problems.

White southern ministers and their congregations, however, did focus more on salvation than on social issues. While it is not the place of this work to analyze the extent to which religion in the American South was otherworldly in focus, it bears repeating that Christianity has struggled with this balance for its entire history. The earliest Christians had to cope with the fact that their messiah did not return in their lifetimes as they had expected, and countless generations since have confronted conflicting messages within the Christian New Testament about the need to make the world better and the need to prepare one's soul for judgment and whether those two needs are indeed pertinent to the same goal.

White southern ministers and their critics grappled with these issues at the beginning of the twentieth century. In 1906, reporting on the often-discussed merger between the northern and southern branches of the Methodist Church, Lyman Abbott wrote in the *Outlook* that southern Methodists would have to rewrite their creed in order to secure such a reunification. Abbott favored such an action because the southern Methodists needed, in his words, to "adapt their creed to the present conditions."[88] In a 1903 *Atlantic Monthly* article, Theodore T. Munger, professor at Andover-Newton Seminary in Massachusetts, summarized a recent census of religious denominations and pointed out that many of them were "based on Scripture read with literal exactness, and the special point usually refers to baptism, prophecy, the form of the Church, eschatology, and not a few involve the knottiest points in metaphysical theology." Munger chose for his example "a sect in Texas that flourishes under the name, 'Old Two-Seed-in-the-Spirit Predestinarian Baptists.'"[89] His choice of the tiny group symbolized Munger's belief that religion in the South was given over to theological debates of conservative, not modern, character.

The notion that white southerners embraced a conservative expression of Christianity, one that emphasized otherworldly concerns, was apparent in Walter Hines Page's 1902 discussion of a southern town he had visited years earlier. According to Page, "the circuit-riding preacher at 'revival' times insisted that the grace of God fell short of saving them that danced and played cards." Page went on to relate a family conversation about salvation in which "a pious Methodist girl of eighteen" asked her mother, "'[I]s it impossible for an Episcopalian to be saved?'"[90] The preoccupation of white southerners with the more obscure points of theological discourse was the subject of William E. Barton's 1903 piece for the *Outlook*, "The Church Militant in the Feud Belt." Barton reported that the Salvation Army was heading into Kentucky to save souls. He advised the missionaries that the "feudists" were "Hardshell Baptists," willing to "welcome" them to stay as long as they liked and to "discuss the five points of Calvinism . . . nightly for a month."[91] C. T. Revere related to readers of *Outing* how residents of the Kentucky town he had visited had a three-way distinction among Baptists, including the "'Feet Washers,'" the "'Muddy Heads,'" (so named because they "anoint[ed] the head with wet earth") and the "'Soup Eaters,'" who "partook of broth at communion."[92] Not all white southerners, however, were well versed in denominational differences. A. T. Hanes, in a letter to the editor of the *Nation*, wrote that he had been told of a Presbyterian missionary traveling in Arkansas who asked a woman whose "log cabin" was "embellished with coon-skins and the hides of other 'varmints,'" whether she knew of any Presbyterians in the area. According to the Hanes, the woman responded, "'I don't think they air [*sic*]; my old man has been huntin' in these here parts for nigh onto twenty years, and he ain't never killed narry one yit.'"[93] And to add some color to his portrayal of Appalachia, University of Chicago sociologist S. S. MacClintock wrote in the *American Journal of Sociology* of a debate between two Kentucky ministers, one of whom "laid his Bible on the floor, jumped on it with both feet, and declared 'he was standing on the Bible.'"[94] The preacher took both his Bible and his language literally. Biblical literalism would be a marker for later modernists to discern fundamentalists, and the South already appeared to have biblical literalism in spades. Southern religion appeared comical in the eyes of northern audiences, a religion that seemed to have nothing better to do than debate seemingly minor theological points or to remain completely ignorant of them.

White southerners themselves helped to fuel the fire by criticizing their region's assumed propensity for conservative religion. Southern academics led the charge. Although he was a transplanted northerner, Berea College president Frost identified himself with Kentucky in similar articles for both the *Atlantic Monthly* and the *Missionary Review of the World*. In them, Frost argued that the lack of educated clergy contributed to the popularity of "'hardshell' predestinarian teaching" in Kentucky, although he did note that among mountain clergy there were "in rare instances even some [examples of] liberality."[95] Professor of English and dean of Trinity College William Preston Few, writing in Trinity's own *South Atlantic Quarterly* in 1905, called faith in the South "a religion that is emotional, given to profession, and sometimes froward in its retention of outworn forms." He went on to state that "from this kind of conservatism has come insistence upon regularity of experience and profession that has seemed to . . . make religion a clog upon Southern progress." For Few, the remedy was to judge "men . . . not by what they profess to be and believe, but by the amount of Christian service they give and by the spirit in which they give it." Such a shift would produce a "more intelligent and Christian charity. . . ."[96] Fellow North Carolina resident Clarence Poe held that such a shift was already under way in 1907. According to Poe, in the South,

> there has been a broadening of religious opinion, and the religious thought of to-day is as far removed from ancient blue-law Puritanism on one hand as it is from modern iconoclastic criticism on the other—an advance that is significant in many ways.[97]

For Frost, Few, and Poe, the label of "Puritan" was something to be shunned.

Occasionally, however, the South embraced the label of Puritanism. Writing just one year later in the *World's Work*, Edwin A. Alderman, president of the University of Virginia, gladly compared the South's religion with that of the Puritans. In Alderman's view, "the fancied home of the cavalier is the home of the nearest approach to Puritanism and to the most vital Protestant evangelicalism in the world to-day." Here Alderman turned to the scientific racism so prevalent at the time and proclaimed that this fine state of affairs was due in part to the South's "conserving power of homogeneity, absence of urban mass, [and] provincialism."[98] While Alderman was a part of the white southern academic establishment, which accepted the notion that education was a necessary cure for southern evils, he held the South up as an example of the virtues of Anglo-Saxon purity and tied that purity to its perceived Puritan heritage. The white southern critics, however, saw their region hopelessly mired in a Puritan age—nothing to be proud of—and later observers of the fundamentalist movement and the Scopes Trial would again turn to the term "Puritan" as a derogatory label for the South.[99]

Joining with men like Alderman, though, author Corra Harris proclaimed her affirmation of conservative religion and her rejection of liberal Protestant thought. Harris, a Georgia native, wrote vaguely autobiographical novels that documented the hardships and virtues of the life of a Methodist circuit rider and his wife, although there is evidence that Harris's real-life union with such a minister was not a happy one.[100] In her first novel, *A Circuit Rider's Wife*, Harris tells the story of a young woman, Mary Elizabeth Eden Thompson, who, like the author, married an older Methodist minister and followed him throughout his career. As she tells Mary's story, Harris includes descriptions of religion in Georgia, distantly respectful of charismatic worship and boastful of the region's ability to hold fast to conservative theology, which in her eyes was true religion. Following her husband's death, the widowed Mary moves to New York City, where she finds herself out of step with the theology prevalent in the modern city. She plans a return to the family's home in Georgia and addresses her late husband to tell him her troubles:

> Up here the best, the wisest people don't know what the truth of God is: they think they can find it in science. Faith is for fools who cannot think. They are not trying to reconcile God to man, but man to God, and trimming down the Holy Ghost to suit his scientific bug faculties.[101]

Harris concluded her first novel with a condemnation of liberal Protestantism and religion in modern New York by saying:

> I do not wonder that so many men and women go wrong in New York. They are orphans, deprived of their Heavenly Father by the very preachers themselves. And it's very hard for orphans to behave themselves. They know what is right, but righteousness does not appeal to them, because it has never been sanctified by love. That is what is the matter with these people. They do not love God, they do not care, or know, or believe that He loves them. They are so sensible, so profoundly reasonable that they are sadly damned by their own little intelligences. They have theories, views, and knowledges that are not going to show up well in the next generation. And that is their crime, to propagate ideas that will destroy the integrity of those who will come after them.[102]

Harris believed that northern clergy, not southern clergy, had strayed from what God wanted and that the sins of the fathers would be visited upon the children who grew up in this modern world. She conflated liberal Protestantism with northern Protestantism, much as later critics would conflate fundamentalism with southern Protestantism. With *A Circuit Rider's Wife* serialized in the *Saturday Evening Post* for the benefit of a national reading audience, she helped to popularize the notion of the South as religiously conservative, and she used that tradition to parry any assertion by liberals that the southern way of religion was outmoded or incorrect.

Harris was not the only southern author to make such claims against the North in fictional form. Thomas Dixon Jr., in his 1903 novel, *The Leopard's Spots*, allowed the Reverend John Durham to entertain a lucrative offer to preach in Boston rather than remain in North Carolina. After the Boston deacon extends the offer and disparages the South, Durham replies:

> "Believe me, Deacon, the ark of the covenant of American ideals rests to-day on the Appalachian Mountain range of the South. When your metropolitan mobs shall knock at the doors of your life and demand the reason of your existence, from these poverty-stricken homes, with their old-fashioned, perhaps medieval ideas, will come forth the fierce athletic sons and sweet-voiced daughters in whom the nation will find a new birth."[103]

Dixon, speaking through Durham, equated northern liberalism with northern Protestantism and argued that southern conservatism was the answer for the country's moral woes.

But whether the writer was a southern woman in favor of conservative religion or a northern man opposed to it, there was near unanimous agreement that the South had either ignored or rejected the tenets of liberal Protestant theology. The only disagreement was whether such a rejection was a wise action or not. For the majority of writers, the South was out of step with the rest of the country, its lack of religious progress was in conflict with the national character, and the conservative religion was a result of educational deficiencies.

Coverage of education in the South was far from wholly pessimistic. To give up on the white Anglo-Saxons of the South would have meant recognizing that the scientific racism at work in intellectual circles was wrong. Northern writers took every opportunity to tie any perceived advancement in educational reform in the South to the efforts of northern reformers and not their southern counterparts. Southern writers, on the other hand, often voiced their self-sufficiency and answered outside critics with indignation.

In a 1905 editorial, the *Nation* noted that without the George Peabody Fund to finance schools in the South, "these new approaches for the educational uplifting of the South would have found the field they are filling far more difficult and more barren than has been the case."[104] Caroline Matthews of Boston, Massachusetts, contributed an article to the *Educational Review* in 1907 in which she sang the praises of northern denominations' fieldwork to improve the schools in western North Carolina. The *Educational Review* was published in New York, edited by Nicholas Butler Murray of Columbia University, and attracted "the leading educators in America" as contributors.[105] According to Matthews, the State of North Carolina deserved praise for working "side by side" with Presbyterian and Episcopalian missionaries and refraining from sectarian conflicts with local churches.[106] Leonora Beck Ellis sang the praises of the University of Georgia, noting that it had had to endure difficult financial conditions because of and after the Civil War.[107] Walter Hines Page, writing for the *World's Work*, noted that South Carolina, Texas, and Virginia were all making progress in 1909 in constructing new schools. "Compared with the older school system in other parts of the country," he wrote, "the facilities in the Southern states are far from complete; but there is an enthusiasm behind the work which will in time make it both complete and efficient."[108] In his piece for the *North American Review*, Winthrop Talbot began with an old adage about how bad southern schools were but managed to say something good about education in the South in 1915. According to Talbot, "it has long been a choice morsel for the social pessimist and critic of democracy that nearly one-fourth of the population of the Southern States is illiterate." Talbot argued that the "Black Belt" referred not only to race but "also schooling." He then reversed course and announced that "each Southern State has cut its percentage of illiteracy more than twenty-five percent during the last census period."[109] And Lyman Abbott published several articles in the *Outlook*, praising the South's efforts to reform its schools, articles that his biographer reports drew intense criticism for Abbott's position.[110] Northern elites had already developed a strong bigotry against the South, a bigotry that they were loathe to shed. Abbott had violated their code by defending the South, and his peers had no problems in voicing their displeasure with someone who had broken rank.

In defense of the South, some contributors wrote to magazines expressing their confidence in the region's schools and the need for northern reformers to stop meddling. Margaret Hancock of Fayetteville, Arkansas, for example, wrote to the editor of the *New Republic* praising the work of Arkansas governor Thomas C. McRae. Hancock described him as a self-made man with no "formal education" who was campaigning on a "'Forward Educational Movement'" for the state. Hancock called her governor "unique" and voiced the "approval in [her] heart."[111] Hancock's support, however, reveals her belief that education was sorely lacking in her home state, a belief that northern critics maintained.

But while there were signs of educational progress, the more pervasive image was one of arrested development and, with it, incomplete civilization. Ignorance pervaded Dixie, most observers agreed, and that ignorance imperiled the region's future and even the nation's future. Some pundits worried that the South had become complacent in its deficiencies and would never try to work its way up. William H. Hand, state high school interpreter of South Carolina, wrote that

> the blighting blackness of ignorance obscures the light of knowledge and too often leaves the ignorant man wholly satisfied with his dismal lot. And one of the most unpromising features of this already gloomy prospect is that in many of the States the illiterate females outnumber the illiterate males. An illiterate mother does not promise much for the child of to-morrow.[112]

Like Hand, Carl Holliday, writing in the *Sewanee Review* in 1903, saw ignorance as a "blighting force" and blamed the South's educational problems for hindering the development of literature in the region.[113] Columbia University professor George Edward Woodberry published similar views the same year in *Harper's Monthly Magazine*. Woodberry saw Edgar Allan Poe as the region's sole contribution to literature and blamed the South for not expecting its writers to produce more.[114] And the *Nation* argued in 1906 that the South, once "freed from its voluntary chains," would "grant freedom of thought and freedom of criticism" to its aspiring literary lights.[115] The South, these writers believed, was suffering from a lack of the civilizing force of education, and that malady was reflected in its illiteracy statistics, its society, and its lack of literature.

The image of the South as poor and violent was already in place before the attention of the world turned to the Scopes Trial in 1925. White southerners exemplified the need for education, and education was equated with a Darwinian view of science. And southern clergy had failed to call their flocks to "book learning" rather than just spiritual education, a spiritual education that centered too much on the next life and not enough on this one.

If the journalists were united in their belief that the South needed to be educated, they were certainly varied in their explanations of how the South had fallen behind the rest of the country in providing academic opportunities for its residents. Race, poverty, religion—all played peculiar roles in the South, roles that northerners would deny existed elsewhere in the country. Religion, in particular, seemed to occupy southerners' attention in different ways than it did their northern counterparts. Outside critics of the South, and even some white southerners, charged that piety in the South centered too much on personal salvation and the correction of drinking habits and not enough on the social betterment of the entire community. They also mistook the prevailing homogeneity of white southern Protestant religion as proof of increased piety in the region. The white South was, the funhouse image showed, a place where colorful, evangelical preachers dominated religion and politics, and their parishioners followed them blindly. The next chapter, "The Long Meter Doxology in the State House: The Teetotaling South," will examine the perceptions of the role of preachers in white southern society and in the most vocal of southern reform campaigns, the temperance movement.

CHAPTER 3

The Long Meter Doxology in the State House: The Teetotaling South

Addressing the New England Society in New York City on December 22, 1890, Henry W. Grady, editor of the *Atlanta Constitution* and advocate of education in the New South, asked his audience to give him a fair hearing by allowing him first to relate the story of some young pranksters. As he explained,

> There was an old preacher once who told some boys of the Bible lesson he was to read in the morning. The boys, finding the place, glued together the connecting pages. The next morning, he read on the bottom of one page, "When Noah was one hundred and twenty years old he took unto himself a wife who was"—then turning the page—"one hundred and forty cubits long, forty cubits wide, built of gopher wood, and covered in pitch inside and out." He was naturally puzzled at this. He read it again, verified it, and then said, "My friends, this is the first time I ever met this in the Bible, but I accept it as evidence of the assertion that we are fearfully and wonderfully made."[1]

Grady's account, while meant to persuade his audience to give him the same faith that the old preacher gave his Bible, contained in it the derogatory image of southern clergy that was popular at the time. The preacher was old, easily confused, obviously not well versed in scripture, and given to extreme biblical literalism. Grady had played into the hands of critics of the South who believed that the region's religion was both different and lacking at once.

Grady was not the only person who gave embarrassing testimony about the ineptitude of white southern preachers. Berea College president William Frost, passing through New York City in an attempt to raise money for his institution, told a crowd assembled at Broadway Tabernacle that Appalachia residents near him had

> a little mission Sunday school up in the mountains, and the "preachers" speak to the congregation by appointment. One of the preachers was told that his next appointment would come on Easter Sunday. He was too proud to acknowledge that he did not know what the day meant, so went to his home and searched through his New Testament for the desired information. He did not find what he sought, but when the day came preached on the subject of Queen Esther.[2]

Frost's subject had so little knowledge of the Christianity on which he was to preach that he could not identify what Christians hold as the most important Sunday. Instead he had managed to find the account in the Old Testament of Esther's heroic rescue of the Jews from the devices of the evil Hamen. The preacher did not understand the focus of his faith.

Northern critics of religion in the South charged that white southerners as a whole subscribed to a notion of religious piety that focused too much on personal salvation and otherworldly concerns and not enough on improving society and bringing about the Kingdom of God on earth.[3] These observers believed that there was a distinctive type of religion in the South, "southern religion," which was more emotional, less thoughtful, and above all, focused on the afterlife. This final characteristic meant to northern critics that white southern churchgoers were not learning proper ethical lessons to apply to their daily lives. Instead of working to help others and improve society, white residents of the South were allegedly concerned only with their personal salvation. And the preachers must not have been leading properly, the reasoning went. They were also, according to public perception, too powerful. In the eyes of the outside media, the white southern preacher was something of an autocrat, a person who could control life from Monday through Saturday with just a few words from the pulpit on Sunday. Preachers in the South probably had no more power than clergy in any other region of the country, but they were the visible representatives of their denominations, and they were respected members of their communities, so they got the lion's share of the glory and the blame.

The varying depictions of the Reverend Sam P. Jones illustrate the stereotype of the white southern pastor. Though he was one of the great revivalists of his day, Jones bore attacks for his style and theology—labeled ignorant, too folksy, and out of step with his times. For the historian, Jones also serves as a barometer for improved northern feelings about white southern clergy. Ironically, Jones died just as the white southern clergy were becoming more involved in the temperance crusade and more esteemed in northern eyes for their role in that movement. Following his death in 1906, Jones was the recipient of almost hagiographic tributes, in part because white southern clergy had made headway in enacting prohibition legislation in several states. The northern commentators for the most part approved of this movement as an example of a way to improve society, and their obituaries of Jones reflected it. At the same time, however, some critics found in the temperance movement much more ominous motives on the part of the white ministers of the South. By the early 1920s, moreover, when national prohibition had been enacted and enforced, the mood turned ugly against the South.

Northern writers started with the premise that the South was more religious than the rest of the country, a premise that white southerners helped them construct. It was a premise that conflated the region's Protestant majority with true religious devotion. The North had just as many if not more religious people (that is, people who professed religious belief of some kind), but the population included Jews, Roman Catholics, and a few others outside the dominant Protestant denominations. In other words, apparent homogeneity in religious belief was taken as proof of increased religious feeling. Such a mistake further underscores how northern and southern writers valued Protestant religious beliefs over any other type of religion.

Examples of white southerners professing their region's supposed excess of religion abound. For example, the Reverend I. T. Tichenor, D.D., writing in 1885 for the *Christian Index*, a Southern Baptist periodical published in Alabama, saw the South's religious ethos as one element of its potential for success. According to Tichenor, "the high moral tone of her people, the strength of her Christian faith, the culture of her highest classes, place the South where no other people stand."[4] North Carolina newspaper publisher Clarence Poe wondered rhetorically in the *Outlook* whether one "will find anywhere in America a section in which religious influences are stronger than in the South."[5] Southern author Corra Harris also publicized her region's propensity for piety. In a series of articles that appeared from 1900 to 1905 in the *Independent* (a formerly Congregationalist journal published in New York City), Harris, writing under the name of Mrs. L. H. Harris, called southern white women "distinctly religious," affirmed that the white southern "temperament" was "not secular" and labeled the South as "missionary ground," a place where religion was active.[6] Dixie residents Tichenor, Poe, and Harris were proud of their region's piety, and they were not afraid to publicize their views.[7]

Nonsoutherners picked up on these assertions and amplified them. J. Cleveland Cady described the proliferation of churches he saw in Appalachia in 1901, calling a particular community "overchurched."[8] The next year, in the same publication, the *Outlook*, Ernest Hamlin Abbott noted the "large . . . proportion of church membership to population of the South."[9] In an article describing the new industries of the South, Walter A. Dyer reported that the workers of the region were "intensely religious, and, as a whole, moral."[10] In *Cosmopolitan* magazine, John Temple Graves confidently asserted in 1908 that "there is not a state south of the [Mason-Dixon] line in which the religious element does not dominate public opinion." The control of two denominations—Baptist and Methodist—was so strong, he continued, that "the opposition of either of these great denominations is fatal to any public measure or to any public man."[11] The sheer number of Baptists and Methodists, Graves was saying, contributed to their control of southern society and politics. Edward Alsworth Ross added that the Bible occupied a vaunted place in the South. "The Bible settles every question," he wrote in the *New Republic*, "and no other book is worth looking into."[12] An "epidemic of church building" had arisen in the region, according to the *Literary Digest*.[13] Writers North and South agreed the area was religious.

But while many writers saw the South as more religious than the rest of the country, that assessment came with a price. As discussed in the preceding chapter, statements about the conservative nature of religion in the South, less desirable to northern observers than "modern" religion, were common. And these statements reflected and perpetuated a belief that there was a single "religion" in the South, a belief that was just not true. Religion in the United States did have certain limited regional variations, but the term "southern religion" presumes that sections of the country possess different theologies, practices, and pieties. Such a generalization is false, but I will use the term "southern religion" to refer to that religion which the commentators of the day characterized as conservative, emotional, and different from an imagined national standard of progressive Protestantism. By "modern religion," I mean that which the commentators of the time described as liberal, thoughtful, and less dogmatic than religion before the advent of modern biblical scholarship and the changes that accompanied it. And, as mentioned earlier, this religion, according to the observers, was that practiced by whites.

Since the South was allegedly home to a form of religion that outside critics saw as inferior, the clergy's ability to impart this "old-fashioned" theology to their congregations was of great interest. Many observers believed that in imparting such views, white southern pastors suffered from intolerance and wielded too much power over society.

Observers were almost uniform in their assessment that southern white Protestantism was rigid and "backward." According to southern expatriate Walter Hines Page, writing under the pseudonym Nicholas Worth, the southerners of his childhood "held fast to a primitive and violent religion, all expecting to go to heaven."[14] Describing Charleston, South Carolina, Greenough White was "struck by the survival of old-fashioned, low-church evangelicalism there."[15] Columbia University professor Holland Thompson, in an article about southern mill towns, described the religion of the region as "old-fashioned," with an undue emphasis on eternal punishment in a "literal burning hell." He added that the occasional revivals that "banish the usual stolidity of the congregations" were of "the old type," complete with a "'mourner's bench'" of the eighteenth century.[16] The *Literary Digest* reported in 1922 that "the preaching is entirely out of keeping with the needs of the day."[17] Writing to defend his region in the unlikely forum of the *American Mercury*, southern editor Gerald W. Johnson admitted that there was truth to the assertion that there was a "noticeable smell of sulphur that permeates religious practice below the Potomac," which was "evidence of a certain irrationality in Dixie."[18] George Milton, a "Democratic editor," argued in the *Century* that the South had "always had a strong evangelical Protestant tinge," which he credited with making the region "a fertile field for sectarian enthusiasms and prejudices."[19] And as usual, Appalachia was singled out as an example of this trend. In 1901, Lyman Abbott, in his "Spectator" editorial column in the *Outlook*, reported that the area's religion was "of the most primitive character."[20] The Reverend Robert S. Wightman, in an article that appeared in the *Missionary Review of the World* and was reprinted in the *Literary Digest*, agreed, saying that the residents of Appalachia needed to "be reclaimed morally, spiritually, socially, intellectually, economically" and objecting to "'preachin' that makes ye get up and holler."'[21] According to the *Pictorial Review*, the "religion of the mountain people," in simple terms, was "primitive in the extreme."[22] These characteristics of southern religion made it suspect in the eyes of journalists, and they were concerned that southern clergy inculcated the wrong values in their too easily led flocks.

In one such example, W. P. Trent, in the Boston-based *Atlantic Monthly*, cited in 1897 the "baleful intolerance" that manifested itself in "the pulpit" as the reason white southern clergy did not lead by example against mob violence.[23] Edward Alsworth Ross accused Appalachian ministers of using religion to repress women. "To prop male domination," he wrote in the *New Republic*, "the preachers have worked the Bible for all it is worth," exploiting "Eve's sin in Eden and St. Paul's 'Let the women learn in silence with all subjection.'"[24] Even before Trent's and Ross's accusations, a writer who, for obvious reasons, signed himself simply "A Southerner," wrote in the *New York Times* that the white clergy in the South defended the status quo, opposed progress, and were responsible for preserving slavery, obstructing new scholarship, and ignoring the problems created by the liquor traffic. The "Southerner" claimed that the average preacher virtually cowed his neighbors: "I know no people so dominated by their clergy, no clergy such resolute and consistent foes of progress. The clergy upheld slavery to the last gasp, and still often defend the system."[25]

Writing in the *Century* nearly thirty years later, William Garrott Brown continued to assert that the white southern clergy were too influential. Brown also indicted the laity, arguing that they did not question what the clergy told them. According to Brown, the laity took "their moral and religious guidance . . . from a ministry whose methods and whose power constitute an important neglected fact of Southern life." Brown claimed that there were too few "college-bred" members of the Baptist and Methodist denominations and that those denominations "inculcate[d] a strict and narrow adherence to the scriptural code of morals," including bans on dancing and stage productions. Brown also noted that "neither [Baptist nor Methodist denomination] requires its ministers to be educated" and that the "preaching is for the most part highly emotional." Brown went on to explain that

> so great is the power which [southern clergymen] thus collectively exercise that if one were to call the plain people of the South "priest-ridden," the strongest objection to the phrase would be that Methodist and Baptist ministers do not consider themselves priests.[26]

Brown was correct that Methodist and Baptist clergy would have objected to the term "priest" because it carried with it a presumption that the clergy could perform sacraments that conveyed saving grace, something that Protestants had rejected centuries earlier. But for Brown and the "Southerner," the South was not a Christ-haunted landscape, as Flannery O'Connor would later describe it, but a preacher-haunted one.[27] "The Southern cleric's pulpit is his throne," liberal Protestant Rollin Lynde Hartt observed in early 1923, associating the clergy of the region with royalty in its ability to pronounce upon matters and influence society.[28]

The power of white preachers in the South was often cited as the reason the region was home to various laws regarding the observance of the Sabbath and banning certain practices such as divorce. As early as 1885, the *Philadelphia Inquirer* noted that white Southern Baptists were debating in their annual meeting in Augusta, Georgia, whether any cause for divorce was to be found in the Bible.[29] Several years later, South Carolina Episcopalian T. W. Bacot proudly wrote to the northern Episcopalian paper, the *Churchman*, that his diocese had applauded the South Carolina law proscribing divorce. The diocesan resolution noted that the diocese was "co-terminal with the *State* of South Carolina," a distinction that may have appeared to concerned observers a mixing of church and state.[30] At the time of Bacot's proud proclamation, South Carolina was the only state in the country where divorce was completely prohibited.[31] The presence of laws requiring that certain activities not take place on Sundays also occupied national attention. The *Atlanta Constitution* reported in 1911 that the City of Atlanta's Park Board had decided to ban swimming in Atlanta parks on Sundays "between the hours of 9 a.m. and 2 p.m.," the traditional time for church services.[32] The fledgling news publication

Time quoted an item from the *American Mercury* stating that the Birmingham (Alabama) Commissioner of Safety had "issued an order . . . that Sunday golf, billiards, and *dominoes* be stopped. . . ."[33] And in 1925 the *Literary Digest* reported that "in North Carolina, South Carolina, Georgia, Alabama, Tennessee, Mississippi, and Arkansas commercialized antagonism to Sunday has not been able to make much headway."[34] To the outside observer, the South appeared to be an area in which the clergy helped enact laws governing divorce and enforcing Sunday observance. While a majority of Americans most likely supported such ideas, the notion that the white religious denominations in the South advocated such laws must have been worrisome to the religiously liberal pundits. Preachers appeared to be autocratic, not democratic, dispensing religious directives on municipal matters. Religious liberals, on the other hand, would have preferred that the clergy allow parishioners to be more autonomous, with each individual making decisions about the appropriateness of an activity. A Christian should use his or her own faculties to determine whether to drink on Sunday (or any day of the week), and the state should not enforce such laws but should ensure that it did not become the handmaiden of theocracy.

Biblical interpretation also varied regionally, according to the published opinions of the time. Although he did not intend to attack his home region, white southerner Thomas Nelson Page shared with a national audience his personal testimony that Dixie took the Bible literally. In a nostalgic article in *Scribner's Magazine* in 1901, Page called religion in the South "the religion of the grim evangelical divines of the last century." He went on to explain that for white southerners this world

> was only "a vale of misery," through which we had to walk with fear and trembling so as to reach in safety the other world where true Life beings. The Bible was the literal word of God, and the only admissible question on any point was what the Bible said.[35]

While he aimed to praise, Page's comments placed the South and its religion squarely into the line of fire by categorizing the theology as otherworldly and thus, to critics, flawed. One such critic, the Reverend John Carlisle Kilgo, president of Trinity College, held that the South's reliance on a religion of salvation meant a diminution of its morality. Kilgo wrote in the *South Atlantic Quarterly* in 1907 that the "Southern people have always had an implicit faith in God and in the Bible as the revealed will of God," but this tendency had meant that "private standards of morality have not been applied to public questions." The average white resident of the South, he charged, "tolerated in the multitude" that which he "would not do himself."[36] And Lyman Abbott's son, Ernest Hamlin Abbott, wrote in his father's magazine, the *Outlook*, that in "most of the sermons and religious addresses [he] heard in the South the conception of religion seemed to be that of a preparation for a world to come rather than a mode of earthly life." The Congregationalist Abbott, descendant of Puritans himself, worried that this focus on the next world removed the need to explore "the relation of the individual with his God and his fellow-men," emphasizing instead "the condition of his soul after death." Abbott wrote that most of the white southern congregations he had witnessed

> seemed to be expected to suspend their reasoning power and put in its place an unquestioning credence, called faith in the formulas, always purporting to be derived directly from the Bible, which set forth the way to attain a happy eternal destiny.[37]

Abbott's use of the phrase "directly from the Bible" implies that he viewed the white southern congregations as reliant on biblical literalism.

Abbott's critique of white southern religion sounds much like earlier Protestant attacks on Catholicism and Puritan charges against the Church of England. Shared among these targets was their opponents' perception that the clergy led their congregations through formulaic worship with promises of reward for correct behavior and an absence of the vital role, in Protestantism, of direct recourse to the Bible as the sole source of God's revelation to humankind. Abbott noted the suspension of "reasoning power," a characteristic that would have raised alarms for liberal Protestants who valued the role of reason in religion. That lack of reason was on the mind of Berea College professor John Smith, William Frost's successor, who, writing in 1922 in the New York Times, described white southern preaching as "spectacular and medieval," with sermons that were merely "monotonous recitals of creeds, isolated verses of Scripture, and denominational differences."[38] The term "medieval," which had been used to describe white southern society as it lynched blacks, arose again as a label for white southern clergy, and it would appear again as the Scopes Trial attracted attention. The South clearly was not modern.

Attacks on the role of the clergy in white southern society did not go unnoticed by the targets themselves. In 1906, the Reverend John E. White, pastor of the Second Baptist Church of Atlanta, told readers of the South Atlantic Quarterly that white southern politicians had helped usurp the power that preachers once held. White argued that "the preacher has lost his public power to a great degree in the common chaos of Southern unsettlement." He went on to state that

> the politicians of our sorrowful period have resented [the preacher's] approach to public influence and the idea has been successfully grafted on to Southern public opinion that the field of politics is worldly or of the devil, therefore the preacher must keep well out of touch with it.[39]

White's fellow southerner, William E. Dodd, wrote from Randolph Macon College (affiliated with the Methodist Episcopal Church, South) in Ashland, Virginia, to

the *Nation* to dispute the contention that white southern clergy were all conservatives. Dodd argued that "men of the most liberal views on matters of creed now
occupy the first pulpits of the South" and cited among his examples John E. White.[40]
John Kilgo, D.D., alleged that "due credit is given that class of preachers who have
persistently wrought to create high and true ideals in all that affects life," even as
he related the story of a minister in the South who told a group of preachers,
"'Brethren, I sometimes fear we are educating too much. What we need is the Holy
Spirit.'"[41] But White's and Dodd's arguments fell on deaf ears, as publishers, writers,
and critics caricatured the white southern clergy again and again. Such caricatures
had small elements of truth in them, but they missed the variety of theological opinions among white southern clergy. Those men, like their nonsouthern counterparts,
varied in their opinions. The heresy trials of several northern Baptists and Presbyterians raised their interest, but so did efforts to improve prison conditions, expand
educational opportunities, and make the South a more "modern" region. But these
efforts went largely unnoticed in nonsouthern publications.

The arrival of the Reverend Sam P. Jones on the national stage did little to
change assumptions about white southern preachers. "Born in Alabama in 1847,"
Jones worked as a lawyer in Georgia until his father, "on his deathbed," extracted
a promise that Jones would give up alcohol.[42] Jones had a conversion experience
and joined the southern Methodist itinerant ministry.[43]

Sam Jones drew national attention when he held a multiday revival in Nashville in May of 1885. Although he borrowed heavily from the techniques of evangelist Dwight L. Moody, who had won praise from midwestern and eastern city
leaders, Jones's popularity with the crowds of converts, churchgoers, and the curious in Tennessee's capital did not extend to northern writers, nor to the *Atlanta
Constitution*.[44] After reporting that Jones had been the subject of an insulting pamphlet circulated in Nashville that characterized his audiences as "'religious cranks,
hypocrites, unlettered men and women, fanatics, defaultors, snuff dippers, mor-
phine and opium eaters, robbers and thieves,'" the *Constitution* went on to state,
tongue in cheek, that "during the coming week, Mr. Jones will doubtless have his
big tent crowded."[45] Reporting during the same revival, the *New York Times* placed
its coverage directly below the aforementioned "Southerner's" condemnation of
religion in the South. The *Times* article listed many of Jones's characteristic sayings—lines like "quit your meanness," "I've never seen a town yet that didn't have
a 'smiling' infidel," and "I never saw a man yet who disbelieved in a hell, who, if
there is one, is not making a bee line for it."[46] Two years later, the same paper
reported that Jones had predicted "an awful disaster" and had "frighten[ed] the
women of his flock in New Orleans," presumably because the city had fallen away

from his standard of Christian practice.[47] In these articles, Jones appeared homey and quaint, an eccentric who condemned modern practices and seemed out of step with life in America.

They also focused on the "southern" character of Jones's evangelism, as well as his language and delivery, which were deemed lowbrow. In 1885, the *St. Louis Republican* described his "thought and expression" as

> intensely southern. He has the conservative ideas of religion which, however much they have been weakened elsewhere, are still strong in the south, and he denounces whatever he considers sin, with the force and fire of denunciation it met from the earliest Methodist circuit riders.[48]

Jones's appeal to white southerners did not pass unnoticed either. A May 1885 article in the *New York Times* noted that "Samuel," in his "youth," had "received a good academic education" and that the "grammar and rhetoric used by him in his sermons are not the result of ignorance."[49] What the piece left unsaid but understood was that Jones had to "dumb down" his language in order to reach the great mass of uneducated southerners who could only comprehend homey and plain sermons. In language that would foreshadow the depictions of Tennessee in the Scopes Trial, the *New York Times* in July of 1885 stated that he was "either the greatest revivalist of the United States to-day or Tennesseans are the most consummate asses living."[50] Writers were also quick to discount Jones's influence. In 1885, when a St. Louis revival was not as successful as Jones would have hoped, the *New York Times* carried the front-page headline "Evangelist Sam Jones Fails to Redeem the Wicked City."[51] Two years later, when Jones failed to fill a meeting hall after charging fifty cents admission, the *New York Times* again placed the coverage of the ill-attended revival on the front page and reported that the "emotional wave" Jones had started had "almost entirely disappeared."[52] But the New York reporters had spoken too soon. Jones continued to attract large crowds and to tour the country.

Into the twentieth century, observers continued to be baffled by the allure of Jones's preaching. In 1902, Calvin Dill Wilson, in the *Critic*, a New York–based literary journal, analyzed the "phenomenon" of the well-known Georgia pastor.[53] Wilson placed himself on the side of the modern world by declaring at the beginning of the piece that "it is the beginning of the twentieth century, and America is a civilized country." But, he argued, the continued popularity of Sam Jones "may well cause one to rub his eyes and wonder whether he is awake," as if, like Rip Van Winkle, the modern observer had been asleep and missed important developments. Once again, the South appeared stuck in time. Why was Wilson so puzzled by Jones's appeal? For Wilson, the confusion lay in "the phenomenon that the platform speaker who draws larger crowds than any other man in America, at least in many portions of it, is one who continually hurls at his hearers epithets that no one would dare utter in a drawing room." From the critic's point of view, Jones was a man who insulted his audience while drawing a crowd, something that seemed inconceivable. Wilson portrayed Jones as an "interesting" speaker whose language was "vivid, apt, homely, plain," but he omitted any mention of faith when he discussed Jones's appeal, instead casting aspersions on his audience members, who "scarcely realize until he is gone that he has dealt brutal insults to every man and woman before him; and many of them never realize it."[54] For Wilson, writing in a northern literary magazine that did not emphasize religion, Jones was a curiosity, his audience gullible, and his mission the subject of critical interpretation of oratory, not theology. His mission was, in short, beyond rational understanding.

The northern press also linked Jones to violence, a continuing theme in outside portrayals of the South and its white citizens. In March 1886, the *New York Times* reported that Jones had been linked to a murder in Georgia "which followed a discussion of the prohibition question." According to the account, Jones had "advised the Prohibitionists to go to the polls on election day, March 22, armed with pistols." Apparently both the "drys" and the "wets" took Jones's words to heart and armed themselves early, and a dispute over the upcoming election resulted in a fatal shooting. In response, Jones noted that an "anti-Prohibitionist" had done the shooting, but added that "'a man literally takes his life in his hands when he goes out to talk prohibition down there.'"[55] Jones also inspired animosity toward himself with his condemnations from the pulpit. The mayor of Palestine, Texas, a front-page story in the *New York Times* noted, assaulted Jones with a cane for comments Jones had made against him during a revival. According to the account, Jones "grappled with the Mayor," managed to grab the cane away, and "the preacher then gave the Mayor a dose of caning."[56]

The incident in Texas was not an isolated one. In 1893, the *New York Times* ran a front-page story entitled "Clergymen Out For Blood," which detailed a feud between Jones and the Reverend Mr. Dobbs, "the Baptist pastor" of Cartersville, Georgia. According to the report, Dobbs had accused Jones of helping to clear a fellow Methodist minister of a "scandal," a charge that Jones denied. "Close friends" of the two men reported that they carried "pistols and [were] ready for self-defense." The disagreement had gotten so bad that "neither Baptists nor Methodists [were] speaking as they pass[ed] by" each other on the street.[57]

More than a decade later, Jones was involved in a "fist fight with Postmaster Walter Akerman" of Cartersville, Georgia, where Jones lived. Jones had "denounced Akerman from the pulpit, called him a 'dirty dog,'" and "threatened to report [Akerman] to President [Theodore] Roosevelt if he did not cease selling wine." Again, Jones did not turn the other cheek but instead "struck back, but bystanders separated the two men."[58] Readers must have wondered about this pugilistic man of the cloth, sharp-tongued and given to physical attacks on his adversaries. Of course Jones had not improved his standing with reporters by insulting them as well. He once turned to a group of reporters covering a revival and "denounced them from the platform: 'You little sap-headed reporters, with eyes so close together that you can see through a keyhole with both of them. . . .'"[59] Clearly, Jones needed a press secretary and public relations firm to help him with the media.[60]

Although in life Jones was the target of scorn, his sudden death on October 15, 1906, brought with it admiring tributes and editorial praise. The change appeared to be sudden, yet it had its roots in the temperance movement. Sam Jones had been instrumental in supporting the temperance effort in the South, a movement that was gaining momentum and legislative victories, and a movement of which the modernist northern writers approved because of its promise for eradicating a chief cause of social ruin. Daily papers nationwide reported his death, paying tribute in editorials to the late evangelist. The *New York Times*, which had once grouped its coverage of Jones with a derogatory article about religion in the South, lauded his "bitter denunciation of saloonkeepers and the liquor traffic" and claimed that he possessed "wit, sarcasm, lively humor, and a faculty for fanciful imagery that won him many devoted admirers."[61] On the front page, the *Boston Globe* called him a "noted evangelist" and commented that he "preached the Gospel more than 30 years and in that time it is estimated that more than 30,000,000 persons heard his deliverances."[62] The *Washington Evening Star* reported that Jones's "labors were frequently attended by the most gratifying results."[63] Even the *Atlanta Constitution* praised Jones, calling him "picturesque" and crediting him with "grip[ping] the consciences of men as more conventional preachers could never have reached them."[64] The daily newspapers of the nation bid the preacher farewell in language they seldom had used to describe him in life.

The weekly and monthly publications followed suit. Fellow white southerner Walter Hines Page used his editorial column in the *World's Work* to honor Jones, although he damned with faint praise Jones's propensity for "old-fashioned" religion. Page noted that Jones "had no new doctrine—he was a preacher of the old-time religion." He continued by noting that Jones scorned "biblical research" (which fundamentalists would later revile) and "was profoundly grateful that he had not been 'prepared' in a theological seminary." But for Page, the important work of Jones's life was his ability to promote temperance. As Page described it, "many remarkable things happened during his crusades." In a Nashville revival, "a prominent wholesale liquor-dealer went from one of his meetings, emptied into the sewer every barrel of his stock, gave his warehouse to the Salvation Army, and headed the movement which built a great tabernacle."[65]

The *Methodist Protestant*, a northern Methodist publication in Baltimore, noted that while the editors "did not approve of his style," Jones "was a tremendous foe of the saloon" and "a bold, brave, courageous, true man of God."[66] The passage of time and his work in the temperance movement had secured for Jones a more favorable place in the American mind. That favorable position was reflected in a hagiographic article in *Cosmopolitan* magazine two years after Jones's death. The author, John Temple Graves, portrayed Jones as a tireless warrior for prohibition in his home state of Georgia, "the very Lion of the Tribe of Prohibition in all the Southern and Western states." According to Graves, Jones "had the remarkable faculty of thundering a face-to-face denunciation into the ears of saloon-keepers, saloon-owners, complacent officials, and timid preachers, without making a personal enemy among them."[67] Forgetting the earlier incidents of violence and their own ridicule of the Georgia preacher, the liberal writers and leaders in the North, for the most part, gazed approvingly on the South's temperance crusade, and Jones's memory was the beneficiary. Jones had gone from a sideshow preacher to a venerated leader in many eyes.

The memory of Sam Jones as valiant temperance leader, rather than religious gadfly, was not created overnight but grew from coverage that northern publications afforded temperance victories in the South. Temperance was gaining momentum both legislatively and in popular support. As antialcohol forces gained strength in the South, northern publications triumphantly reported their victories and praised the region for its strong stand against demon rum. During the first decade of the twentieth century, the alliance between white southern clergy and temperance workers received hopeful praise from observers, both northern and southern. But that praise would turn to condemnation after the nation adopted the Eighteenth Amendment and prohibition settled over the land. As public sentiment began to turn against prohibition, so did the rhetoric about the South's role in bringing it about.

Why the nation turned away from the liquor trade in the period before Jones's death is not within the scope of this book.[68] Instead, the balance of this chapter will focus on how press coverage of southern temperance victories helped shape the image of a region that would sacrifice alcohol at all costs. But the coverage also provides an interesting illustration of the anxieties in the more urban cities of the North.

It is no coincidence that the temperance movement picked up great speed just as the United States was admitting huge new waves of Eastern European and Italian immigrants and as the scientific racists were expounding their theories about why these new Americans were inferior to the older stock. Just as the believers in Anglo-Saxon purity looked to the southern mountaineers for proof of racial potential, the temperance movement looked to the South for an example of how a ban on alcohol could improve a society dominated by Anglo-Saxons but fraught with imagined terrors of black ravishers and real examples of mob violence. It also meant a crackdown on Appalachian "moonshine," which was thought to contribute to the region's flaws.

Again the popular image of the South had a basis in reality. Although states in the South were not the first nationally to go dry, the South as a region did vote for prohibition on a state-by-state basis earlier than the rest of the country. Each victory in the South was accompanied by national attention from a variety of publications.[69] In 1899, *Popular Science Monthly* noted that Louisiana, South Carolina, and the City of Atlanta were all experimenting with some type of restriction on the sale of liquor.[70] The next year, Lyman Abbott's liberal-leaning *Outlook* reported that the North Carolina dispensary system was operating well.[71] In 1903, the *Outlook* told its readers that Tennessee had "achieved the enviable position of suppressing the saloons . . . by the honest sentiment of the people."[72] In a 1905 article in the *Atlantic Monthly*, Frank Foxcroft worried that states that had adopted some style of prohibition laws were repealing them, but he expressed praise for the "Southern states" in their work to increase no-license areas, jurisdictions in which no licenses could be granted to sell or serve alcohol.[73] And in 1907, Edward Lissner told readers of the New York–based *Harper's Weekly* that "politicians in the South have come to a realization that the prohibition movement in their region is one which must be taken with the utmost seriousness."[74] A magazine reader in the early twentieth century would have had a hard time ignoring the references to the South's affinity for temperance.[75]

As journalists reported on the prevalence of dry sentiment south of the Mason-Dixon Line, they also noted the role that religion played in popularizing prohibition and securing its legislative enactment. The *New York Times* coverage of the Georgia statewide prohibition vote noted that the lawmakers sang "Praise God from Whom All Blessings Flow." The *Atlanta Constitution* reported that the supporters of prohibition sang the same Long Meter Doxology in Alabama when that state when dry.[76] But the singing of hymns was not the only way white southern clergy and church members made their presence known in the prohibition movement. Writers both North and South had noticed and documented their involvement since the turn of the century. In an 1899 article, white southern reformer and Presbyterian minister Alexander J. McKelway noted that the movement to establish a dispensary system in North Carolina was "a moral movement." McKelway explained that ministers had used their churches as a means of disseminating prodispensary sentiment and circulating prodispensary petitions. According to McKelway, "the movement spread like wildfire."[77] In *Putnam's Magazine* in 1909, S. Mays Ball described the efforts in Georgia to enact statewide prohibition and credited two Atlanta ministers with helping to get the legislation enacted, Dr. Len G. Boughton and Dr. A. R. Holderby. According to Ball, Broughton was "a prominent Baptist minister who fought strenuously for prohibition" and "there [was] usually something doing when Dr. Broughton [began] action."[78] In the *Atlantic Monthly*, John Koren wrote in 1915 that "the dominant religious forces of the South, peculiarly fitted to be a vehicle for temperance propaganda, lent their full strength to the movement against the saloon."[79] The role of religion in the South's politics again came to the attention of northern readers, many of whom supported the dry cause. Some praised the involvement of white southern clergy even though it may have smacked of bringing church into the matters of state.

Writers outside the region were especially interested in the Georgia legislature's decision to enact prohibition legislation. In 1907, one year after the Atlanta race riots, the Georgia state legislature very publicly and reverently voted in favor of statewide prohibition. The House passage of the bill followed Senate approval, and the governor had already indicated that he would sign the measure. On July 31, the Georgia House overwhelmingly supported prohibition, and the coverage of the event further strengthened the perception of the South as both dry and religious. Major daily newspapers gave attention to the victory. As noted earlier, the *New York Times* reported that "as soon as the final vote was taken the great crowd burst into 'Praise God from Whom All Blessings Flow.'" The prohibition supporters then carried the House sponsor of the bill, the Honorable Seaborn Wright, "through the Capitol singing 'Gloria in Excelsis.'"[80] And the *Washington Evening Star* noted that after celebrating in the capitol, the protemperance "crowd proceeded to the Grady monument, where the Doxology was sung and speeches made by all leaders of the fight for the bill."[81] By patterning their victory celebration after Protestant liturgy and singing a doxology, the temperance backers showed that religious beliefs formed the basis of their position.

Northern denominational newspapers also made note of the growing prohibition sentiment among white southerners. The New York–based Methodist *Christian Advocate* gladly informed its readers of the Georgia triumph and added that "prohibition is gaining ground all through the South." It numbered efforts in Mississippi, Alabama, and Texas among the accomplishments of southern prohibition forces.[82] In November 1907, the *Christian Century* (formerly a Disciples of Christ publication turned "'undenominational'") called on the North to follow the South's example. "The South," the *Christian Century* argued, "has banished the saloon to save its industries and its homes. The North must do the same thing. . . ."[83] The same week, the northern Episcopalian newspaper, the *Churchman*, wrote from New York City that the most "striking changes" in the effort to advance prohibition had come from the South.[84] The northern *Methodist Protestant* called its readers' attention to the victory in Alabama of statewide prohibition.[85] Clearly, there was no shortage of press attention to the banning of liquor in the South.

Many outside observers, as well as most white southerners, believed that prohibition would lead to an easing of racial tensions. The goal of curtailing alcohol consumption among blacks provided a way in which North and South could agree on race. As Frank Foxcroft noted in his 1908 *Atlantic Monthly* article "Prohibition in the South," there was widespread belief that alcohol corrupted blacks, dragging them even lower into their supposed, but really white-imposed, inferiority. "Drunkenness," Foxcroft boldly proclaimed, "unquestionably demoralizes labor and incites to crime." He continued by explaining that

> the frightful race riots in Atlanta, which sprang from the dives and were carried to such excesses of unreasoning ferocity by men who were inflamed by drink, may well enough have been in the minds of the Georgia legislators when they enacted state prohibition.[86]

Foxcroft was indeed correct that the race riots were on the Georgia legislators' minds when they gathered at the Grady memorial, symbol of the New South and the scene of so much violence the previous year.

The belief that black men who drank became even more likely to commit criminal acts was not new. The Southern Baptist publication, the *Baptist Argus*, published in Louisville, held the saloon-keepers of Atlanta responsible for the riots of 1906, arguing that sales of liquor had made black men more likely to rape white women and made white men more likely to lynch black men.[87] The Reverend John E. White, liberal pastor of the Second Baptist Church of Atlanta, predicted in the *South Atlantic Quarterly* that enactment of prohibition would allow the South to turn its attention away from "the negro question" and instead focus on "the South's responsibility for the negro's moral welfare."[88] P. H. Whaley, writing for the widely popular *Collier's*, held that prohibition in the South resulted from the rise in "negro" crimes committed while drunk, which also led to lynching. The very safety of white women, Whaley argued, was at stake.[89]

But the leading role that the pastors had played in enacting prohibition in the South would come back to haunt them. Not everyone agreed that prohibition in the South, or anywhere in the country for that matter, was such a good idea. Voices of dissent rang out from the beginning of the temperance movement, and these voices grew louder as the antisaloon forces won successive legislative victories. The dissenters explored the tension between individual choice and the common good.

As early as 1893, a nationally circulated magazine published comments critical of white southerners' efforts to limit the sale of alcoholic beverages. Writing in the *North American Review*, the Honorable W. G. Chafee, mayor of Aiken, South Carolina, decried the "paternalism" of the dispensary system recently put in place in his home state. Chafee was happy with the resulting "marked decrease of drunkenness," but he worried about the "so-called Reform faction," headed by South Carolina governor Ben Tillman.[90] Greenough White, writing in the *School Review*, agreed with an assertion he credited to John Fiske that "there is more Puritanism in the South today than in New England."[91] Commenting in *Century* on the South's battle with the saloon, William Garrott Brown noted that the South was a place where "the government stretches its authority to the uttermost in the endeavor to enforce absolute moralities." "Government," Brown wrote, "is for the time being well-nigh puritanized."[92] Here Brown used the term "puritanized" in a derogatory fashion. Government in the South to him resembled the Massachusetts Bay Colony's polity—a government that was democratically elected but heavily influenced by the views of the clergy. Observers outside the South joined in with their doubts that prohibition was actually working in Dixie. S. Mays Ball, writing in 1909 in *Putnam's Magazine*, asked rhetorically, "Prohibition in Atlanta? Well, there isn't any."[93] R. W. Simpson Jr. wrote in *Harper's Weekly* in 1909 that "in a word, there isn't any prohibition." Simpson believed that temperance efforts would work only in rural districts, not in urban ones.[94] Two years later in the same publication, R. E. Pritchard told readers that "prohibition in the South is a failure." According to him, the antiliquor legislation bred "a defiance of law. . . ."[95] His words call to mind the characterizations of the South as a lawless place—southerners would obey laws against neither lynching nor selling demon rum, even if they had been the ones to enact those laws in the first place. The *Hartford (Connecticut) Courant* told its readers in 1913 that "the prohibition issue has been 'a ubiquitous trouble-maker' in Tennessee for years," and cited the recent political battles there that resembled the feuds for which the mountains had become famous.[96] White southerners, even when they followed the lead of their temperate northern brethren, could not escape the perception that their efforts were incomplete, ill advised, or futile.

Once national prohibition was enacted, the South bore the brunt of a new volley of criticisms. Observers in the North doubted that the national effort to prohibit the sale of alcohol would be any more successful than the state efforts in the South, and they blamed white southerners for imposing their solution to racial problems and their crusading morality on the rest of the country. A writer from Maine told the *New York Times* that she did not believe that federal prohibition would work "if the present conditions in the South are any indication."[97] Two weeks later, the *Times* condemned Virginia's efforts to enforce prohibition, citing recent shootings of unarmed bootleggers by law enforcement officials. "Administered by the relentless Drys," the editor warned, "the prohibition law is the chief and crowning law, and to break it is to commit the sum of all villainies." The *Times* went on to note that Virginia officials were having a difficult time enforcing the prohibition law.[98] Another New York City newspaper, the *Herald*, informed its readers in 1922 that North Carolina and Georgia were "'generally regarded as the wettest'" states in the country since the enactment of the Eighteenth Amendment.[99] The South could pass but not enforce its own prohibition laws.

Several observers called the South to task for imposing its solution to racial problems and moral dilemmas on the rest of the country. In the *World's Work* in 1924, four years after the enactment of national prohibition, John J. Fleming penned an article opposing it. According to Fleming, the reason that temperance efforts gained so much ground in the South was "the inability of the large Negro population to use liquor intelligently," which led white southerners to embrace a ban on its sale, which later became a national ban.[100] But author Edgar Lee Masters, writing in a 1919 letter to the editor of the *New Republic*, was far less charitable in his analysis of the southern contribution to national prohibition. Masters began by stating his hope that he would be remembered as "one who took the pains to record his contempt of the party and the men who turned a republic into a . . . theocracy." He condemned the temperance supporters for their "ignorance . . . littleness . . . fanaticism . . . [and] twisted intelligence." Masters then went further, noting,

> as a laughable irony the South, which went to war, tried to break up the Union in order to preserve the glorious principles of local self-government as applied to the practice of keeping the negro in slavery, is the very South that has been so great an influence imperiling the Republic. First they wanted to keep the negro in slavery, and then they wanted to deprive him of booze. Ham has done the trick for us![101]

Masters's comments demonstrated his belief that the South had turned into a theocracy, where the clergy controlled the government, and that this clergy-run area had also managed to force the rest of the country to accept its method of keeping blacks in line—to take away their liquor. His ringing condemnation of Dixie implied that the region was hypocritical in its application of states' rights and obsessed with the oppression of blacks and the furtherance of religiously motivated laws.

Masters was not alone in his assessment. The always fiery H. L. Mencken averred that the Methodists "gave us Prohibition," and the *Independent* contended that prohibition had carried in the South because of a belief that "liquor was the work of the devil."[102] Religion's influence in politics was too powerful in the opinion of these writers. Quoting an opponent of prohibition, Rollin Lynde Hartt told readers of the *World's Work* that "prohibition [was] 'a movement to put the church in control of the state. . . . [T]his is pure theocracy, such as was the ideal of the Middle Ages.'"[103] Prohibition had moved the South not forward, as proponents wished, but backward to medieval times, carrying the rest of the country with it.

By 1919, six years before the Scopes Trial, the South had already been firmly cemented in the national consciousness as the place where religion was supreme, religion was different, and religion was powerful. The reform movement that led to the passage of national prohibition only helped to enhance the image of the South as religiously different. In this case, the South seemed an area in which enthusiastic but often uneducated ministers exhorted their listeners, who the popular consensus agreed were illiterate rubes, to seek their own salvation. The white southern clergy cared little, liberal observers agreed, about the condition of southern society, the region's propensity for mob violence, or its need to strengthen schools. Instead, the critics portrayed the pastors as paternalistic, interested in enhancing their own power, and obsessed with the demonic power of alcohol. The South's efforts to enact temperance measures had drawn praise from northern and southern commentators who believed that alcohol consumption led to personal and economic ruin. But its means of enforcing the laws, and its insistence that other regions follow its example, led many journalists to characterize the temperance movement as yet another one of the South's aberrant behaviors. As the organizers of the World's Christian Fundamentals Association prepared for their meeting in Philadelphia in May of 1919, they could hardly have foreseen that their movement would be categorized as regional—that is, southern—but all of the elements for a conflation of fundamentalism and "southern" religion were already in place. The Scopes Trial was unnecessary to understanding the white South as other. That perception was firmly held in many minds already, and the Scopes Trial merely added more proof to an already closed case. The conflation of fundamentalism and "southern" religion would happen very quickly.

CHAPTER 4

"Salesmen of Hate": Fundamentalism Becomes Southern

I n 1910, Congregational minister, magazine editor, and liberal Protestant Lyman Abbott had just received in the mail his first complimentary installments of a multivolume set entitled *The Fundamentals*, a collection of essays covering a range of topics of relevance to Christians. These books were written by clergy and theologians, some of whom would start the fundamentalist movement. Praising them in his magazine, the *Outlook*, Abbott told his readers that the volumes were "distinctively constructive, not polemical" and that their authors "render[ed] a valuable service to the Church." Abbott explained in true liberal fashion that the books were helpful because "laymen should understand the difference between the older and the newer thinking in theology." However, their authors had set forth "views . . . which . . . we regard as archaic, and in light of the modern knowledge, untenable."[1] Abbott's language clearly indicated that *The Fundamentals* was part of the historical record and not something for modern Christians to accept and embrace.

But fifteen years later, the fundamentalists had taken on a much more sinister appearance in the eyes of many Americans. Satirist and pundit H. L. Mencken summed up this new view of the fundamentalists in his scathing denunciation of

William Jennings Bryan, the populist leader and spokesman for creationism, following Bryan's death in Dayton, Tennessee, shortly after the conclusion of the Scopes Trial. According to Mencken, the fundamentalists

swarm in the country towns, inflamed by their pastors, and with a saint, now, to venerate. They are thick in the mean streets behind the gas-works. They are everywhere that learning is too heavy a burden for mortal minds, even the vague pathetic learning on tap in little red schoolhouses. They march with the Klan, with the Christian Endeavor Society, with the Junior Order of United American Mechanics, with the Epworth League, with all the rococo bands that poor and unhappy folk organize to bring some light of purpose into their lives.[2]

In just six short years after the fundamentalists made their public appearance, their depiction had changed from that of a group of conservative, quaintly outdated band of theologians into one of a radical, fanatical, and intolerant mass threatening American freedom. And they had managed to be tied to the South along the way.

Fundamentalism did not burst into national prominence with the Scopes Trial in 1925. It had earned media attention more than five years earlier as many major publications gave space and analysis to the newly emboldened conservatives bringing their beliefs before denominational assemblies, councils, and the lay public. The Northern Baptist Convention's annual meetings in 1922 and 1923 received press attention, as did the Reverend Harry Emerson Fosdick's struggles with conservatives within the northern branch of the Presbyterian Church. For the most part, the media coverage of these doctrinal battles was balanced and detailed, with both sides represented in written accounts, especially in the early 1920s. But by 1924, when the issue of evolution had become prominent in the debate and fundamentalists showed increasing strength, northern observers were less charitable toward the fundamentalists.[3]

These same observers, moreover, had begun to label the South as fundamentalist in a negative way even before the Scopes Trial. The emergence in the South of a new incarnation of the Ku Klux Klan, bent on enforcing what it saw as conservative Christian values, and its spread to the rest of the country made the South again seem violent and religiously different. The antievolution movement found fertile ground in the South, and several southern states' enactment of antievolution legislation provided additional examples to northern journalists (and disgruntled white southern liberals) of the South's alien and dangerous nature.[4] The racial and religious message of the Klan, combined with the attack on what liberals believed was modern education, firmly pinned the label "fundamentalist" on the lapel of the South without regard for evidence—statistical or theological.

As noted previously, historians have long debated what fundamentalism is, how it formed, and what it meant in the early years of the twentieth century. For the purposes of this book, the fundamentalists constituted a group of intensely theolog-ically and politically conservative evangelicals who coalesced in the early twenti-eth century in northern urban centers in reaction to the assertion of liberal Chris-tians that religion should take on the trappings of America's dominant culture. Fun-damentalists reacted to changes in American culture, especially the labor unrest after the First World War. After 1919, the movement became formally organized and espoused a militant rejection of modernity, calling for a return to conservative Christian dogma, with emphases on biblical inerrancy; the reality, depth, and per-vasiveness of sin; the divinity of Jesus; and dispensational premillennialism.[5] They believed that these were the traditional pillars of American Protestantism (mistak-enly so in the case of dispensational premillennialism) and that they should guide and inform American society. Holding such beliefs, fundamentalists disagreed with liberal (or modernist) Protestants, who held that in light of recent biblical schol-arship and certain changes in American society, religion was more malleable and that culture should inform and guide it. The fundamentalists' tactics were particu-larly militant, in large part because they saw liberal Protestantism as a mortal threat to Christianity.

Fundamentalists appeared at a time of great upheaval in American society and American intellectual life. Race riots, labor strikes, the mass return and demobi-lization of American soldiers from Europe, and the women's suffrage movement all signaled deep currents at work reshaping the American cultural landscape.[6] Many groups fought against these changes, including antievolutionists, the Ku Klux Klan, and anti-Catholic nativist groups, each with its own target and motives. Member-ship in these groups was not mutually exclusive, and journalists often lumped their adherents together indiscriminately. For instance, fundamentalists did play a role in the antievolution movement—those who opposed the teaching of Darwin's the-ory of evolution in public schools—but not all fundamentalists were antievolution-ists, nor were all antievolutionists fundamentalists.[7] But for liberal-leaning journal-ists, editors, and academics, the distinctions among these groups blurred over time. After a while, the media tended to portray them as cut from the same cloth—a fab-ric of uneducated, violent, intolerant people who opposed modern life and the changes it brought with it. And before the Scopes Trial, the media had concluded that the uneducated, violent, intolerant white people of the South were in fact fun-damentalists, every one.

Fundamentalism did not always suffer in press accounts. The organizational beginning of the movement—the first meeting of the World's Christian Funda-mentals Association in May 1919 in Philadelphia—drew over a thousand atten-dees and helped propel the movement to a more prominent position in seminaries, denominations, and eventually, national media. The *Philadelphia Inquirer* noted the group's antipathy toward "modern ideas," citing its belief that Jesus did not advocate "the survival of the fittest," which was a slur on evolutionary theory and represented a misunderstanding of Darwin's theory.[8] The paper also reported that conference organizers were surprised by the attendance. The "noon meeting" drew "hundreds of persons [who] crowded into the auditorium as soon as the doors were thrown open to general admission."[9] The *Inquirer* ran two more stories over the course of that week, each of which was impartial.[10]

Similar examples of balanced reporting of early modernist/fundamentalist skirmishes were not confined to Philadelphia. For instance, the newly launched news magazine *Time* reported in 1923 that Dr. Cornelius Woelfkin of Park Avenue Church in New York City had squared off against Dr. John Roach Straton and Dr. J. Frank Norris over the issues of evolution and theatergoing.[11] *Time* took no stand on the matter, merely reporting the two sides' upcoming meeting in the Northern Baptist Convention's annual meeting in Atlantic City in late May. The magazine continued this tradition of neutral coverage when it discussed the General Assembly of the Presbyterian (North) Church's upcoming meeting in Indianapolis. After defining the terms "Fundamentalist" and "Liberal," *Time* went on to summarize the crux of the argument between the two sides:

> Liberals believe themselves to be more fundamental than the Fundamentalists, because their religion does not center on smaller matters of scripture like unscientific geography or unproved miracles, but on a Being who was so Divine that men could see God in Him. While the Fundamentalists see their whole scheme of salvation slipping if science and higher criticism of the Bible are accepted, the Liberals see the whole scheme of salvation rendered ridiculous if unscientific stories (and to them non-essential) in the Bible are held to be prerequisite to Christianity.

The author of the article presciently observed that "science" was part of the debate: "Both sides of the controversy are interested in science, one claiming ideas like evolution and the reign of law as revelations that can be made friendly to the truths of Christianity, the other holding them to be irreconcilable with Christianity as taught in the Bible."[12]

Time was not alone in its evenhanded assessment of the simmering dispute. The *Nation*, normally aligned with all things liberal, commented on the 1923 Presbyterian General Assembly meeting and the liberals' insistence that the Bible was not inerrant. The editorial correctly reminded liberal Protestants that "belief in evolution touches the average Protestant Christian less closely than doubt as to the perfect inerrancy of the Gospel stories or of the ancient creeds."[13] The magazine editor admonished modernists for having strayed too far ahead of their denominations in their efforts to make Protestant theology contemporary. The *Nation* reissued this admonition several months later when it warned that

despite some vagaries, in its general conception of God, the universe, and salva-
tion, Fundamentalism is undoubtedly in the main stream of Christian tradition while
Modernism represents a religious revolution as far-reaching as the Protestant
Reformation.[14]

The modernists, pundits warned, had gotten too far in front of the general public. One month later, in January 1924, another New York publication with a liberal leaning, the *New Republic*, argued in favor of the fundamentalists' belief that people who did not subscribe to the creeds of a denomination did not belong to that particular community. According to the editorial, "these creeds have in the past supplied the keystones for the arches which carried the superstructure of denominational Christianity."[15] In this respect, the coverage of the fundamentalist/modernist debate was correct in its assumptions. The doctrinal beliefs that fundamentalism embraced were closer to the traditional Protestant evangelicalism that a majority of U.S. residents embraced. The liberals had a vague understanding of the Christian concept of sin, and their relegation of Jesus to a mere human role model and their insistence on progress were not historically associated with Christianity. But to many liberals, the sheer number of evangelical believers was not important; only their interpretation of the gospel was.

But at the outset, the media remained on the sidelines. The increasing number of denominational disputes led other journals to include lengthy and thoughtful articles about the divisions between modernists and fundamentalists. Reporting in 1923 on the pending heresy trial of a Texas Episcopal minister for denial of the Virgin Birth, the *New York Times* succinctly presented both sides' arguments.[16] In March of 1924, former Harvard University president Charles William Eliot, writing in the Boston-based *Atlantic Monthly*, concluded that America was divided into three "parties or sections in regard to religion": fundamentalists, modernists, and people who knew little about religion. Eliot then described fundamentalists as those who believed in biblical inerrancy (he did not use the word *literalism*) and tended to be "Calvinistic" in their doctrines. He defined modernists as adherents of "modern Biblical Criticism," and gave a long list of modernist views on various Bible stories.[17] Eliot's use of the word "inerrancy" rather than *literalism* is important. He recognized that fundamentalists were not literal followers of the Bible but they believed it was inerrant in matters of faith. Fundamentalists understood then and still understand the use of allegory, poetic imagery, and metaphor in the Bible, distinctions that literalists would not make. Eliot also correctly recognized the strong flavor of Calvin's belief in predestination at work in fundamentalist theology. In another example of objective reporting, the *Survey* ran side-by-side affirmative and negative arguments in response to the question "Does fundamentalism obstruct social progress?"[18] In the earliest reports of fundamentalism, the movement was presented as a thoughtful reaction to changes in Protestant theology, and fundamentalists tended to be viewed as closer to traditional evangelical American Protestantism than progressive, liberal Christianity was.[19]

But even as such evenhanded critiques appeared, they were overtaken by negative journalistic sentiment against the fundamentalists. As the fundamentalists began to win more of their battles with the modernists, as liberal minister Harry Emerson Fosdick was forced to leave his pulpit for his liberal views, and as anti-evolution legislation began to wend its way through state legislatures, the novelty of the controversy wore off for reporters, and their tone and their words turned squarely against the fundamentalists. Well before the fateful days in Tennessee, critics of fundamentalism had already applied to the fundamentalist movement many of the same damning monikers the South had suffered.

As early as 1922, the fundamentalists' reputation for being intolerant and rhetorically violent was sufficient to lead one religious liberal, Unitarian minister Albert Dieffenbach, to brand them "'the religious Ku Klux.'"[20] Dieffenbach's perception of the fundamentalists as the theological equivalent of Klan members was most likely shared by his fellow liberal Protestants and quite a few northern elites as well. *Time*, which had been following the various disputes carefully, wrote in June 1924 that fundamentalists in the northern branch of the Presbyterian Church had as their chief goal "to kill modernism once and forever."[21] Already journalists were noticing the violent rhetoric of the new breed of religious conservatives. Occasionally, reporters believed that the fighting words of the fundamentalists were indicators of a violent nature. The *Century*'s editor, Glenn Frank, writing in May 1923, worried that "were Jesus to return to earth, I should have fear for His safety were He to fall into the hands of the fundamentalists."[22]

More common, however, was the view that the fundamentalists were merely rhetorically violent, although that rhetoric was not lost upon the critics who saw fundamentalists as intolerant and even dangerous. Rollin Lynde Hartt, Congregationalist minister and advocate of liberal Protestant thought, called on readers of the *World's Work* to pay attention to the gruesome details of fundamentalist homilies of the Reverend Dr. I. M. Haldeman. Haldeman was a "vigorous writer and pastor of the First Baptist Church of New York City."[23] Hartt described him as one

> who declares that Christ will return "with garments dipped in blood, the blood of others," and "enunciate His claim by terror and might." He will "tread and trample His fury till the blood of men shall fill the earth." He "will come to His glory, not as the Saviour meek and lowly, but as a king, an autocrat, a despot, through the blood of a trampled world."[24]

A year earlier, the *Literary Digest* had also quoted the rhetoric of Haldeman, reporting that observers believed that "its awfulness, its bloody sweep over the world, surpasses the most gruesome pictures in the Book of Revelation."[25] One year later, the same publication noted that one fundamentalist had told a reporter, "'We're going to rip them [the liberal Protestants] up,'" hardly a comforting statement to people who believed in the amelioration of social problems through education and charity and who eschewed notions of a final judgment.[26] A Methodist pastor related to readers of the *World's Work* how he lost his ministry in part because he believed that the writers of the Bible were mistaken in their belief that God would kill innocent people.[27] Always the subject of controversy, Baptist minister J. Frank Norris, preaching at John Roach Straton's First Baptist Church in New York City, warned that recent earthquakes were signs that the end of time was nigh. The *New York Times* reported that Norris entitled his sermon "How New York Will Be Destroyed in One Hour" and that he claimed that there were no earthquakes in Jesus' time.[28]

The fundamentalists' violent portrayal of the end of time continued to attract the attention of observers, some of whom were unable to understand completely how this rhetoric contrasted with their own views of the Kingdom of God on earth. The premillennial rhetoric was necessarily pessimistic, but the observers of it used their own optimistic, postmillennial-influenced opinions to issue a critique of the fundamentalists' exceptionalism. Former Harvard president Charles Eliot said that "the Fundamentalists are prophesying the speedy coming of Christ at the head of an invincible army to drown civilization and society in blood, as a necessary preliminary to setting up on earth a better Church and a better State."[29] He correctly observed that the dispensational premillennial belief included the possibility of a thousand-year reign under Christ, but he did not emphasize the distinction that the ideal state had to be divinely established, not humanly, as the liberal Protestants believed. Eliot had seized upon their warlike rhetoric, even if he did not completely understand it.[30]

Fundamentalist rhetoric on doctrinal matters other than the second coming attracted the attention of nonfundamentalist observers and led them to label the new religious conservatives as bellicose. Writing in the *Nation*, Heywood Broun, literary critic for the *New York Tribune*, portrayed John Roach Straton as a person so focused on revenge that he would dare to ask God to destroy New York City. In the satirical piece, Broun had Straton beg that the Almighty "'smite them hip and thigh'" for the crime of "watch[ing] a baseball game" on a Sunday.[31] In 1923, the *New York Times* reported that Texas fundamentalist and firebrand J. Frank Norris had told a congregation that the fundamentalists were on a "crusade" to purge Baptist ranks of nonfundamentalists.[32] Rollin Lynn Hartt returned to do battle with the fundamentalists in a 1923 *New York Times* article, in which he described the leaders of the movement as "bellicose" and "old-fashioned."[33] The controversy over the continued appointment of liberal Baptist minister Harry Emerson Fosdick to First

Presbyterian Church in New York City brought more critical comments about the fundamentalists. Fosdick was eventually forced out of the Presbyterian pulpit but not without more scorn for the conservatives from the press.[34] The *New Republic* called the fundamentalists "a party militant," "true reactionaries" who were conducting "a mass attack" in "each denomination." Further comparing the fundamentalists to an invading army, the *New Republic* explained: "In each field they have inscribed banners with slogans suitable to the denomination and, wearing their atavistic rituals upon their shields, they have attempted to carry the central position of the church by storm."[35] And Harvard Divinity School professor Kirsopp Lake, writing for the *Atlantic Monthly*, noted how the fundamentalists "recruited" new members from "'Bible Schools' which offer a cheaper education for those wishing to be ministers than can be found in universities or in the theological schools that take only college graduates."[36] Clearly, said these writers who covered the first fundamentalists, the new religious conservatives were a militant army that recruited its members from the less educated and pressed its doctrines by force on the various American denominations, ignoring the American tradition of democratic debate and consensus.

The fundamentalists also heard that they were uneducated. In 1922, the *New Republic* held that "millions of Christians have accepted the results of scientific research and have abandoned more or less of the old interpretations," while "millions have shut their eyes or turned away."[37] "Turn[ing] away" for the magazine meant staying in ignorance. *Time*'s coverage of the disputes in the northern Presbyterian Church suggested that the effort to wipe out modernism would involve the "ousting" of "a group of educated ministers like Henry Sloane Coffin, Henry Van Dyke, [and] William Pierson Merrill."[38] Describing modernist ministers as "educated" was a code used to distinguish them from the presumably uneducated fundamentalists. Writing for the *New Republic* in 1924, John Dewey, the well-known American philosopher, took up the theme of fundamentalism as ignorance. He placed the fundamentalists in the past, decrying their rejection of modern interpretation of the Bible. The new conservatives, he wrote, "proclaim the infallibility of men who lived many centuries ago in periods of widespread ignorance, of unscientific methods of inquiry, of intolerance and persecuting animosity."[39] It was no accident that the *New Republic*, edited by Comtean-influenced Herbert Croly, published Dewey's disparaging remarks about the fundamentalists. Education and progress were paramount for Comte and his disciples, and the fundamentalists' insistence on unchangeable creeds seemed to these observers to be the height of ignorance and backwardness.[40]

Adherence to what the modernists perceived as outdated creeds was not the only characteristic that qualified the fundamentalists as uneducated, ignorant bogeymen.

Northern observers also worried about the movement's embrace of antievolution legislation in several state legislatures. The journal *Current Opinion* reported that Julian Huxley, "grandson of [the] famous scientist" Thomas Huxley, found it paradoxical that in a country in which so many people were educated "an anti-biological and anti-scientific movement should be virulent."[41] For Huxley, and for many of the cultural elite in the American North, rejection of evolution went hand in hand with ignorance and an unwillingness to support education. Indeed, commenting on populist leader William Jennings Bryan's embrace of the antievolutionist movement, Henshaw Ward wrote in the *Independent* that all the Great Commoner had "accomplished was to horrify most educated Christians and to give pleasure to all who sneer at religion." Ward went on to engage Bryan in an imaginary conversation with Dr. William E. Hatcher, the white biographer of John Jasper, the nineteenth-century African American preacher who was famous for his sermon "The Sun Do Move!" which referred to the biblical account of Joshua 10:12–14, in which God stopped the sun so that Joshua could defeat his enemies. Jasper used the evidence that God had stopped the sun to prove that the sun, in fact, did move.[42] In his attack on Bryan and fundamentalism, Ward used racism in demonstrating that Bryan believed what a "Negro" years ago did. Bryan and Jasper, for Ward, were the models of Christians who refuted science and thus showed themselves to be hopelessly ignorant.

The periodicals from the years preceding the Scopes Trial contain further examples of "ignorance" among the allies of creationism and fundamentalism, especially as the antievolutionist movement gained ground in the South. In July 1923, *Time* told the story of how a University of Tennessee professor "assigned a book on evolution as outside reading" in violation of "the school's policy." The article suggested, tongue in cheek, that Knoxville's "official" designation as the "seat of higher learning in Tennessee" was in question as a result of the uproar over evolution.[43] Two weeks later, the magazine reported the professor's dismissal for the same offense.[44]

Just a few months later, liberal Protestant Rollin Lynde Hartt published a piece in the *World's Work* in which he documented the antievolutionist movement and its growth. For Hartt, the movement was merely a cover for fundamentalists who sought to end academic freedom. Hartt employed prominent liberal Shailer Mathews in his efforts to demonstrate the antievolutionists' ignorance. (Mathews served as dean of the University of Chicago Divinity School and published frequent works in support of modernist theology.)[45] He quoted Mathews as saying, "'It is only those who are ignorant of both the origin and nature of the Bible and of the facts in our universe who are terrified lest science should make them lose their faith.'" But while Hartt found such an argument persuasive, he complained that with the "Fundamentalists . . . such contentions are without effect."[46] Reason, Hartt believed, could not influence the fundamentalists; they were unable to understand it. Dr. T. V. Smith of the University of Chicago also saw creationists and fundamentalists as ignorant and unable to comprehend reason. In an article for the *Scientific Monthly*, Smith told his fellow scientists that evolution was so unpopular among the general public because the "task of raising the general level of intelligence" was "slow." He went on to label William Jennings Bryan a man of decreasing intellectual stature and importance: "It is indeed altogether probable that even as a religious prophet— as a politician he has, you remember, been dead or dying these many years!—he speaks to and for a constantly declining number of people." Smith also warned that, despite his contention that Bryan's audience was diminishing, he was popular in "most of the south." Smith went on to describe a preoccupation that he believed Bryan held with the other world. For Smith, that interest was "medieval."[47] By inference, the South was still, for this University of Chicago academic, a place teeming with uneducated people who were ready to follow Bryan like lemmings into a sea of ignorance. And *New Republic* contributor Chester T. Crowell accused the fundamentalists of hypocrisy, arguing that they were "chasing evolutionists out of the classrooms where history and philosophy are taught but employing them in the medical schools."[48] The words of Crowell, Smith, and others like them were harsh, but northern observers would use even sharper words of disdain for the South's educational level when the Scopes Trial occupied the nation's attention in July of 1925.

Ignorance was not the only shortcoming the fundamentalists were accused of during the years before the Scopes Trial. The perceived fundamentalist propensity for heresy trials and insistence on creedal statements of faith and doctrine led many observers to call them "medieval" and liken their methods to the Inquisition, just as the reporters had called the South medieval for its views on lynching and education and for the role of the clergy in influencing public policy in the region. Critics of the fundamentalists linked justice with reason and injustice with a lack of reason. The addition of the charge of "inquisitor" allowed the opponents of fundamentalism to link the fundamentalists' religion with violence and oppression. Writing in early 1923, A. Wakefield Slaten told readers of the *Educational Review* that denominational colleges, which he labeled outlets for "overflow student population" from large state schools, were requiring their professors to sign statements that attested to their belief in the creeds of the denomination. Slaten spoke against such a practice and called the effort the "inquisitorial removing of teachers from their chairs."[49] Slaten's use of the term "overflow" to describe the students of denominational colleges indicates that he believed that they were not of sufficient intellectual ability to attend more rigorous institutions. The fundamentalists and their students were, in his mind, intellectually deficient and authoritarian in their college government.

Slaten was not the only writer to employ images of the Inquisition. In the May 1923 edition of *Century*, editor Glenn Frank summed up his feeling about the "fundamentalist movement in theology" by explaining that "it represents a renaissance of the mania for persecution that marked the Inquisition." He added that "its insignia should be the creative mind dormant and the creed-making instinct rampant."[50] In early 1924, *Scribner's Magazine* carried similar comments from Henry S. Pritchett, president of the Carnegie Foundation for the Advancement of Teaching. According to Pritchett, the fundamentalists brought to mind "the story of Copernicus" and led him "to recall the condemnation of Bruno and Galileo, and to reflect how intolerance in theology dealt grievous wounds to religion."[51] Pritchett's use of Galileo came more than a year before the detractors of the South would use the same Italian scientist as an example of how religious attempts to stifle scientific education were dangerous and antimodern.

The comparison of fundamentalists to inquisitors continued throughout 1924 and into 1925. Rollin Lynde Hartt published a book in 1924, *The Man Himself: The Nazarene*, in which he provided a modernist biography of Jesus. As a conclusion, he argued against the tenets of fundamentalism and argued that they led to an "Age of Torture."[52] Howard Chandler Robbins, dean of the Cathedral of St. John the Divine in New York City, explained in the May 1924 issue of the *Forum* that "the fundamentalist joyously takes his place beside the sixteenth century divines and adopts their presuppositions." He claimed that "the modern fundamentalist is a stout-hearted hater of heretics," and that "by his [Spanish inquisitor Tomas de] Torquemada-like activities he has given color to the popular impression that his motto is 'Keep the hell fires burning.'"[53] The next month, the liberal journal the *Outlook*, now edited by Lyman Abbott's son, Ernest Hamlin Abbott, also invoked Galileo and the Inquisition, arguing that the fundamentalists were like those who attacked Galileo and that "they had their predecessors in the Sanhedrin [the Jewish court which handed Jesus over to the Romans] . . . whenever light breaks forth, they try to shut it out." For the *Outlook*, the "light" of knowledge was battling the "darkness" of ignorance. The magazine took some comfort that the fundamentalists "can no longer burn at the stake or crucify, but they can pass resolutions."[54]

As doctrinal disputes embroiled certain denominations, religious newspapers also joined the list of publications that saw in the fundamentalist movement a modern-day variant of the medieval inquisition. The *Universalist Leader*, published by the Universalist Church, which had not had such a dispute within its ranks, said that the opponents of liberals wanted "to reestablish medieval theology" including "all the . . . dreary dogmas of the Dark Ages."[55] And the New York City Episcopalian publication, the *Churchman*, covered with interest the campaign of conservatives at Southern Methodist University to "dislodge from the faculty Mims Thornburgh

Workman, associate professor of Biblical History and Literature." The *Churchman* article, which ran the month immediately before the Scopes Trial, called the efforts "a new epoch in the history of the inquisition."[56]

Their characterization as inquisitioners made the fundamentalists targets of parody as they waged their campaigns against heresy within their denominations. In the May 1924 issue of the *Century*, John F. Scott published a spoof of the conservatives, using Lewis Carroll's *Through the Looking Glass* as his model. In Scott's parody, Alice travels into "Literal-Land," where she watches as a heresy defendant is found guilty and sentenced to be whipped. The "'executioners'" take the defendant outside, tie him to a whipping post, and then, along with the "prisoner" sing "alternate verses of a disciplinary hymn":

EXECUTIONERS:
"The Bible is infallible, which you must not deny.
Adam named the animals, and Enoch did not die.
Take care you do not change it, for that would surely breed
Distrust of our authority! Now won't you say the creed?
Will you, won't you, will you, won't you, will you say the creed?
Will you, won't you, will you, won't you, won't you say the creed?"

PRISONER:
"I cannot see your argument; it has no sense at all.
To sin by eating apples is not a serious fall.
There is no hell hereafter for which I feel the need,
But if there were, I tell you now, I would not say the creed!
Would not, could not, would not, could not, would not say the creed.
Would not, could not, would not, could not, could not say the creed."

EXECUTIONERS:
"Arius was a heretic, Apollinaris, too.
They sought to think things for themselves, much the same as you.
The Apostles at Nicaea—please give this careful heed—
Drew up our sacred document. Oh, won't you say the creed?
Will you, won't you, will you, won't you, will you say the creed?
Will you, won't you, will you, won't you, won't you say the creed?"[57]

Scott reported that by the time the executioners had finished the song, they were too exhausted to carry out the punishment. As the liberal journalists saw them, the fundamentalists were a band of zealots who demanded strict adherence to their beliefs and punished "heretics" mercilessly. For the most part, they were ludicrous in their beliefs and their insistence on universal acceptance of their doctrines.

But that humor was tempered with fear. In the midst of all the excitement about evolution and its role in schools, another foe of modernity appeared in the

South and then spread to the North. Reincarnated in the fall of 1915 by William Joseph Simmons, a former Southern Methodist circuit rider, the new Ku Klux Klan found increased enrollment first in the South. According to one account, when Simmons and his followers first met on Thanksgiving night 1915 on Stone Mountain, Georgia, they had "a Bible open to the twelfth chapter of Romans" and "proclaimed the new Knights of the Ku Klux Klan."[58] The choice of scripture was, at first blush, an odd one, but the new Knights had a reason for choosing Paul's admonition to the Romans to do the will of God. For them, the precepts "be not conformed to this world but be ye transformed by the renewing of your mind" and "be not overcome by evil" (Romans 12: 2 and 12: 21, King James Version) meant that they had to work against the corruption they saw in society. The Klan attracted members who wanted to preserve Anglo-Saxon cultural authority, and it soon involved itself in a campaign of violent oppression of blacks, Jews, Catholics, and people it deemed to be of questionable morality.

It did not take northern journalists long to publish accounts of Klan activities in the South and of the Klan's religious motivations, especially after the Klan began to expand its membership in the early 1920s. Worried over the Klan's new appeal and the recent election of Tom Watson as Georgia's newest U.S. Senator, Charles P. Sweeney warned the readers of the *Nation* in 1920 that anti-Catholicism was flourishing in the South and that "we might some day expect to see the burning of Catholics at the stake and such other of the monstrous delights of inflamed ignorance as are now practiced on the Negro population." Sweeney concluded his warning by calling for "serious reflection by the whole people, for freedom of conscience and of action are menaced while [intolerance] continues to advance."[59] Just over a year later, Albert De Silver, writing also in the *Nation*, reported on the new "descriptive folder" which the Klan was handing out to interested potential members. According to De Silver, the same Klan that proclaimed itself in the brochure a "friend" of "the Negro" was responsible for attacks in the name of chivalry on blacks in Trenton, South Carolina; Jacksonville, Florida; Dallas, Goose Creek, Fort Worth, Houston, Waco, and Deweyville, Texas; and Birmingham, Alabama.[60] In 1922, the *Atlantic Monthly* published an article in which the author tried to explain why people joined the Klan. According to Leroy Percy, the Klan used "religious intolerance" as its "chief appeal" in the South.[61] The widely read magazine *Ladies' Home Journal* told its audience in January 1924 that the Klan was a form of "religious and race hatred" and that it had spread beyond its birthplace of the South. The *Journal* warned that the Klan contained within it "the germs of a new civil war" and cautioned that it could not "endure and grow without plunging this country into a worse political chaos than it has ever experienced in the past."[62] And W. E. B. Du Bois, writing for the *Nation* in 1925, charged that the Klan in Georgia was part and parcel of a religious yet violent society that valued white people and openly abhorred blacks. Du Bois called religion in Georgia "fundamental," an obvious reference to the fundamentalists who were gaining in national prominence, and saw little hope for liberal ideals in that state. He linked the violence of the Klan with the religion of the fundamentalists and declared that Georgia was home to both of these opponents of modernity. "No, there is little hope," Du Bois mourned, "in Georgia for religion despite a light here and there. . . . They lynch and murder body and soul."[63]

But as repulsive as reporters found the new Klan, they were even more horrified to learn that white southern clergy were actively involved in the movement. Such a connection merely reinforced in the northern mind the belief that white southern clergy had forgotten their calling as Christian ministers and had stepped out of their proper role in society. As early as 1922, the *Atlantic Monthly* published allegations that white southern preachers were involved in the workings of the Klan. Leroy Percy explained that the Klan "appeal[ed] to religious intolerance" and that among its members in the South were "Christian men [and] pastors of churches."[64] In 1923, Leonard Lanson Cline, reporter for the *Baltimore Sun*, reported in the *Nation* that in the town of Bastrop, "in darkest Louisiana, . . . The Reverend Leon W. Sloan is pastor of the Baptist Church. Gossip names him also a Klansman, and he will not deny that there is more than one nightshirt in his closet." Cline believed that the involvement of men like Sloan allowed the Klan, "with the approbation of the evangelical church," to carry out "its meanest and most brutal desires."[65] For Cline, clerical involvement in the Klan was an example of religion gone hopelessly astray, mutated into evil, and commanding far too much respect within its warped society. The same week, *Time* announced that five Kentucky ministers had "signed resolutions endorsing the Ku Klux Klan."[66] Magazines were also quick to report how the Klan made overtures to potentially friendly clergy by donating money to certain churches, and more than one observer also linked the Klan to the temperance movement and its clergy leadership.[67] The southern clergy, the writers argued, were actively participating in the wrongdoings of an errant culture.

The most strident condemnation of clergy involvement in the Klan came when *World's Work* writer Robert L. Duffus began a series of articles in which he offered an even less charitable picture of the white southern clergy's participation. According to Duffus, the Klansmen were "Salesmen of Hate" who drew their inspiration from Protestant theology. Duffus painted a picture of the Klan as an organization that was widespread in the South and "flourished best in communities where educational standards were low and social life raw or primitive." He also explained that the Klan's expansion went hand in hand with the expansion of "the 'fundamentalist' movement," which he believed was of particular appeal to "the Puritanical South." His linkage of the Klan with the fundamentalists and of fundamentalism with the South occurred in 1923, a full two years before the Scopes Trial and a year before Du Bois's charge. The religious appeal of fundamentalism and the Protestant emphasis of the Klan, Duffus argued, helped to bring in the support of the white southern clergy, and "the clergymen were shown the Klan's highly moral ritual and code, the business men and professional men were flattered as men of influence, and the politicians were made dizzy with dreams of power."[68] For Duffus, the Klan was the devil who knew how to appeal to his audience, and the white southern ministers, like white southern businessmen and politicians, could be wooed easily with the right words. Here the clergy seem not so much evil as inept, weak, and uneducated, unable to recognize the snake in the grass. Duffus's bumbling Klan-member clergymen and Cline's hateful clergy are representative of the opinions that northern observers had of white southern pastors in the early twentieth century. Both stereotypes had their antecedents in earlier portrayals of the clergy in the South as it failed, in northern eyes, to improve education and society in the South and even at times worked against them.[69]

As if the rise of the Klan and its connections with the South and its clergy were not enough to convince observers of the region's faults, a new wave of violence erupted at roughly the same time. This new bloodshed helped to emphasize the image of the South as violent.[70] Once again, the region appeared to outsiders inherently vicious, and it seemed to mock the foundations of American freedom. Once again, the South was an embarrassment to the United States.

An increase in lynchings and racial violence in the region in 1919 drew vehement condemnation. The *Nation* was incensed that the "Negro" had gone "so willingly to war for the United States" but it found "real and terrible transgressions" at home to rival those of Germany and Russia. "The State of Georgia," the editors wrote, "again carries the banner of shame, leading all others states with eighteen lynchings," and a mob in Texas had killed "a child under sixteen who was pregnant."[71] Just a few months later, the *New York Times* reported that white men were burning black churches in Georgia, as well as schools and a lodge hall.[72] In July, the *Nation*, clearly exasperated with the situation in the South, merely ran a collection of headlines from southern newspapers that announced a public lynching in Mississippi with comments from Governor Bilbo that he was "powerless to prevent it."[73] Later the same month, the *Outlook* told readers that the increase in southern mob violence was accompanied by a "renewal of the form of lynching that includes torture and burning at the stake."[74]

The murder of Henry Lowry was one example of the torture and burning the *Outlook* had warned was taking place. Reporting on Lowry's lynching in Nodena, Arkansas, on January 26, 1921, William Pickens told readers of the *Nation* that Lowry had come to Arkansas from Mississippi to work for a white planter who had extensive land holdings in Arkansas. The planter, Mr. O. T. Craig, apparently had great power over his tenants, even opening their mail and permitting "such 'justice'" as he desired. As Pickens explained, the "Constitution does not follow [blacks] into the backwoods of Arkansas." The planter soon caught Lowry in a "debt-slave system" in which the landlord could invent figures that allowed him to continue to require a tenant's work in exchange for the housing, food, and other particulars the landlord had supplied. Lowry and Craig argued, and Lowry shot and killed Craig and his daughter. (Lowry later claimed that Craig fired the first shot.) A mob then followed Lowry through several states, captured him, and lynched him in Nodena, publicizing in the afternoon papers of nearby Memphis "the exact hour when the lynching and where the burning was to take place," and then "'celebrated' with a good dinner."[75] Lowry's murder also made the front page of the *New York Times*, and the editors commented that the lynch mob was composed of "bitterly and savagely angry Tennessee men" who "fed before they killed."[76] The *Washington Evening Star* called the crime "ghastly" and said that "for sheer, inhuman savagery, sickening to the hearts of a public grown too used to horrors, this deed of a so-called civilized community could furnish new ideas in human sacrifice to the peoples of the most distant jungles."[77] Lowry's death provoked much the same condemnations that earlier lynchings had.

Shortly after the press coverage of Lowry's lynching, another sensational story appeared in the national media that served to remind observers of the South's violent nature. A white plantation owner, John Williams, was accused by one of his workers, Clyde Manning, of operating a peonage farm in Georgia and forcing Manning to execute eleven workers who Williams believed had given information to federal authorities about his employment practices.[78] Manning turned state's evidence against his former enslaver, and a white jury, on the basis of Manning's testimony, convicted Williams, although the jury helped Williams escape the death penalty through a legal loophole. Press reaction to the brutal killings was swift and sensational. The *New York Times* and other papers ran almost daily updates of the trial and told their readers the lurid details of how Williams forced Manning to chain men together and throw them off bridges and how Manning, at Williams's order, told one man to dig a hole, on the pretense that it was for a new well, and then struck him on the head with the shovel and buried him in his newly dug grave.[79] The *Times* told its editorial readers that the peonage system—in which black men were forced to work off real or imaginary debts, usually in perpetuity—was common along the Mississippi River and in Arkansas and called for "a thorough investigation by the Department of Justice of charges of peonage in the South."[80] The *New Republic* questioned why any editorial board would be pleased with the conviction of Williams on Manning's testimony, since whites were still oppressing blacks and had never held that "whites may with impunity murder their colored servants for profit or convenience."[81] And the *Nation* ran an article about the killings entitled "Slavery in Georgia, A.D. 1921."[82]

The waves of violence continued to roll across the South, and condemnation continued to run on the pages of magazines and newspapers. In 1921, Walter White, chairman of the NAACP, told the *New Republic* about violence in the Florida town of Ocoee, in which as many as fifty blacks were killed by Klan members because they had voted in local elections. White noted that a young white girl had described the lynching as "'the fun we had when some niggers were burned up.'"[83] The *New Republic* worried a few months later that Americans were growing accustomed to southern mob violence, citing a number of incidents in Texas.[84] In May 1922, a white mob in Kirvin, Texas, went on a killing spree following the death of a white girl, and the *Chicago Tribune* related the story to readers, as did the *New York Times*, which noted in its headline that the "Grandfather of Their Victim [was] Present and [gave] His Consent Before the Fire" was started.[85] In January 1923, white mobs lynched blacks and burned an entire town, Rosewood, Florida, to the ground, earning the South a place on the front pages of the *New York Times* and the *Washington Post*.[86] Violent "yokels" in Missouri lynched a black man for touching a white woman, according to *Time* magazine.[87] And following the abduction and subsequent murder of five men in Mer Rouge, Louisiana, the *Boston Herald* bemoaned the lack of grand juries and convictions in lynching cases in the South.[88]

The Lowry lynching, the peonage murders, and the continuing violence in the South helped to remind the nation, according to northern commentators, that although the United States had entered the twentieth century two decades earlier, the South seemed hopelessly mired in the early nineteenth. In the mind of the national media, the South was still at the forefront of mob violence and inhuman savagery.

The South's perceived embrace of violence and of antievolution legislation, combined with its affinity for the Ku Klux Klan, led outside observers to complete the syllogism that fundamentalists were ignorant, intolerant, and warlike in their rhetoric; the South was ignorant, intolerant, and just plain violent; therefore white southerners must be fundamentalists. The connection had already been made that the two were linked, both implicitly and explicitly. Reporters had called the South fundamentalist outright, and they had insinuated as much as well. To someone making a cultural reading of fundamentalism and a cultural reading of the white South, the two appeared to be identical.

If anyone reading American magazines and newspapers had missed this connection, however, the coverage of the Scopes Trial in the summer of 1925 brought the conclusion home to millions of Americans. The old slurs against the South—

that it was medieval, inquisitorial, and uneducated—arose again in the prose reporters sent to their editors. This time the slurs were both against the forces of fundamentalism that the critics saw at work in the region and against the South itself.

The Scopes Trial was an early example of the media circuses that Americans have come to associate with sensational journalism, and the planners of the trial knew they would attract media coverage and tourists to their town. John Scopes, a high school biology teacher in Dayton, Tennessee, informed a few business-minded citizens of the town that the textbook he used contained a discussion of the evolutionary theory that was banned by the Tennessee legislature in 1924. Scopes agreed to test the law and be arrested for the offense of teaching evolution in a public school, and the American Civil Liberties Union soon came to his defense. In the end, a jury would find Scopes guilty, but the judge would set the minimum fine. The Great Commoner, William Jennings Bryan, would aid the prosecution, die suddenly after the trial, and forever be tied to fundamentalism in the American imagination. And the South would suffer the consequences.

In the summer of 1925, the allies of each side arrived in Dayton to prepare for the trial. The press arrived, too, sending back to home offices lively and colorful accounts of the preparations and the actual legal proceeding itself. These accounts demonstrate the degree to which northern journalists had internalized the belief that white southerners were fundamentalists, and fundamentalists were white southerners.[89]

Charges that the Scopes Trial was medieval and patterned on the Inquisition dominated the coverage of the events in Dayton. The reporters drew upon a common language already used to describe the South and the fundamentalists. As the two sides prepared for the trial, the *Nation* argued that the antievolution law in Tennessee "returns to the days of the Inquisition when men were burned alive for daring to think, when an official church tried to cry halt to science."[90] The insinuated comparison between the Inquisition's executions at the stake and the South's practice of lynching lurks not far from the surface of the *Nation's* assessment of the situation in Tennessee. On the same day that the *Nation* made that comparison, the *Outlook* compared the fundamentalists with those who opposed the Protestant Reformation, i.e. medieval people or Catholics. "Freedom of inquiry," the *Outlook* opined, "was one of the most insistent demands of the Reformation."[91] The fundamentalists, garbed in antievolutionist clothing, were like the Roman Catholic Church in its perceived efforts to suppress free speech and free thought. The *Outlook's* assessment was ironic because the fundamentalists saw themselves as the true Protestants, the ones who were carrying on Martin Luther's and John Calvin's struggle to free Christianity from the influence of the Catholic Church.

The comparisons continued as the trial grew closer. The *Independent* called the antievolution law "the deliberate medievalism of a few ignorant men" and reminded its readers to note that Torquemada, like the fundamentalists, was guilty of "obscuring and befogging the light of truth."[92] In July 1925, the *Nation* called for an open debate on the evolution question, arguing that "any other course will take us straight back to the Middle Ages, when scientific truth was determined by vote of ecclesiastical councils and the wisdom of Greece and Rome was lost amid casuistry, obscurantism, and the Inquisition."[93] Inherent in this criticism and anti-Catholic rhetoric was the notion that the clergy had taken over the lawmaking functions of the State of Tennessee. While the magazine did not say so outright, it suggested that Tennessee had become a theocracy in which the clergy acted to inform the government of God's rules and intentions. Other magazines did likewise. *Collier's*, a very popular journal, told its readers, "[T]o understand Dayton, remember Galileo and the Inquisition, or our own witch-hunting Puritans."[94] The voice of liberal Protestantism, the *Christian Century*, likened John Scopes to victims of inquisitions, men like Copernicus, Bruno, and Galileo.[95] Moreover, in an editorial entitled "The Fanatics Also Serve," *Collier's* reported that, compared to the Scopes Trial, "the medieval inquisition was not more impertinently tyrannical."[96] For these commentators, the Scopes Trial and the state that had enacted the legislation that brought about the trial were examples of a modern-day inquisition at work.[97]

The charges of inquisition carried with them an attack on the role of the white clergy in the South. No longer the ignorant boobs of Henry Grady's address who could not read their way through the Bible nor the preacher who had never heard of Easter in William Goodell Frost's fundraising appeal, the white southern clergy now appeared to observers as squarely in charge of lawmaking in the South, lawmaking that failed to separate church and state. In an article for the Episcopal Church's New York newspaper, the *Churchman*, Forrest Davis claimed that Tennessee was "inspired by . . . the devout pastors" to try to "save its Bible religion from alien contagions by shutting out the modern world."[98]

Objecting to William Jennings Bryan's "proposition to delegate to state legislature or church council the determination of scientific orthodoxy," Ohio Wesleyan University professor Edward L. Rice complained in *Science* that such an idea "savors of the Middle Ages rather than of twentieth century America." Rice also observed that "Mr. Bryan wields an influence not to be ignored."[99] The power Bryan and the fundamentalists held over the Tennessee legislature was, for Rice, frightening and needed to be held in check. At least one historian has argued that Bryan did wield tremendous influence with fundamentalists, helping to push them into the fight against evolution.[100] Ernest Hamlin Abbott, editor of the *Outlook*, also warned about the Tennessee antievolution law, charging that if the Tennessee law were upheld, "the world would be returned to the position it occupied before the Reformation. The seat of dogmatic authority would be the legislative chamber instead of the

Vatican; there would be no other essential difference."[101] Abbott's editorial relied on anti-Catholic sentiment to drive his point home. If Tennessee were to win and Scopes to lose, Abbott insinuated, "priests" would have too much authority, and Tennessee would resemble the Vatican.

As the trial drew closer, the innuendos of theocracy and outright accusations of failure to separate church and state grew louder and more insistent. The *New Republic* unambiguously accused the antievolutionists of "seek[ing] to identify the American state with the truth of certain specific religious doctrines, and to reverse the fundamental principle of American liberty which is the separation between church and state."[102] The same week that the *New Republic* made its charge, the *Christian Century* published an editorial entitled "The Established Church of Tennessee." Using contemporary sociological theory, the nondenominational religious paper explained:

> If fundamentalism were a sect—as it is, in some important respects—it would be at once obvious that the purport of the law [against teaching evolution] is to make [fundamentalism] the established church of Tennessee with every teacher its priest and an altar in every schoolhouse.[103]

According to the *New York World*, the Scopes Trial was really a struggle over whether "'the State of Tennessee may consistently, with the American doctrine of separation of Church and State, establish the Bible of the Fundamentalists as the official standard of truth in its public schools.'"[104] The *Outlook* reported that Dayton was home to a "tremendous preponderance of believers in the anti-evolution law."[105] After the trial was over, the Episcopal *Churchman* suggested, tongue in cheek, that the solution to the Tennessee dilemma was to have a "thoroughly Fundamentalized America" and then "no one but a Fundamentalist would wish to remain in America."[106] And *Harper's Monthly Magazine* accused the fundamentalists of believing that they had heard "the *vox Dei* [voice of God] speaking through the electorate of Tennessee."[107] Tennessee appeared to the rest of the country as a place that wanted to force its religious views on everyone—something antithetical to the notion of a federated democracy as northern observers understood it.

The trial also brought charges that the South was against civilization—a loaded term that seemed to insinuate that the region rejected the liberal views of the importance of education and the value of deductive reasoning. For Herbert Croly, editor of the *New Republic*, the Scopes Trial placed Tennessee squarely against "civilization."[108] The more "educated" and usually upper-class white southerners raced to distance themselves from the trial. The Reverend James Sheerin wrote in the Episcopalian publication *Southern Churchman* that "civilization and religious faith are set back a generation by a trial which reflects credit on no one bringing it to pass or helping to prolong it."[109] The *Southern Churchman's* northern counterpart, the *Churchman*, characterized Dayton as an uncivilized place, saying that "the world, which thunders past in the North and East, has been deflected into these hills never to depart" once the trial had finished.[110] And the editor of the *Christian Century*, Charles Clayton Morrison, charged that there was "booming medievalism" in Tennessee, a state that he argued was "engaged in sweeping back the tides of modern education."[111] Because Tennessee had decided to prosecute someone for teaching evolution, critics charged that the state had placed itself against civilization. For them, *civilization* was synonymous with liberal tenets of education and a belief in progress.

Northern observers indicated that to be opposed to civilization meant more specifically to be "uneducated" and resistant to education. Many of them clearly explained that they saw the people of Tennessee as uneducated. How else, they reasoned, could the state pass such an antievolution law and then prosecute one of its own employees for violating that law? *The New Republic* commented that "Tennessee is not noted for the high educational level of its inhabitants, nor for their familiarity with modern developments in thought." The author of the article, Royce Jordan, went on to claim that the state had taken so long to pass an antievolution bill because "a large proportion of the inhabitants had never, until comparatively recent times, even heard of the theory."[112] The *New Republic's* editor, Herbert Croly, equated belief in evolution with intelligence, averring that "all people everywhere" who were "intelligent" believed in evolution.[113] And to hammer the point home, the same periodical published an article by Frank R. Kent, a columnist with the *Baltimore Sun*, who asserted that the "isolation and illiteracy" of the region's people were in part tied to their "rigid" religion, which "absorbs all the thought they have aside from their work."[114] Fellow *Sun* columnist and longtime foe of both the South and fundamentalism, H. L. Mencken wrote in the *Nation* that Tennessee had "escaped the national standardization" and its antievolution law was designed to induce complacency and conformity to Tennessee's parochial mores, not national educational standards.[115] The *Los Angeles Times* lampooned "Nashvillians, Memphicists, and Chattanoodles," saying that they believed evolution was a disease "worse than the measles or the mumps and the mountain folk cannot be blamed for placing it on the black list."[116] The *Christian Century* opined that the fundamentalists were like all the other manifestations of the "static mind throughout history."[117] George F. Milton, editor of the *Chattanooga News*, complained that "Tennessee . . . is struggling under the handicap of ignorance."[118] Southern expatriate Joseph Wood Krutch feared that the Scopes Trial would mean that "the control of learning will pass into the hands of the uneducated, and youth will leave the schools more ignorant than when it entered them."[119] And the *New York Times* accused William Jennings Bryan of making "ignorant and intolerant assaults upon those who accept evolution as the method of creation."[120] The labeling of fundamentalists and antievolutionists as ignorant continued well after the end of the trial in Dayton. In November 1925, Rollin Lynde Hartt, writing for the *Forum*, equated fundamentalism with a lack of education and liberalism with an education.[121] *Scientific Monthly*, reporting in December 1925 on Scopes Trial judge John T. Raulston's recent address to Calvary Baptist Church, whose pastor was fundamentalist leader John Roach Straton, quoted Raulston as saying, "'I will say that if more learning will cause us to lose our faith in the deity of Christ and our hope in resurrection, then I pray to God to leave us in our state of ignorance.'"[122] The pigeons had come home to roost. The fundamentalists were ignorant, and they sought refuge in a place famous for its ignorance (the South), in a subsection of which that was even more notoriously ignorant (Appalachia).[123]

The press coverage of Dayton and the Scopes Trial also tied the region's lack of education to an alleged propensity for violence among the town's residents and their affinity for the Ku Klux Klan. Writing for the *Forum*, John Porter Fort told readers that at a mass meeting in Dayton, a barber had "'bitten' an argumentative opponent" of creationism. According to Fort, the "'man-biting' barber" told his opponent that "'you cannot say that my family came from monkeys'" and then bit him.[124] The depiction of the barber harks back to the coverage of the mountain feuds and bitter theological debates for which Appalachia had already become famous. Now these debates were center stage, and the combatants ridiculed nationally.

The assumed violence of the region was also echoed in the comments about the fundamentalists and Tennesseans' membership in the Ku Klux Klan. The *New Republic*, commenting before the start of the trial, told its readers that "fundamentalism means a deliberate choice of ignorance . . . the Ku Klux civilization is predominant."[125] The *Nation* called the region "a fine soil for fundamentalism, [and] the Ku Klux Klan. . . ."[126] Modernist Rollin Lynde Hartt impugned the intelligence of the South and of the fundamentalists, saying, "Among the fundamentalist rank and file, profundity of intellect is not too prevalent, nor is the understanding of politics in the larger sense of the word. From that rank and file comes the membership of the Ku Klux Klan."[127] Shortly after the Scopes Trial, *Time* gave attention to an effort in Virginia to enact antievolution legislation. According to the article, prominent among the backers of the Virginia proposal was the Ku Klux Klan.[128] The increased appearance of white hoods and attempts to ban evolution curricula from public schools in the South led outside observers to conclude that the region was still as ignorant, uneducated, and violent as it had ever been. Such a conclusion ignored the fact that intelligent people, people who had received first-rate educations, could and would disagree over important matters. The media and the cultural elite wrongly perceived any attack on the teaching of evolution as proof of ignorance.

By the time the dust had settled in Dayton, it was hard to find a journalist or publication that did not profess that white southerners and fundamentalists were one and the same. The fundamentalists' crusade within certain denominations, their perceived alliance with the antievolutionists, the success of the antievolution campaign in the South, the emergence of the Klan, and new waves of racial violence within roughly the same few years made it hard for the cultural elite to sort out who was reacting against which form of modernity. The fundamentalists rejected liberal Protestant thought and Social Gospel–style reform efforts. The antievolutionists fought against the teaching of Darwin's theory of natural selection in public schools. The Klan fought against modernity in general and African Americans in particular. And the South, which had never really seemed to embrace northern notions of modern society, became the battleground for these forces. It was an easy generalization for the North to make: the white South had violently lynched and rioted, it had appeared to reject the value of public education, it elevated its ministers to prominent levels and then proceeded to ignore biblical injunctions to aid the poor. The fundamentalists had waged war rhetorically against their fellow Christians, they had rejected theological seminaries in favor of Bible schools, and they had denied the value of social progress and instead insisted on a violent Armageddon to come. The South and the fundamentalists appeared to be one and the same. The two were inextricably entwined in the national imagination.

CHAPTER 5

"Gundamentalist": J. Frank Norris and the South's Fate

J uly 1926 was a busy month for press coverage of white southern clergy. On July 28, the Baltimore-based *Methodist Protestant* informed its readers that the Reverend Dr. Ashley Chappell, a Methodist Episcopal Church, South, pastor from Asheville, North Carolina, had been acquitted by a denominational court of a "charge of immorality." According to the news item,

> Dr. Chappell was seized with an acute ailment while taking a walk in Memphis during the General Conference last May, and went into the nearest house for relief. This proved to be a disorderly house, which was raided by the police shortly after he entered it. The church at large, as well as his own brethren, will be gratified at his complete vindication.[1]

Another southern man of the cloth, J. Frank Norris, was not so fortunate in his media exposure, although the charge was far more serious. Norris, a Southern Baptist preacher and a leader of the fundamentalist movement, was arrested July 17 in Fort Worth, Texas, and charged with shooting a man to death. While Dr. Chappell's unfortunate choice of houses received only brief mention in one denominational newspaper, Norris's crime garnered front-page headlines in New York, Chicago, and Boston.[2]

Northern opinions of Norris had been strongly critical of the Texas Baptist, and his alleged crime, of which he was later acquitted, helped to sharpen attacks on Norris and his fundamentalist brethren, southern as they were now believed to be. The mounting opinion of the popular media that the South was a perfect home for violent, intolerant, uneducated fundamentalists had begun before the Scopes Trial of 1925. It was fed by the belief that white southerners as a whole were violent, uneducated, and unreasonable, and the notion gained more than a foothold in the national imagination after the Scopes Trial. No longer interested in whether white southerners actually held fundamentalist beliefs or what fundamentalists did believe (Scopes had firmly equated fundamentalism with antievolutionism), commentators pronounced the South the hotbed of fundamentalism and condemned both the movement and the region for their perceived failings. Like many other stereotypes about the South, the region's perceived propensity for conservative theology had some basis in truth, but the reporters and writers did not use statistical evidence to prove their points. Nor did they identify northern fundamentalists as transplanted southerners, which many of them were. Instead, they ridiculed, harangued, and chastised the South for being out of step with the rest of the country. Yet again, they focused on the clergy as the source of the problem. The movement's disappearance from the national scene prevented fundamentalists from being able to counter these attacks.[3]

As if the tragicomic escapades of Norris were not enough, national attention focused on the South yet again two years later when Democrat Al Smith ran for the presidency against Herbert Hoover. Smith's 1928 campaign was marred by charges of papal influence (Smith was a Catholic) and slurs against Smith's stand on prohibition. Leading the anti-Smith Democrats in the South was James Cannon Jr., bishop of the Methodist Episcopal Church, South, an argumentative and relentless opponent of Smith. The campaign, one of the dirtiest in U.S. history, broke apart the "Solid" South, as southerners in several states deserted the Democratic Party and helped vote Hoover into office.[4] While the coverage of the Smith attacks did not include specific charges of fundamentalism at work, it did portray Cannon and southerners as bigoted enemies of non-Protestants and of politicians who questioned the efficacy of prohibition. The specter of the South's past foibles loomed large as southern Protestants, including fundamentalists, turned out to defeat "Rum, Romanism, and Ruin."

Several historians have pointed out that fundamentalism beat a hasty retreat from public view during the late 1920s and early 1930s.[5] From the perspective of the secular press, fundamentalism appeared to capsize and sink after the public humiliation the movement endured during the Scopes Trial. But even as the bow of the great ship of conservative religion began to submerge, several northern commentators sounded the alarm that fundamentalism was not yet gone. In November 1925, the *New Republic*'s editor, Herbert Croly, gave extensive attention to a new book published by Harvard Divinity School professor Kirsopp Lake. Lake, Croly warned, saw the fundamentalists as able to "win [control of Christianity] speedily and completely." Among their strategic assets were "energy, determination, organization and a more intelligible and familiar mental and moral posture."[6] Despite the fact that Lake had written his book *The Religion of Yesterday and To-morrow* (1925) before the events in Dayton, Tennessee, when the fundamentalist "threat" was still very much apparent, Croly still saw later some danger of the fundamentalists reemerging. Magazine readers also saw the fundamentalists as a lurking danger. Writing in response to an article by fundamentalist John Roach Straton in the February 1926 issue of the *Forum*, John Ingraham of Fillmore, California, recalled the comparisons that others had made about the fundamentalists. Straton had suggested a museum exhibition on the Bible's Creation story, and Ingraham answered with a few suggestions of other exhibit images to include

> A picture of the burning of a witch, with the Bible command, "Let no witch live."
> A picture of the burning of Servetus, with the caption "For Jesus' sake, Amen."
> A picture of the Cortez expedition converting the savages to Christianity.
> Pictures of the Inquisitions, with samples of the torture wheels, racks, dungeons, etc., used in the work of saving souls for Jesus.
> Pictures of the massacre of the Huguenots.
> Pictures of the burning of books and the suppression of education.[7]

It had been almost a year since the Scopes Trial and the death of William Jennings Bryan, but the fundamentalists were still tagged with the image of intolerant persecutors of rational thought. The *Washington Post*, reporting on a Ku Klux Klan gathering, assumed that a speaker who advocated the placement of "'the Bible and the American flag . . . in all of the public schools,'" espoused "fundamentalism."[8] Fundamentalism was now equated with extremism, and it had a location, south of the Mason-Dixon Line. Indeed, the term "fundamentalism" now crossed academic boundaries and was applied to conservative thought outside religion. William B. Munro, writing for the *Atlantic Monthly*, condemned "fundamentalism" in politics.[9] Newspapers made the term even more ambiguous, using it to refer to the followers of a political candidate or the advocates of states' rights.[10]

Fundamentalism also became the butt of even more jokes. The *Forum* invited its readers to submit their own definitions of fundamentalism and published some of the entries in its December 1926 issue. One reader, Mrs. Chloe Cluston Bly, offered "'a Fundamentalist is one who would drag man back from to-day's dawn to yesterday's candle-light.'" An unidentified reader called the movement "'the rear aspect of Protestantism in intellectual transition.'" Yet another, Paul Langdon of

Fort Wayne, Indiana, said, "'A Fundamentalist is a besieged Christian anxious to dictate the terms of surrender to Science.'" But the contest's most acerbic entry came from a southerner, the Reverend J. S. Hodges, D.D., of Denison, Texas, who wrote,

> A Fundamentalist is one who is located at the bottom. He holds to his moorings, too timid to break away and fearful of all new adventures and discoveries. Theories weigh little with him and hypotheses miss his mark. Fiction appeals not to him. He is no gambler. His element of risk is zero. He takes no step in the dark, scales no mountains, discovers no North Poles, and swims no Channels. He is "sot" in his ways and fears all change for it might bring grief. It applies to his religion, business, citizenship, and recreation.[11]

For these readers, fundamentalism in the late 1920s was merely a source of amusement, a movement of uneducated and intolerant people who were, happily, fading away.

Despite the humor, not every religious liberal considered the war won and the enemy defeated. Albert C. Dieffenbach, Unitarian minister and editor of the *Christian Register*, publicized his belief that the fundamentalists still posed a danger to Christianity as he understood it. In a three-part series in the *Independent*, Dieffenbach used the liberal-leaning publication to generate a wider audience for his new book, *Religious Liberty: The Great American Illusion*, (1926). He argued, "Protestantism is in eclipse. Christianity enters a new dark age. . . . victory rests with the Fundamentalists." He accused the Baptist denominations in America, "both North and South," of being controlled by "the hands of the great inciters and fanatics." The fundamentalist takeover of the Baptists, Dieffenbach believed, signaled their takeover of other denominations. And he closed his argument by linking the Ku Klux Klan to the persistent and threatening conservatives. "The Fundamentalist Ku-Kluxers," he wrote, "and night riders in this church made the most pathetic and terrible spectacle that ever brought disaster to religion. And what is worse, they won!"[12]

Other publications picked up Dieffenbach's warning and carried it themselves. The *Literary Digest* summarized his book and cited his claim that "the Fundamentalists 'have won control of the churches with a total membership running into more than thirty millions of souls.'"[13] The *Churchman*, the denominational newspaper of the Episcopal Church, also lauded Dieffenbach's book and called its readers' attention to Dieffenbach's warning about the imminent demise of religious liberty under the fundamentalists.[14] The *Independent* cited Dieffenbach's claim that fundamentalists "abound" in the South and were prone to "violence, narrowness, and the supreme arrogance of the ignorant."[15] Reviewing Stewart G. Cole's book *History of Fundamentalism*, Maynard Shipley noted in the *New York Times* that "Southern and Midwestern Fundamentalism" were associated with the Ku Klux

Klan and that there was a question in his mind whether fundamentalism was "completely at an end."[16] The fundamentalists, these observers believed, were threatening the very foundations of American religious liberty, just as white slave owners and secessionists had done before the Civil War, and they had to be stopped. Far from being a movement on the brink of extinction, fundamentalists were still very dangerous and poised to make certain civil liberties extinct.

The battlefield in this combat, northern observers and the fundamentalists agreed, was to be the South. As one historian has observed, the fundamentalists saw the South as a region in which they could make great gains. Although they were hampered by sectional differences, northern itinerant fundamentalists found a home in the South.[17] They made no secret that the South looked promising, and several publications picked up this development. Covering a session of the Methodist Episcopal Church, South's, Baltimore Conference, the *Washington Post* noted that the opening speaker, the Reverend D. A. Beery, delivered a "vigorous defense" of fundamentalism.[18] The *Literary Digest* informed readers in 1927 that an "ambitious program" was "to be initiated in the South," which would "put [Hell] back in its proper place in the teaching of religion, and the theory of evolution [would] be driven out of the schools. . . ." The article noted that the World's Christian Fundamentals Association had recently held its ninth annual convention in Atlanta and that some newspapers in the South, including the "stout Fundamentalist paper, the Memphis *Commercial Appeal*," supported efforts to ban the teaching of evolution from public schools.[19] Miriam Allen de Ford, writing for the *Nation* in 1926, equated the continuing efforts to ban evolution with fundamentalism and placed them all in the South. According to de Ford, the State of Mississippi, the State of Texas, the State of Arkansas, the City of Atlanta, and the "University of Louisiana" had all blocked efforts to teach evolution in public schools. Such actions placed them in the "Fundamentalist" category of her analysis, and she warned that "the avowed purpose" of the fundamentalists was "to establish a fundamentalist theocracy in America."[20] The *New York Times* carried coverage of the antievolution victories in the South, claiming that the "religious fundamentalists gained a complete victory" in Arkansas, and the *Columbus (Ohio) State Journal* called the movement "'sinister,'" claiming that the "'real motive'" was "'a union of Church and State.'"[21] The *Nation* seemed to agree with the latter claim, informing its readers that "professing atheism is a dangerous business in the State of Arkansas."[22] In the *American Mercury*, an article about Arkansas's debate over evolution insinuated that Baptists and Methodists participated too much in lawmaking. According to the author, Clay Fulks, "pragmatical parsons infest the Arkansas region" and "incite" the laity "continuously against intelligence wherever it shows its head."[23] In 1929, Dr. Christian F. Reisner, preaching in New York City in 1929, told his audience that Bryan was "'great,'" adding that his last years "were 'spent among the extreme Fundamentalists of the South who shut him off from the sound views of modern Christians.'"[24] And to add a little local color to the national news, the *New York Times* quoted Tennessee lawmaker "'Uncle Billy' Matthews, oldest member of the [Tennessee] House" who said that "'if the doctrine of evolution is right, then our Bible is wrong.'"[25] While the northern fundamentalists were just beginning to understand the South's potential, journalists had already placed it in the fundamentalist column, even if they were not entirely sure what that meant.

Journalists continued to highlight the South's propensity for violence and intolerance even as they documented the gains that fundamentalists made in the region. According to a profile in the *American Mercury*, white southerners were still engaging in mob violence even as they praised the Lord and passed the hat for fundamentalist revivals. Alabama native Sara Haardt described how residents in her home state could easily shift between evangelistic revivals and mob violence. "Hardly a week goes by," Haardt wrote, "that some evangelist doesn't hold forth to capacity houses in every town throughout the Solid South." After describing the excitement of the revival, she went on to explain how the mood would become more ominous:

> Afterwards, while the excitement is still running high, a party of masked men plant burning crosses before the doors of Jewish suspects, and others near the statue of Robert E. Lee as a warning to motorists that petting parties must cease in that neighborhood.[26]

In her profile of North Carolina in the same magazine, Nell Battle Lewis related how North Carolinians had turned the Baptist State Convention into a theological blood sport, calling it "the liveliest sporting event in the commonwealth." Since no one had punished Wake Forest College professor William Louis Poteat for teaching evolution, Lewis wrote, "the Fundamentalists set out to get the Doctor's scalp." She held out little hope for Poteat's school, which she called "as green an oasis of liberal thought as can be found in the Bible Belt." According to Lewis, soon "the armies of the Lord will fall upon it and reduce it to aridity."[27] Owen P. White, also writing in the *American Mercury*, characterized fundamentalists as worshiping a vengeful God, preferring "the implacable Jehovah to the benign God." "They adore the harsh doctrine which calls for an eye for an eye and a tooth for a tooth," White continued, and "they lust for the punishment of the other fellow." He went on to claim:

> According to some of the Texas theologians Christ is even armed. I don't know whether he is supposed to carry a squirrel-rifle, a bow and arrow, or a nigger shooter, but at any rate He must have some kind of weapon that is suitable for work at long range. I say this because of an experience I once had when I got

up and walked out of a revival just when the preacher had on a full head of steam and was going his best. He saw me, with another young man, rise from my seat, step into the aisle and start for the exit. The flow of his remarks stopped immediately; he paused for a moment to give full effect to what was coming, and then bawled out: "Behold the sinners! The vengeance of the Lord is upon them and they will be shot in the back before they reach the door!"[28]

Writing in the *Independent*, Edgar W. Knight called the fundamentalists "shock troops" who were led by "bigots and narrow religionists—including the Rev. Dr. Frank Norris, well-known 'gundamentalist' of Texas."[29] The fundamentalists in the South were violent in practice, violent in rhetoric, and violent in theology, Lewis, Haardt, White, and Knight agreed.

The decades-old notion of southern religion's being different continued to play a role in accounts of the region. The *Christian Century* ran a story in 1929 claiming that "the churches have also been the strongest forces in fostering the spirit of isolation" and that "in no other section of the world has a strict, literal orthodoxy been so unanimously preached as it has been in the south."[30] The "strict, literal orthodoxy" here was an obvious attack on fundamentalist theology. In another article in the *Christian Century*, John Beauchamp Thompson, a resident of Texas, observed that "not all southerners are fundamentalists, but the masses are." He added that southern prayers "are often, if not always, based upon Old Testament theology."[31] Joining the chorus singing the fundamentalist nature of southern religion, Gerald W. Johnson argued in the *North American Review* that Virginia was settled by "Puritans" who were different from the "Massachusetts Puritans" only in that "the Massachusetts Puritans could read and write."[32] The South clearly had a bad case of fundamentalism, fundamentalism that was innate and regional.

Other observers attributed the strength of fundamentalism in the South to the region's continued and very real educational and social deficiencies—a more charitable assessment of fundamentalism, one that made white southerners less morally culpable. French Strother, writing in the *World's Work*, blamed the "bonds of ignorance" for the region's persistent and "stubborn conservatism in religion."[33] In the same journal, Vanderbilt University professor Edwin Mims agreed, ascribing the South's embrace of the antievolution movement to the fact that "the South still has a great mass of uneducated people—sensitive, passionate, prejudiced—and another mass of the half-educated, who have very little intellectual curiosity or independence of judgment." These attributes, Mims argued, meant that southerners were likely to be whipped into a frenzy by a "demagogue."[34] And Tennessee native Lillian Perrine Davis mourned in the pages of the *Sewanee Review* the effect of the Scopes Trial on the innocence of the Tennessee mountaineers, whom she believed were fundamentalists. According to Davis, until the foolish ones seeking political capital took their faith and fouled it with the un-American evolution law, they were a beautiful example of the survival of things which, after all, have had a great deal to do with the progress and development of the English-speaking peoples.[35]

But whether the white South was fundamentalist because it was uneducated, allegedly racially pure yet socially backward, or just plain violent, the region was firmly perceived as a natural home for this extremely conservative movement in American Protestantism. True, the South was home to more violence than the rest of the country and its schools were lagging, and true, the fundamentalists employed violent rhetoric and rejected modern culture, but the image that appeared was more like a reflection in a funhouse mirror.[36] The features were there, but they were grossly distorted.

Interestingly enough, the caricature contained even more accuracies than the media observers noticed. According to at least two historians, many of the most famous fundamentalists were indeed men who had either been born or reared in the South.[37] But contemporary reporters, in their rush to place fundamentalism in the South, ignored the southern roots of fundamentalists living in their own back-yards. The Reverend John Roach Straton, for example, preaching from his pulpit near Central Park in New York City, was repeatedly identified as "Pastor of Calvary Baptist Church in New York City," rather than a fundamentalist reared in the South.[38] The very few articles that did include a mention of Straton's regional heritage were by authors who used it to their advantage, portraying him as a product of the uneducated, violent, and backward South. Haywood Broun's article in the *Nation* "A Bolt From the Blue," which in its closing lines referred to Straton as a "Southern gentleman," ridiculed Straton's outrage over Sunday baseball games.[39] Stanley Walker, writing in H. L. Mencken's *American Mercury*, called Straton the "Fundamentalist Pope" and noted that he "understands thoroughly the minds of the bucolic Baptists of the South . . . and he knows what a rural legislator will do when the pastors crack their whip."[40] Typically, however, even Straton's opponents merely called him "pastor of Calvary Baptist Church in New York City and militant leader of the Fundamentalists."[41] Likewise, William Bell Riley was typically described as "Pastor of First Baptist Church in Minneapolis, Minnesota," despite his Kentucky roots.[42] Neither Riley nor Straton were strangers to media coverage; they were not "stealth" southerners hiding behind enemy lines. Articles about them ran in the *Independent*, the *Literary Digest*, and the *New York Times*, and Riley authored articles defending fundamentalism in *Current History* and the *Independent*.[43] The critics of fundamentalism did not want to investigate the roots of the movement; they believed that they had already found them in the South. In jumping to this conclusion, they failed to consider where fundamentalism had a stronger initial following: the Northeast and the Midwest. Such a conclusion was unthinkable—fundamentalism belonged to an uneducated and intolerant region that was in need of assimilation. The presence of former southerners did not matter now; what mattered was only the perception that white southerners were fundamentalists.

But one man who was both a white southerner and a fundamentalist garnered media attention on both counts. A Baptist preacher from Texas provides an excellent example of the distortions the media funhouse created. No other southern fundamentalist earned national attention or media attacks more than J. Frank Norris. According to one historian, those who knew Norris saw him in one of two lights, either as "the hero they loved" or "the villain they dared not dismiss."[44] Norris was born in Alabama in 1877 but grew up in eastern Texas and attended Baylor University.[45] The Baptist preacher had a long history of controversy and violence, having watched his father murdered and himself having been charged with (and later acquitted of) perjury and arson.[46] His brushes with the law and his outrageous statements in many ways resemble the caricatures that earlier reporters had drawn of Sam Jones, but Norris eclipsed Jones in notoriety. Norris managed to make a name for himself in fundamentalist circles, and he drew the attention of liberal northern writers who disapproved of his rhetoric and tactics.

Liberal Protestant and prolific writer Rollin Lynde Hartt had already reported on Norris's propensity for personal attacks on those he suspected of heresy. In a 1923 article in the World's Work, Hartt described how Norris had read a book by Southern Methodist University professor John A. Rice and "fell upon Doctor Rice with great fury, branding him as an 'agnostic,' an 'infidel,' and an 'atheist.'"[47] Norris's continued attacks on men within and outside of his own Southern Baptist denomination earned him such titles as "one of the most militant leaders of the Fundamentalists," and "the Texas Cyclone."[48] Commenting on Norris's visit to Calvary Baptist Church in New York City in March 1922, the New York Times called him the "Texas Tornado" and noted that he had promised to "'give 'em hell from the first word to the benediction.'" Norris called New York "'a modern Nineveh, a modern Babylon, a modern Rome.'"[49] The Texas preacher's penchant for talking about hell earned him more attention from the New York Times in 1923, as Norris declared, "'Hell has not changed although men have tried to put out the fire.'"[50] But his slaying of a man in his study in July 1926 brought upon Norris even more violent nicknames and more caustic criticism. And the fundamentalist pastor's involvement in a killing was just one more piece of evidence, outsiders believed, that white southerners were violent and fundamentalist at once.

In July 1926, Norris shot and killed Mr. D. E. Chipps, a lumberman who had come to Norris's study to demand that Norris stop his attacks on Fort Worth mayor

H. C. Meacham, a Roman Catholic whom Norris accused of funneling tax revenues to projects that would benefit Meacham's business and a Roman Catholic church and school.[51] Norris shot Chipps and claimed self-defense. The slaying and the subsequent trial provided journalists with an abundance of material to shape into condemnations of southern fundamentalists.

Daily papers had a field day covering Norris's first sermon following his arrest for murder. "Slayer Preaches to Packed Church" screamed the front-page headline of the *New York Times*.[52] The *Minneapolis Morning Tribune*, the hometown paper of midwestern fundamentalist leader W. B. Riley, used the same wire story under the large headline "Pastor Kills Man in Church," and the rival *Minneapolis Journal* told its readers "Texas Pastor Kills Enemy in Church."[53] The wire story reported that Norris chose Romans 8:1 for his text, "'There is no condemnation to them that are in Christ.'"[54] The accused killer's choice of scripture seemed designed to vindicate his actions, but it also implied to a more secular reading public that Norris considered himself above the civil law. To more theologically minded observers, Norris must have appeared antinomian in his outlook—believing that saving grace placed him beyond the reach of moral obligations. The *Times* made sure to remind its readers that Norris had had a "stormy career" as a "'hellfire and damnation preacher'" and that he had "found New York steeped in sin—so lost to godliness that later he predicted it would be destroyed by an earthquake as prophesied in Revelations [*sic*]."[55] This reminder, coupled with the story's details about Norris's attacks on modern life, served to paint Norris as a rural rube who could only comprehend the big city as a place of sin.

While the *Times* portrayed Norris as a hellfire and brimstone rural zealot, the *Chicago Tribune* chose to focus on the support the preacher received from his congregation. The paper noted that the attendance was "eight thousand" and that "scores of men and women went to the altar and shook Dr. Norris' hand."[56] The *Los Angeles Times* noted that many telegrams to Norris contained "frequent" "Scripture verses" and proceeded to quote three telegrams, all from southerners.[57] The *Boston Globe* also noted the strong support of the congregation that had posted Norris's $10,000 bond. Capitalizing on the image of a pastor accused of murder preaching in a hot Texas church in July, the *Globe* provided a description of the service in its account:

> An American flag hung motionless in the sultry atmosphere which drove those within the church to fan vigorously even during prayer. The pastor freely used a large purple-edged pocket handkerchief as he preached. Many of his usually vigorous gestures were absent. "Who is he that condemns?" asked the minister. . . . "If God is for us, who can be against us. All things work together for Him who is called to God."[58]

Here was a man accused of murdering another man, preaching to a crowded church that those who followed Christ could suffer no earthly condemnation, the day after he got out of jail. The fundamentalists indeed appeared to be a violent lot who declared themselves beyond the reach of secular justice. Much like the men who took part in the South's lynching parties and suffered no punishment, Norris and the white southern society that shielded him appeared lacking in justice and compassion while abounding in violence, lawlessness, and defiant ignorance.

Monthly magazines as well portrayed Norris as a fundamentalist who believed he was above the law. Owen White, writing in the *American Mercury*, commented that Norris's church was a "place wherein 8000 children receive instruction every Sunday morning" despite the fact that Norris "lately killed a man in the church."[59] *Time* labeled Norris's brand of fundamentalism "the humid (often illiterate) phrases and hot war-whoops of a revivalist-Genesis-trumpeter" and said that among his congregation "the prevailing belief . . . is that whatever Baptist Norris does is done for the Lord, and is by Him blessed."[60] These comments and the overwhelming attendance at Fort Worth Baptist Church were reminders of the perception outside the South that white southern clergy had an amazing power over their flocks. Norris could kill someone, claim self-defense, and still draw huge crowds. He appeared to be so powerful that *Time* called him "the Baptist tsar from Texas."[61] But Norris did not use his immense power for good causes, as northern liberal Protestants and social reformers saw it. He engaged in a conservative brand of religion that sought personal conversions followed by behavioral changes and a neglect of social issues. Writing for the *New Republic*, Nels Anderson described Norris's theology and his hold over his audience in the following manner:

> His congregation grew on a diet of hell-fire religion, of hate for sinners in the concrete rather than sin in the abstract. He drew them around him by attacking sinners in high places, by periodically unearthing scandal or by making occasional startling exposures. By these witch-burning orgies he has been able to hold their interest and loyalty.[62]

Several publications also made reference to the Ku Klux Klan when reporting on the Norris murder trial. The *Washington Post* and the *Atlanta Constitution* both ran the same Associated Press wire story, which mentioned "references to the Ku Klux Klan during the trial." Before the trial, *Time* had reported that Norris was a "Ku Klux Klan member" who had "vigorously denounced race tracks, Catholics, and other things and persons."[63] The *New York Times* noted that an "ex-Klansman" had been seated on the jury, and it reported to readers that the Texas Grand Dragon of the Ku Klux Klan supported Norris.[64] While his biographer has found no evidence that Norris was a Klan member, he acknowledges that Norris was certainly "sympathetic" to the Klan and its aims.[65]

Even after the trial was over and the jury had acquitted him, the notoriety that the shooting initiated followed Norris for the rest of his life. In November 1926, in an article on controversial evangelist Aimee Semple McPherson, Bruce Bliven wrote in the *New Republic* that her strange disappearance and reappearance should be excused. "After all," he argued, "even committing a murder was to J. Frank Norris of Texas, and to his congregation, only a casual incident in the fight against modernism."[66] Southern educator Edgar W. Knight gave Norris the nickname "'gundamentalist'" shortly after his acquittal.[67] The *Churchman* called him "Frank ('Two-gun') Norris."[68] When Norris went to preach at the Northern Baptist Convention in Chicago in 1927, the *New York Times* helpfully reminded its readers that "Dr. Norris is the pastor who shot a man at the doorway of his church study."[69] In 1929, when Norris's church suffered from not one but two mysterious fires, the *New York Times* brought up his past murder trial and previous arsons at his church.[70] In marking Norris's death in 1952, *Time* magazine sounded frustrated when it wrote that he "got off scot-free" on the murder charges.[71]

To these observers such a minister seemed more like an incarnation of evil than a man of the cloth. For many liberal Protestants in the North, and indeed for many fundamentalists in both the North and the South, J. Frank Norris was at odds with an accepted view of a Christian minister. He made personal attacks through words, he shot a man to death, and he claimed to be above the law. Norris to these observers was dangerous and wrong. He symbolized the violence, ignorance, and impulsiveness of the fundamentalist movement, and he helped to further the perception that southerners were naturally fundamentalist. He also personified the popular image of the white southern clergy that had been developing for many years. He was charismatic and influential and seemed to have an absolute control over the minds of his large congregation. He fought personal vices, yet he ignored social problems, problems that liberal Protestants and education reformers believed were holding the South back. And he proclaimed himself a recipient of saving grace, which placed him among the elect. In the media circus, Norris seemed to possess all of the attributes of southern fundamentalism the popular media had described. His continued legal escapades and fiery rhetoric kept him in the national spotlight for many years, allowing him to serve as the foremost example of the southern "propensity" for fundamentalism.

If the South had not already done enough to ensure its image as "other" in the eyes of the northeastern and midwestern journalists, the presidential election race of 1928 provided yet one more example of meddling southern clergy and anti-Catholic opinion in the region. Led by Methodist bishop James Cannon Jr., Democrats in the South opposed to Al Smith, the wet Catholic governor of New York, waged a campaign of slander, whispers, and outright bigotry against him. Historians have debated whether Smith's loss to Herbert Hoover was largely due to his stand against prohibition or his religion, but recent studies have leaned toward the latter.[72] Cannon's rhetoric against Smith in the 1928 presidential race became another example of southern intolerance in the eyes of reporters and pundits.

Smith's candidacy began long before 1928. He was a popular and colorful personality, a man who had risen through the ranks of New York's Tammany Hall to become governor of the state and was a close contender for the Democratic ticket in 1924. As a consequence, newspapers and magazines had plenty of time to discuss whether Smith would run successfully in the South. A few southern observers were even bold enough to predict a Smith win. George Washington Hays, writing in 1926 in the *Forum*, argued that Smith would secure the 1928 nomination and would carry the South. A former governor of Arkansas, Hays drew on notions of southern fairness, Anglo-Saxon racial purity, and populism to explain his position. "I am convinced," he concluded, "that every fair-minded man and woman will readily concede that he has kept his religion in the background in all of his political activities."[73] Writing in the *Nation* three months later, Hays repeated his assertion of southerners' ability to tolerate different faiths, stating that he spoke for "the average Southerner" when he "state[d] that the principles of Democracy are too great and mean too much to us ever to be sacrificed for anything so un-American and so petty as religious bigotry."[74] His predictions would turn out to be true for Arkansas— it voted for Smith, as did South Carolina, Georgia, Alabama, Mississippi, and Louisiana—but Smith lost in Virginia, North Carolina, Tennessee, Kentucky, Florida, Missouri, and Texas. Texas resident Ruby A. Black, however, shared Hays's confidence in Smith. She held up her hometown of Thornton as an example of a place where citizens who were "Dry and Fundamentalist" and "anti-Catholic" would vote for a wet, Catholic Democrat. Black believed that "if they are Democrats first, and Protestant Prohibitionists second, they are probably subconsciously, if not consciously, preparing their minds to pick somebody who can be elected, regardless of prohibition or religion."[75]

Far more common, however, were opinions that questioned Smith's southern viability or that outright predicted his defeat. There had been fair warning of Smith's vulnerability. As early as 1923, a group of southern delegates to the Anti-Saloon League's annual meeting "issued a declaration that they would urge voters to vote the Republican ticket if the Democrats nominated a Wet (such as Governor Smith or Senator Greenwood) for President in 1924."[76] George Milton echoed the warning in 1924, telling *Outlook* readers that the "South won't be satisfied with a 'wet' candidate, or even a 'moist' one." He added that because Al Smith was Catholic, the Ku Klux Klan would play a role in the contest. "There is no use," he lamented, "discounting the Ku Klux Klan in politics," adding that it was "representative of a large body of Southern belief which has imbued itself with the belief that the Catholic Church is seeking control of the American Government, that it is corrupting the schools, and so forth."[77] Following the 1924 defeat of John W. Davis, who had secured the Democratic nomination after a divided national convention, the *World's Work* editorialized that "the Smith-[William G.] McAdoo feud [of the 1924 Democratic Convention] has taken a religious character which it will never lose." The magazine predicted that "the Protestant and Catholic elements will lock horns for another four years" and that the Democratic Party would be "a party, at the end, even more demoralized than it is at the present time."[78]

Not everyone agreed that a Smith candidacy and loss in the South would be bad. The *Nation* argued in November 1925 that "anything that would make the South change its political adherence, even in one election would be so beneficial to political thinking and development in that section of the country that [a Smith candidacy] might easily prove to be a blessing in disguise." Indeed, the editors believed that the "threat" of the South's voting for a Republican if "the Democrats would nominate one who is both a Roman Catholic and a wet" had been made so many times it was hard "to take it seriously."[79]

But despite the *Nation's* optimism about the threats, the general consensus remained that a Smith nomination would mean a Democratic defeat in the South. And constantly at the front of the list of Smith's faults was his Roman Catholic religion. The *New Republic* called it Smith's "one notorious and at present fatal disqualification." Discounting southerners who predicted a Smith win, the magazine argued that it was folly to believe that "these fanatics, in so far as they reside in the South, will vote for any Democrat, whatever his religion may be, against any Republican." "These tactics are," the editor continued, "in our opinion, a mistake."[80] Southern Catholic judge Pierre Crabites, a native of Louisiana, agreed. Describing the average southerner, he wrote

> I have in mind the farmer, who is at heart an evangelist, a missionary and a local Billy Sunday. He says, as he leans over his plow, "No, a foreign-born citizen cannot be President of the United States. This Smith is a Catholic and a foreigner. Nobody will force him on me as long as I can shoulder a gun."[81]

Crabites cited the religious homogeneity of the South as one reason Smith had little chance there. "The Southern Protestant," he observed, "has in many cases passed his entire life in a neighborhood where no Catholic resides."[82] He predicted that "before the fight is over, [Smith's] faith will be brought into the thick of the fray. It is already within the range of sharpshooters."[83]

Despite Crabites's prediction, Smith's campaign continued, and the list of dire warnings about Smith's religion grew longer. Mississippi, according to Louis M. Jiggitts, in an *Independent* article, would reject Smith, as would the rest of the South. Warning of Klan involvement in an election, he used Mississippi as an example of the entire region, arguing that "the same hostility that exists in Mississippi to a candidate both Catholic and wet, exists also in the other Southern States."[84] Referring to the South's likely leaning in the election, the *New Republic* predicted that "without religion to interfere, he would run a good chance of being the next President of the United States." "But," the editors continued, "as an unexplained, unmitigated Catholic, he is sure to be defeated."[85] William Crawford in a 1927 *Outlook* article wrote that "two facts make the question as to whether the South will support Smith a debatable subject. First, Alfred E. Smith is a Roman Catholic. Second, Alfred E. Smith is listed in the public mind as a wet." Mentioning the old English law that only a member of the Church of England could hold the throne, Crawford wrote that "it was surprising how many people believed that this law had been transplanted to America." In 1923, "when Al Smith was first spoken of as a candidate," Crawford continued, "I received thousands of letters asking me if it was not against the law for a Catholic to be president." Crawford went on to state that "it is my opinion that Smith will lose a larger number of Southern votes because of his religion than the political leaders are willing to admit."[86] Dixon Merritt, also writing for the *Outlook*, agreed, citing Ku Klux Klan power in Alabama and Mississippi.[87] These commentators all agreed that the religion of the Democratic nominee was a drawback in the South.

As the election drew closer, the comments about Smith's southern problem continued. In March 1928, the *Independent* told editorial readers that Smith was "not popular in a majority of Southern States," and that the Klan, although "weakened," was working against him, with the help of "dry organizations."[88] In June, the *Forum* published a letter to the editor arguing that "there is a general impression that the South is the great reservoir of religious prejudice," an impression that few journalists seemed to want to dispel.[89] The handwriting was on the wall, but Smith and the Democrats did not seem interested in reading it.

By an unfortunate coincidence, the 1928 Democratic National Convention was held in Houston, Texas, a city that provided a colorful backdrop both for detractors of the South and for coverage of anti-Smith sentiment. The *Nation* informed readers that it was "no fault of the Democratic Party" that shortly before the convention's opening "a Negro [was] taken from jail [in Houston] and lynched."[90] Even with the national spotlight on it, the South continued to offer up examples of its famed violence and religiosity. Lewis Gannett told in the *Nation* of "prayer meetings in the churches" in Houston about the Smith nomination, though once again the South was failing to enforce prohibition. "Texas boasts that it gives the Wets all the liquor they want," he wrote, "and the Drys all the laws they want."[91] The

South may have had the religious backing for temperance, but it was still the region that both prayed for prohibition and drank to its demise. Commenting about the South's racial policies on display in Houston and the Democratic Party's position on them, the *Nation* said that the Democratic Party "bleats at conventions about the democracy of Thomas Jefferson and then makes a mockery of every one of its pretensions by denying fundamental American rights" to African Americans in the "reactionary South."[92] Highlighting the religious intolerance of the city, Lewis Gannett described a "mass meeting" in which the "'representatives of seven million churchwomen' assured one another that God would block Al Smith's attempt to 'steal the United States from the Christian [meaning Protestant] people.'" Despite the fact that "every one of them knew that Al Smith would be nominated," these women "compared the Al Smith promises of Northern votes to Satan's offer of the kingdoms of the world, shouted about 'the greatest crisis since the Civil War,' and the 'days of Pentecost.'"[93]

Inside the convention hall, the South offered up for the press even more examples of its aberrant nature. The Mississippi delegation came to blows with each other while trying to decide whether to join the parade of Smith delegates after the nominating speech was finished.[94] The *Los Angeles Times* described a "melee" in the Georgia delegation, a "smashed" North Carolina "standard," and a "conflagration" among the Alabama delegates.[95] Indeed, seven states ("Mississippi, Virginia, Tennessee, Nebraska, Alabama, Georgia, and Florida"), according to the *New York Times*, declined to march in the victory parade.[96] The same Mississippi delegates spent three hours in caucus trying to determine whether to back Smith, with one delegate reportedly shouting, "'For God's sake, don't let Mississippi vote for Al Smith.'"[97] And immediately following Smith's nomination, several southern clergymen announced that they would hold a conference in July 1928 in Asheville, North Carolina, to discuss the defeat of Al Smith.[98]

One of those clergy was Bishop James Cannon Jr. of the Methodist Episcopal Church, South, a native of Virginia and a man who never walked away from a fight and who, like J. Frank Norris, was dogged by scandal.[99] Cannon's motivations for fighting so hard for prohibition and so vehemently against a wet Catholic like Smith are still a matter of debate, but the focus here will fall not so much on Cannon's reasons but his actions and words against Smith and how his comments played in the press.[100]

Cannon had risen to prominence in the Anti-Saloon League, and he used the national press to promote his view that prohibition, as enacted by the Eighteenth Amendment, must remain the law of the land. He warned early on, in 1924, that Methodists in the South would vote Republican in order to preserve prohibition.[101] In 1926, he used *Collier's* to argue that prohibition would remain, saying, "We're going to stay dry."[102] The next year, he repeated his warning at least twice that prohibition could split the Democratic Party in the South.[103] Not content to fire only warning shots, in 1928, when Smith was leading in the race to be the Democratic nominee for president, Cannon penned a devastating attack on him for the *Nation*. Alleging that Smith was "personally, aggressively, [and] irreconcilably Wet," Cannon asked rhetorically, "Shall Dry America, a country with prohibition imbedded in its Constitution, elect a 'cocktail President'?" Cannon argued that Smith's habit of daily consumption of "four to eight" "cocktails and highballs" disqualified him from being president. He tied Smith to the Catholic Church hierarchy's position against prohibition and claimed that this made him "ecclesiastically wet."[104] This last charge shows that Cannon clearly meant to bring Smith's religion into the campaign. Under the guise of speaking about Smith's stand on prohibition, Cannon reminded his audience of the nominee's non-Protestant faith, a faith Cannon knew to be a divisive issue in the overwhelmingly Protestant South. Again, the South functioned as a funhouse mirror—reflecting the general antagonism of the nation against Roman Catholicism but exaggerating it almost beyond recognition.

As the campaign heated up and Cannon's rhetoric increased, the question of whether the clergy should enter into politics arose. Once again, the South in the eyes of the national media appeared to allow its clergy, who were already suspect, too much influence in secular matters. In March 1928, the *Review of Reviews* warned that Bishop Cannon and his followers were "in no compromising mood."[105] Commenting on the July 1928 gathering of southern clergy in Asheville, North Carolina, which declared its opposition to Smith, the *Literary Digest* reported that "the political activity of religious leaders began to loom large at the Asheville conference of Southern drys." According to the *Digest*, most newspapers around the country opposed Cannon's involvement in politics, including the *New York World*, the *Chicago Journal of Commerce*, the *Milwaukee Journal*, the *St. Louis Star*, the *Helena Independent*, and the *Sacramento Bee*.[106] Describing Cannon in an article for *Outlook*, Dixon Merritt likened him to "Attila the Hun" and said that Cannon was so combative that "he maintained a clipping service on every man of any account in the Virginia Conference [the hierarchical structure of the Methodist Episcopal Church, South, in Virginia] because a fight with any of them was always imminent."[107] Not only was Cannon constantly combative, he was a "strict constructionist in most things," which made him absolutely inflexible on the alcohol issue, exhibiting a "life-long, sledge hammer devotion to prohibition."[108] In his portrait of Cannon, Merritt was drawing on familiar themes about the South and its clergy: that southerners were prone to fight over the smallest details, that they were vengeful, and that they would not bend on matters of religion and morals.

Cannon's activism raised the question of clerical interference in politics, a charge often associated with the South. "Another Southern scholar," unnamed in the *Review of Reviews*, reported that "many who oppose [Smith] on account of his Catholicism cloak their real objections under the cry of prohibition."[109] Incensed about the use of Smith's religion as a campaign issue and the involvement of Protestant clergy, George W. Hinman Jr. decried the practice in the *Outlook*. He accused the ministers of using the prohibition campaign to allow them their "first real taste of the apple of temporal dominion" and argued that they now "lust[ed] for still wider dominion." He concluded that "the lust of the clergy for temporal power . . . is the real menace. . . ."[110] "Protestant Ministers in South Blamed for Keeping Alive Religious Hatred," ran the headline in the *New York Times* in July for a story reporting that "bigotry is now more rampant and religious intolerance more evident than ever before."[111] In a debate in Charlottesville, Virginia, in August, Dr. John H. Latane of Johns Hopkins University predicted that the "political parsons are riding for a fall, for the people of America are not going to submit very long to ecclesiastic domination."[112] In September, the *Literary Digest* reprinted a *Macon Telegraph* editorial that condemned the preachers' tactics against Smith. The *Telegraph* stated that a preacher who would engage in such a campaign "is a crusader, a witch-burner, an intolerant bigot."[113] In October, Owen P. White wrote in *Collier's* that the Reverend Bob Jones, the famous Pentecostal evangelist from Alabama who would found Bob Jones University in South Carolina, used revivals to stir up anti-Smith sentiment in the South. According to Smith, Jones told a crowd that "'God's callin' on Dixie to save America from the foreign domination of the cities of the North.'"[114] Jones equated the influx of European immigrants with a Roman Catholic plot to run the United States, and he believed he had to use his pulpit to stop it. Of course, by doing so, he once again raised the issue that the southern clergy used their influence in ways that critics outside (and occasionally inside) the South saw as improper because it was not directly tied to efforts to bring about the Kingdom of God on earth. When the clergy used their influence to secure reforms that ameliorated social problems, such as when they assisted with enacting prohibition, they received more favorable treatment in the press.

White also reported on a Baptist minister from Atlanta, Dr. Arthur J. Barton, who claimed that if Smith were elected, it would mean "'that the floodgates of immigration will be opened and that ours will be turned into a civilization like that of continental Europe.'" Not only that, Barton charged, a Smith win would mean that "'you will turn this country over to the domination of a foreign religious sect . . . and Church and State will once again be united.'"[115] In Birmingham, White reported, the Reverend Dr. Collier spoke to a tent meeting and raised the specter of immigration and foreign domination by the Catholic Church. Speaking of Smith supporters, Collier argued, "'They can't elect him . . . there ain't enough people in the United States who love the dirty foreigners and their dirty political parties better than they love Jesus.'" Collier went on to predict that

> God'll be with us in November, and then that dirty foreign gang, who don't like the laws we make in our own land, can get aboard their ships and sail back to Europe while we stand on shore on the *statues of Liberty* [sic] and sing Praise God from Whom All Blessings Flow.[116]

Echoing their predecessors in the Georgia and Alabama prohibition battles, these southerners continued to sing the Long Meter Doxology to emphasize their religious stance in political arguments. Just for good measure, White also interviewed a Baptist minister from Raleigh, North Carolina, who added, "'Every man who votes the straight Democratic ticket this fall will be voting to crucify his country on a black, bloody cross builded [sic] by the foreign element.'"[117] White concluded that Smith's religion was the real reason he was doing so poorly in the South, not his stand on prohibition. According to White, an Alabama "layman" said, "'It's his church they're after, and as these people who go to these meetings are afraid of their religious intolerance, they hold up the rum issue as a screen from behind which they can take a shot at Rome.'"[118] Quoted in the *Literary Digest*, the *Christian Index*, the "official organ of the Baptists of Georgia," confirmed this observation when it declared that "'multitudes of Protestants are afraid of the Roman Catholic Church because of what the Popes have said in regard to the relations of Church and State.'" In other words, Protestants in Georgia were afraid that the clergy of the wrong sort (Catholic) would wield too much power over the state should Smith win. Continuing, the denominational paper argued, "'All the Roman Catholic laymen of the United States are a mere cipher'" about their beliefs and political preferences. The "'coterie of Spanish and Italian ecclesiastics'" held their intentions secret, and this was why "'many American Protestants are not at all quiet in their mind in regard to the future.'"[119] "'Of course it's religion,'" Virginia Democratic state committee chairman Murray Hooker told a *New York Times* columnist about the lack of support for Smith in his state. The reporter, Richard V. Oulahan, noted that Cannon had denied religion as a factor in his opposition to Smith but that "everybody knows what is at the bottom of the antagonism to Smith in Virginia."[120] Oulahan added that "stories are told . . . of clergymen of the Baptist and Methodist Churches circulating anti-Smith pledge cards among their congregations" and that some "country clergymen call on their congregations to divide up—'All who are for Al Smith and Satan' . . . and 'all who are for Herbert Hoover and righteousness.'"[121] J. Frank Norris could not resist jumping into the debate. He actively opposed Smith, citing his religion repeatedly, which drew more criticism of Norris and the region. Norris offered to debate Smith in either New

York or Texas, requesting specifically to "discuss religious issues."[122] The Reverend Dr. Dan B. Brummitt of the northern branch of the Methodist Church told his readers in the *Northwestern Christian Advocate* that Norris was merely a "'notoriety-seeker'" and referred to him as "'Two-gun' Norris."[123] The comments of Norris, Jones, and others helped cement the notion in many minds that the South was home to religious intolerance, intolerance often associated with fundamentalism. These clergy were openly saying that Catholics could not be trusted because they did not separate church and state, an ironic belief, as the northern media had once and still did accuse the South and its Protestant clergy of the same sin.

In the end, seven states defected from the Democratic column, and Smith lost. Commentators analyzed the results, with many of them agreeing that bigotry in the South led to Smith's defeat. For example, the *New York World* cited "bigotry" and "Prohibition" as the reasons the South failed to remain "solid" in its politics.[124] Several southern newspapers with Democratic leanings, including the *Richmond Times-Dispatch* and the *Charleston News and Courier*, also cited the issue of Smith's religion in his defeat.[125] According to one editorial, "Prosperity, Protection, Prohibition, and Prejudice are the p's that lots of folks in the voting queues seemed to have minded."[126] The *Christian Advocate* "regretted" "Protestant opposition [that] was based on intolerance and bigotry."[127] Reporting in the *New York Times* on the South Georgia Methodist Conference's recent resolution thanking "God for the defeat of Governor Smith," Julian Harris wrote that there was "no question that parsons, prejudices, [and] prohibition" had contributed to the Democratic loss. The *Times* editorial page argued that "bigotry and fanaticism" had won the day in the South and that the region voted "based largely on a harmful superstition."[128] Several months later, commentators were still bemoaning the involvement of the southern clergy in Smith's defeat and the role Smith's religion played. Minister J. A. MacCallum told readers of the *North American Review* that Protestant ministers who had long held political power claimed the moral high ground of separation of church and state during the 1928 campaign. Singling out Cannon and his fellow southerners, MacCallum charged that "the readiness of a multitude of the clergy to surrender their intelligence to the sway of the emotions in an orgy of blind partisanship . . . [was] one of the most sorrowful revelations of our time."[129] According to Virginius Dabney, Cannon's role in the anti-Smith campaign had done "more to foment intolerance . . . in the late campaign than any other individual in the United States, with the possible exception of that great Christian warrior, Imperial Wizard Hiram Wesley Evans, " leader of the Ku Klux Klan.[130] Never one to pass up an opportunity to attack Cannon, H. L. Mencken compared Cannon to a Methodist pope, calling him the "ranking American ecclesiastic."[131] For his part, Cannon continued to defend his political activities, arguing that "the ministry and church cannot view with indifference any legislation which would retard or check the advancement of morals, health, and happiness." For Cannon, the notion of keeping the clergy from commenting on legislation was "anti-christian."[132] In a rebuttal, Heywood Broun replied that it seemed to him "a serious thing that a prominent American politician and cleric should openly advocate the abolition of our traditional separation of church and state."[133]

So in 1928 and on into the 1930s, the same exchanges that had been taking place over the past forty years continued. Southerners defended their region, made excuses for it, or generally attacked northern opinions, while northern writers continued to find examples of southern backwardness. In 1928, writing for the *Montgomery (Alabama) Advertiser*, editor Grover C. Hall sounded the death knell of conservative Protestantism, saying, "To-day nothing seems more obvious to me than that the evangelical tradition is fighting a losing fight in the Southern States."[134] James M. Cain, a southerner, told readers of the *Bookman* that the South was "not insanely anti-Catholic," nor was it "backward in cultural development."[135] Vanderbilt University professor Donald Davidson argued that Dixie had engaged in "intellectual evolution" since the Scopes Trial.[136]

Yet try as they might to defend their region, the southern apologists could not prevent outside observers from finding additional examples of southern deficiency. Sam H. Reading of Philadelphia wrote in April 1928 to the editor of the *Forum* arguing that southern author Corra Harris was in reality not a writer but a "humorist" because she argued that "Southern people are more normal in their vices." What "degree of normalcy," he asked, was there in the "burning of a live human being at the stake and fighting among themselves over the possession of particularly choice portions of the well charred anatomy"? He continued, "since 'they are also more polite,' I wonder if they say, 'Thank you,' to the families of their victims?" He went on to ridicule the South's storied fear of evolution and its brutal prison conditions. A southern woman's defense of her region was, for Reading, a laughable enterprise, given the history of lynching, anti-evolution laws, and the penal system of the South.[137] In 1930, the *New York Times* reported on a feud of words between the governor of Texas and the *Chicago Tribune* over fundamentalism in the South and lawlessness in the North. The *Tribune* had referred to the South as the "'fundamentalist belt of primitives,'" which prompted Governor Moody to remind the Windy City that it had been home to Al Capone and the Valentine's Day Massacre.[138] And the nondenominational *Christian Century* continued to argue that Southern Baptists and Methodists continued to be "responsible almost wholly" for the South's "behavior."[139]

The South was still, in the eyes of outsiders and to some of its own native sons and daughters, an outdated, violent, overly conservative backwater that time had not managed to influence. Despite their well-meaning efforts, these critics had not managed to change the South or their own perceptions of it. The South did not conform to the definition of "America." Instead, it was an example of what could go wrong in America if education and progress did not carry the day. It was only natural that fundamentalism had taken root there, and it was only natural that fundamentalism would apparently die there.

CONCLUSION

Like so many other aspects of white southern life and culture, J. Frank Norris's appearance in the secular press of his day resembles an image in a funhouse mirror. The mirror reflects aspects of Norris that undoubtedly existed—that he was violent, that he ignored social problems—but these features become so distorted in the press that Norris looks comical and ludicrous.

The caricatures of Norris and his slightly more respectable colleague James Cannon Jr. did not appear overnight. Nor were they an immediate result of the Scopes Trial. Instead, the image of J. Frank Norris—white southern fundamentalist, murderer, powerful and paranoid preacher—arose as much from popular perceptions about the South in general and about fundamentalism as it did from Norris's own actions. The image of Bishop Cannon—white southern Methodist, Anti-Saloon League crusader, and vicious opponent of Al Smith—fit nicely with what the non-southern audience had come to expect of southern clergy. The portrayals of these men in the popular media owed much to the intellectual climate of the North and the schools of thought that influenced it. Observers of white southern culture and thought were largely influenced by notions of Auguste Comte and Emile Durkheim, as well as the liberal Protestantism so prevalent in the seminaries and denominational journals of the Northeast. These observers believed that the South was a region that violated their notion of the national character. Although it was largely populated by whites (and even contained pockets of what these scientific racists called "pure Anglo-Saxons" in Appalachia), the South, in their view, had rejected the American guarantee of free speech, the importance of education, and the use of an impartial judicial system. As white southerners from the late nineteenth century on continued to lynch blacks, post alarming illiteracy rates, and use societal pressures to silence dissenting voices, they unwittingly helped outside observers, and indeed some insiders as well, to portray the region as a land without justice, a land of violence, an uneducated land, and a land that represented a blot on the American character.

That this process occurred during a time when millions of Italians and Eastern Europeans were streaming into the United States is no coincidence. Residents of the United States struggled to define what it meant to be an "American" and who was distinctly not American. Historian John Higham has chronicled the manner in which Americans in the North marginalized the new immigrants, for example, perceiving the Jew as parvenu, complete with "pervasive vulgarity and . . . general social climbing . . . upsetting the stability and simplicity of American society on a grand scale."[1] The "custodians of culture," as Henry May refers to them, were also using the South as an example of the way in which American ideals were threatened from within as well as from without. In struggling to define an America that excluded the perceived threats from the new immigrants—violence, religious intolerance (in this case, an allegiance to either Roman Catholicism or Judaism), and illiteracy—the northern elite managed to write the white South out of America as well.[2] Such an effort stands in contrast to other historians' contention that certain religious groups have defined themselves as American by virtue of their variance from the mainstream, and it also calls into question the assumption that religion aligned itself with American culture immediately following World War II. Instead, in this case, the self-appointed mainstream distanced itself from what it perceived as religious and cultural outsiders in the South.[3]

The South, over the decades between 1880 and 1920, rightly earned a bad reputation in the eyes of the North. It did have abysmal educational facilities. It did lynch at a much higher rate than the rest of the country. And it did embrace almost homogeneous (and more conservative) Protestant thought while fostering its own brand of anti-Catholic nativism and anti-Semitism. But the coverage of the daily newspapers, weekly magazines, and monthly journals amplified these traits and created an image that, although based in fact, distorted the conditions of the South. For example, reporters and editors saw embedded in the white southern propensity for lynching signs that the South embraced medieval practices. The examples that northern observers and southern critics reported evolved from trends into character traits of every white southerner, regardless of his or her position on lynching. Moreover, the commentators built such a case that the white southern clergy were either powerless to effect social change or so powerful as to command state assemblies to do their bidding that a parody bordering on travesty emerged. White southern clergy were both inept and theocratic at the same time in the eyes of these observers. While the pastors of the South may indeed have held a special place in society, most were neither as bumbling nor as power-hungry as the popular literature of the day would lead us to believe.

Like white southerners, the fundamentalists suffered at the hands of the northern press, which, after a brief honeymoon, was little interested in their doctrinal beliefs and instead portrayed them as intolerant usurpers of religious liberty. Once the fundamentalists became associated with antievolution legislation, the die was cast, and instead of calling attention to the theological disputes the religious conservatives had with their denominations, with their seminaries, and with American culture, writers chose to emphasize their violent rhetoric, their insistence on the need for religion to dictate culture, and their embrace of a notion of science that intellectuals had labeled ignorant. The fundamentalists became a parody of themselves, the butt of jokes, and were perceived as comical yet dangerous even before the Scopes Trial.

The characteristics of white southerners had been well established in the public mind, and the addition of the fundamentalists to the equation quickly led to a branding of the South as fundamentalist. Largely because of the success of antievolution legislation in the South, and also because of the region's famous affinity for conservative religion, the commentators on culture quickly painted the South as fundamentalist. The South was violent; the fundamentalists spoke in violent ways about Christ's return and talked about waging war within their denominations. The South was uneducated; the fundamentalists rejected Darwinian theory and asked public schools to teach a theory of creation that many scientists believed was not only untenable but also ignorant. The white South embraced legislation governing personal behavior and spurned social uplift movements; the fundamentalists condemned personal vices and rejected the notion of social reform because they believed the world was too utterly fallen to be salvageable through human actions. The syllogism was easy to complete, and the reporters and editors leapt to link the South with fundamentalism. Once the assumption had been made, it was easy to use the Scopes Trial and J. Frank Norris as ready examples of the South's fundamentalism.

The association of the white South with fundamentalism served several purposes. First, it located the movement outside the region where it had, in fact, originated.[4] By placing the movement outside the North, commentators could shift the source of such an antimodern movement away from their perceived home of modernity and to a place they believed was naturally antimodern. The threat to liberal Protestantism, which these observers believed was a part of the American character, was thus localized and, in their minds, more contained. The association of the two also allowed northern critics of the South to continue their campaign against the region. Not only was it home to violent mobs, illiterate adults, and theocratic (but bumbling) clergy, it also, they reasoned, was home to a "dangerous" religious movement that threatened the separation of church and state.

The association of a geographic area with certain cultural characteristics is certainly not new to American history or imagination. Historian Peter S. Onuf has

shown that sectionalism has existed since the Revolutionary War and that this sectionalism served to allay fears that a strong central government would overpower
local interests.[5] The persistence of regionalism throughout U.S. history demonstrates how strongly appealing these notions were and how willing Americans were
to believe that their fellow citizens could be different.

The South, as several historians have demonstrated, had done much since the
Civil War to industrialize, to educate, and to nurture culture in the way that the
North had dictated.[6] Yet it was still dogged with negative stereotypes, stereotypes
that grew in part out of fact and were accepted as fact even by some southerners.
Georgia resident Robert Preston Brooks told readers of the *Forum* in 1926 that his
home state still needed much work. In his words,

> A poverty-stricken people will inevitably be ignorant and backward. Ignorance
> accounts for low political ideals, religious intolerance, anti-scientific agitation,
> Kluxism, lynching; it explains the fact that Georgians are not a reading people;
> that we are a poor field for publishers, that we have no nationally known maga-
> zines, that our libraries are few and inadequate. These social defects cannot be
> eradicated by ridicule and denunciation. Education seems the only remedy.[7]

Despite all of its efforts, the white South was still down at heel, playing catch-up
to the North's standards and, at the same time, thumbing its nose at its northern
relatives. It fought both to define itself as different and to embrace the national heritage that it shared with the North. It was a conflicted place as it tried to industrialize rapidly and yet maintain its strange version of race relations. Even more conflicted than the South's image of itself, however, was the North's image of the South.
It was "priest-ridden" yet Protestant, embracing "Puritanism" and "medievalism,"
home to fundamentalism and "pure Anglo-Saxon stock." The South became, through
its association with fundamentalism, a location where northern intellectuals and
southern critics could work out their own doubts about the country's future and
define the national character in opposition to the trends they saw there. As much
as the northern critics of the South would have hated to admit it, they needed the
South to serve as their bogeyman, an entity that embodied their fears and doubts
but that they could contain, restrict, and subjugate in order to maintain an illusion
of unity and safety.

This book has highlighted several areas in which scholars need to improve or
refocus their efforts. The field of journalism history needs desperately to be revived.
The towering works in the field are now almost four decades old, and yet few historians seem interested in challenging the assumptions or the narratives that Frank
Luther Mott and Theodore Peterson provide. When Mott and Peterson wrote, history was largely narrative, and subtle analysis of the influence of culture, race, class,
gender, and education are absent from their works. An enterprising academic today

could explore more fully the role that liberal Protestant, positivist, or progressive notions played in the editorial contents of U.S. magazines in the late 1800s and early 1900s. An examination of archived letters to the editor would provide an excellent barometer of reader response. Historians tend to rely heavily on these periodicals for their evidence, yet no one is delving into the ideological issues of or public response to these primary sources.

Despite the lack of such understanding, secular magazines and newspapers provide an important resource for historians of religion in America, a resource of which they have not fully availed themselves. Historians of religion have long relied on denominational newspapers and unpublished sermons to make their pronouncements about religion's relationship to culture. Missing from this analysis is a consideration of secular publications' perception of the battles being fought over how religion and culture should address each other. Accounts that rely too heavily on denominational sources make certain doctrinal battles appear larger than life or at least narrow the context in which current readers can place them. As American religious historians learn to trust secular sources for their research, they will begin to place the influences of religion upon culture and of culture upon religion in a broader context, a context that will invite further discussion and interest in the field. This book attempts to place debate over the South's fundamentalism into a national context, and in the process it calls into question assumptions about religious regionalism.

The book also raises questions that future historians will need to address. Why was the South such a fertile ground for fundamentalism? Why did men like John Roach Straton, reared in the South, make their careers in the North, and why did they enjoy such a following in urban areas? Is there really any regionalism left in the field of fundamentalist history, or should we view the itinerant northern fundamentalists that William Glass describes as national circuit riders rather than regional ones? How did Americans respond to the depictions of white southerners and fundamentalists?

These questions await further study, but this work has demonstrated that the South's reputation was earned honestly but distorted unfairly. Since the arrival of evangelical abolitionist thought in the 1840s, the South and the North have often been at odds. The characterization of the South as fundamentalist was only one chapter in a long history of animosity and reconciliation, exclusion and inclusion, that has come to symbolize the struggle over cultural self-definition in this country.

APPENDIX

Table A

CIRCULATION OF SELECTED NEW YORK PUBLICATIONS

	1880	1890	1900	1910	1920	1931
The American Mercury (est. 1924)	—	—	—	—	—	62,074
The Century (est. 1870)	n/a	198,300	150,000	125,000	51,610	(Combined with The Forum
Christian Advocate	64,000	52,500	40,500	35,000	47,000	36,100
The Churchman	17,000	23,000	19,000	17,500	15,000	n/a
Collier's (est. 1887)	—	n/a	170,000	500,000	1,064,294	2,257,290
Current Opinion (est. 1888)	—	n/a	n/a	n/a	37,583	n/a
Educational Review (est. 1891)	—	—	5,000	2,000	2,500	(Ceased 1928)
Everybody's Magazine	n/a	n/a	n/a	500,000	339,185	(Ceased 1929)
The Forum (est. 1886)	—	n/a	45,000	n/a	n/a	82,171
Harper's Weekly	120,000	85,000	80,000	70,000	(Ceased 1916)	
Harper's Monthly Magazine	n/a	n/a	n/a	125,000	80,689	120,947
The Independent	20,000	n/a	n/a	n/a	87,958	n/a
The Literary Digest (est. 1890)	n/a	n/a	50,000	198,650	900,000	1,602,377
McClure's (est. 1893)	—	—	369,265	425,000	522,641	(Ceased 1928)
The Missionary Review of the World (est. 1887)	—	10,000	13,000	9,000	9,473	6,436
The Nation	8,000	8,268	9,498	6,500	33,687	37,127
The New Republic (est. 1914)	—	—	—	—	37,000	25,000
The North American Review	7,500	50,000	20,000	20,000	24,571	n/a
The Outlook (est. 1893)	—	—	79,076	106,656	106,618	85,536

continued on next page

	1880	1890	1900	1910	1920	1931
School and Society (est. 1911)	—	—	—	—	n/a	4,556
Science (est. 1883)	—	3,000	4,000	n/a	n/a	13,337
Scientific Monthly (est. 1913)	—	—	—	—	n/a	9,208
Scribner's	116,666	100,000	175,000	200,000	91,898	73,517
The Survey (est. 1897)	—	—	n/a	12,583	13,686	n/a
The World's Work (est. 1900)	—	—	—	104,000	n/a	(Combined with Review of Reviews 1932)

Table B
CIRCULATION OF SELECTED BOSTON PUBLICATIONS

	1880	1890	1900	1910	1920	1931
The Atlantic Monthly	12,000	n/a	14,000	25,000	94,855	129,798
The New England Magazine (est. 1884)	—	n/a	20,000	30,000	(Ceased 1917)	—
The Universalist Leader	n/a	n/a	18,000	9,000	7,500	n/a

Table C
CIRCULATION OF SELECTED CHICAGO PUBLICATIONS

	1880	1890	1900	1910	1920	1931
The American Journal of Sociology (est. 1896)	—	—	n/a	1,750	n/a	2,600
Christian Century (est. 1884)	—	n/a	n/a	10,250	n/a	n/a
School Review (est. 1893)	—	—	2,500	7,000	3,300	n/a
Time (est. 1923)	—	—	—	—	—	300,172

Table D

CIRCULATION OF OTHER SELECTED PUBLICATIONS

	1880	1890	1900	1910	1920	1931
The Methodist Protestant (Baltimore)	3,850	5,000	6,000	3,600	6,500	5,100
The Sewanee Review (Sewanee, Tenn.; est. 1892)	—	—	500	400	400	325
The South Atlantic Quarterly (Durham, N.C.; est. 1902)	—	—	—	750	700	250
The Southern Churchman (Richmond, Va.)	4,000	5,200	5,500	5,100	4,900	6,850

SOURCE (ALL TABLES): N. W. Ayers and Sons *Directory of American Newspapers and Periodicals.*

NOTES

Introduction

1. Grover C. Hall, "We Southerners," reprinted in *Scribner's Magazine*, January 1928, 83–84.
2. For an overview of the history of fundamentalism, see Ernest Sandeen, *The Roots of Fundamentalism: British and American Millenarianism, 1800–1930* (Chicago: University of Chicago Press, 1970); George M. Marsden, *Fundamentalism and American Culture: The Shaping of Twentieth-Century Evangelicalism, 1870–1920* (New York: Oxford University Press, 1980); and Virginia Brereton, *Training God's Army: The American Bible School, 1880–1940* (Bloomington: Indiana University Press, 1990). For a look at fundamentalism after the Scopes Trial, see Joel Carpenter, *Revive Us Again: The Reawakening of American Fundamentalism* (New York: Oxford University Press, 1997).
3. Cullen Murphy, writing in consultation with Timothy L. Smith, defined evangelicals as "Christians of whatever denomination who are determined to rest their faith and religious practice on the authority of the Bible; who believe that the New Testament promises eternal life through a morally transforming experience of the Holy Spirit that Jesus described to Nicodemus as being 'born again'; and who are, for these reasons, intensely committed to missionary work ('evangelicalism'), both in their own towns and neighborhoods and around the world." Murphy, "Protestantism and the Evangelicals," *Wilson Quarterly* 5, no. 1 (1981): 105.
4. George M. Marsden, *Understanding Fundamentalism and Evangelicalism* (Grand Rapids, Mich.: William B. Eerdmans, 1991), 4–5.
5. It is important to note that the battle between liberals and conservatives took place largely in the context of American Protestant denominations. American Catholics had their own differences that can be labeled as liberal and conservative viewpoints, but these disputes took place, for the most part, over the proper role of American Catholic clergy with regard to the Catholic hierarchy in Rome. Regardless of whether Catholic clergy embraced a liberal or conservative stance regarding the American Church and Rome, they were in agreement over the points of theology named above, but with a Roman Catholic understanding. For instance, Catholics did not and do not use the King James Bible, a favorite of Protestant conservatives. Moreover, Roman Catholics do not subscribe to the notion of dispensational premillennialism, nor does the majority of American Protestants.
6. See Marsden, *Fundamentalism and American Culture*; and Nancy T. Ammerman, "North American Protestant Fundamentalism," in *Fundamentalisms Observed*, ed. Martin E. Marty and R. Scott Appleby (Chicago: University of Chicago Press, 1991), 19–27.
7. For fundamentalism's antimodern period, see Marsden, *Fundamentalism and American Culture*, 4. Samuel S. Hill Jr. writes on the fundamentalist/evangelical distinction: "Like the larger company of Evangelicals, fundamentalists are committed to

evangelization and the cultivation of personal piety. But while Fundamentalism affirms those activities in themselves, it is much more concerned with, and defined by, correct belief than correct practice. Christian doctrine is defined in the most precise and absolutist ways, and only a fractional degree of flexibility, or better, none at all, can be honored, regardless of one's experiential claims. Fundamentalism is therefore exclusive; only those who preach and believe in line with the truth as the Bible presents it—*interpretation* is no issue here at all—are worthy to be called Christians" (italics in original). Hill, "Fundamentalism in Recent Southern Culture: Has It Done What the Civil Rights Movement Couldn't Do?" *Journal of Southern Religion* 1 (1998): http://jsr.lib.virginia.edu/essay.htm.

8. For an example of the new work challenging the fundamentalist/Pentecostalism split, see Matthew A. Sutton, "'Between the Refrigerator and the Wildfire': Aimee Semple McPherson, Pentecostalism, and the Fundamentalist-Modernist Controversy," *Church History* 72, no. 1 (March 2003), 159–88.

9. For more on the Holiness movement, see Briane K. Turley, A *Wheel within a Wheel: Southern Methodism and the Georgia Holiness Association* (Macon, Ga.: Mercer University Press, 1999).

10. H. L. Mencken, "The Sahara of the Bozart," in *Prejudices: Second Series* (New York: Alfred A. Knopf, 1920), 136–54.

11. Theodore Peterson, *Magazines in the Twentieth Century* (Urbana: University of Illinois Press, 1956), 4; Frank Luther Mott, *American Journalism: A History: 1690–1960* (New York: Macmillan, 1962), 519; David Paul Nord, "Reading the Newspaper: Strategies and Politics of Reader Response, Chicago, 1912–1917," *Journal of Communication* 45, no. 3 (1995): 67, 88.

12. Royce Jordan, "Tennessee Goes Fundamentalist," *New Republic*, 29 April 1925, 259.

13. Albert Bushnell Hart, "The Conditions of the Southern Problem," *Independent*, 23 March 1905, 646.

14. For an excellent examination of southern progressive thought, see Dewey Grantham, *Southern Progressivism: The Reconciliation of Progress and Tradition* (Knoxville: University of Tennessee Press, 1983).

15. "Free Speech in the South," *Independent*, 15 January 1903, 137.

16. Frederick Morgan Davenport, "The Religious Revival and the New Evangelism," *Outlook*, 8 April 1905, 897; Robert L. Duffus, "How the Ku Klux Klan Sells Hate," *World's Work*, June 1923, 174–83.

17. See David W. Blight, *Race and Reunion: The Civil War in American Memory* (Cambridge: Belknap Press of Harvard University Press, 2001); and Nina Silber, *The Romance of Reunion: Northerners and the South, 1865–1900* (Chapel Hill: University of North Carolina Press, 1993).

18. For other opinions on linkage of these notions and the timing, see George B. Tindall, "The Benighted South: Origins of a Modern Image," *Virginia Quarterly Review* 40 (Spring 1964): 281, 288; Tindall, *The Emergence of the New South, 1913–1945* (Baton Rouge: Louisiana State University Press, 1967); and Fred Hobson, *Tell about the South: The Southern Rage to Explain* (Baton Rouge: Louisiana State University Press, 1983), 183–84.

19. Ronald L. Numbers provides a detailed discussion of the various theories of creationism in his book *The Creationists* (New York: Alfred A. Knopf, 1992).

20. Corra Harris, A *Circuit Rider's Wife* (Philadelphia: Henry Altemus, 1910). For an examination of Harris's popularity, see Karen Coffing, "Corra Harris and the *Satur-

day *Evening Post*: Southern Domesticity Conveyed to a National Audience, 1900–1930," *Georgia Historical Quarterly* 79, no. 2 (1995): 367–93.

21. Blight, *Race and Reunion*, 266.

22. See "Who Is Fundamental?" *Time*, 19 May 1923, 20.

23. Examples of secondary scholarship on the religious conservatism of the South include Donald G. Mathews, *Religion in the Old South* (Chicago: University of Chicago Press, 1977); John B. Boles, *The Great Revival, 1795–1869: The Origins of the Southern Evangelical Mind* (Lexington: University Press of Kentucky, 1972); and E. Brooks Holifield, *The Gentlemen Theologians: American Theology in Southern Culture, 1795–1860* (Durham, N.C.: Duke University Press, 1978).

24. Indeed, Christine Leigh Heyrman insightfully argues that the South's conversion to evangelicalism a century earlier was not inevitable. See Heyrman, *Southern Cross: The Beginnings of the Bible Belt* (New York: Alfred A. Knopf, 1997).

25. For more about Social Gospel efforts in the South, see John Patrick McDowell, *The Social Gospel in the South: The Woman's Home Mission Movement in the Methodist Episcopal Church, South, 1886–1939* (Baton Rouge: Louisiana State University Press, 1982).

26. For competing theories on when Americans realized that their world had drastically changed, see Henry F. May, *The End of American Innocence: A Study of the First Years of Our Own Time* (New York: Alfred A. Knopf, 1959); and Frederick Lewis Allen, *Only Yesterday: An Informal History of the 1920s* (New York: Harper and Brothers, 1931). May places the changes in the years immediately preceding World War I, while Allen argues that the shift took place after, and as a result of, World War I.

27. Nell Irvin Painter, *Standing at Armageddon: The United States, 1877–1919* (New York: W. W. Norton, 1987), 149.

28. I am not, by far, the first historian to notice these concurrent developments. For other authors who saw this debate arising during a time of increased non-Protestant immigration, see James C. Klotter, "The Black South and White Appalachia," *Journal of American History* 66 (March 1980): 832–49; and Silber, *The Romance of Reunion*, 143–56.

29. The sociological theory of H. Richard Niebuhr informs my discussion of the two camps. For more on the distinction between the two sides of this debate, see Niebuhr, *Christ and Culture* (1951; expanded ed., New York: Harper Collins, 2001).

30. George Marsden has explored this topic in *Fundamentalism and American Culture*, as has Nancy Ammerman in "North American Protestant Fundamentalism."

31. Gillis J. Harp, *Positivist Republic: Auguste Comte and the Reconstruction of American Liberalism, 1865–1920* (University Park: Pennsylvania State University Press, 1995), 4–21.

32. Daniel L. Pals, *Seven Theories of Religion* (New York: Oxford University Press, 1996), 91–92.

33. Emile Durkheim, *On Morality and Society: Selected Essays*, ed. Robert N. Bellah (Chicago: University of Chicago Press, 1973), 159. "Le dualisme de la nature humaine et ses conditions socials" was originally published in 1914.

34. Pals, *Seven Theories of Religion*, 111.

35. Ferenc Morton Szasz, *The Divided Mind of Protestant America, 1880–1930* (Tuscaloosa: University of Alabama Press, 1982), 132.

36. Matthew Schneirov, *The Dream of a New Social Order: Popular Magazines in America, 1893–1914* (New York: Columbia University Press, 1994), 257–63.

37. For more on the University of Chicago School of Sociology, see chapter 2.

38. For more on Herbert Croly, see David W. Levy, *Herbert Croly of "The New Republic": The Life and Thought of an American Progressive* (Princeton: Princeton University Press, 1985).

39. See Grace Elizabeth Hale, *Making Whiteness: The Culture of Segregation in the South, 1890–1840* (New York: Pantheon, 1998), 199–239.

40. Norris was by no means the first white southern preacher to attract the attention of the national press. Chapter 3 will address the influence of Sam Jones, and chapter 5 will connect the two men's legacies in the popular media.

41. For example, in *Roots of Fundamentalism* Ernest Sandeen views fundamentalism as primarily a doctrinal movement, with no mention of the South. George Marsden sees it as a social movement growing out of the Northeast and Midwest, and reasons that the South was predisposed to fundamentalism (*Fundamentalism and American Culture*, 103). While this generalization is most likely true, it does not explain why or how the average American, with little or no knowledge of religion in the South, came to view the South as fundamentalist. Both Marsden and Paul Conkin note that many of the early fundamentalist leaders were southern-born, yet a careful examination of contemporary coverage of these men does not yield any mention of their birthplaces. See Marsden, *Fundamentalism and American Culture*, 258n; and Paul Conkin, *When All the Gods Trembled: Darwinism, Scopes, and American Intellectuals* (Lanham, Md.: Rowman and Littlefield, 1998), 68. Virginia Brereton in *Training God's Army* concludes that it was an educational movement. Only Glass looks at the South in detail, but he focuses on how the movement came to the South and not how it became known as southern. See Glass, *Strangers in Zion: Fundamentalists in the South, 1900–1950* (Macon, Georgia: Mercer University Press, 2001).

42. For examples, see Mathews, *Religion in the Old South*; Boles, *Great Revival*; and Holifield, *Gentlemen Theologians*. Historians of the South in general have been largely involved in debates about the extent to which the South exists or existed as a distinct culture. See C. Vann Woodward, *Origins of the New South, 1877–1913* (Baton Rouge: Louisiana State University Press, 1951); Edward L. Ayers, *The Promise of the New South: Life after Reconstruction* (New York: Oxford University Press, 1992); and Edward L. Ayers, Patricia Nelson Limerick, Stephen Nissenbaum, and Peter Onuf, eds., *All Over the Map: Rethinking American Regions* (Baltimore: Johns Hopkins University Press, 1996).

43. For examples of the newer scholarship, see Beth Barton Schweiger's *The Gospel Working Up: Progress and the Pulpit in Nineteenth-Century Virginia* (New York: Oxford University Press, 2000); Paul Harvey, *Redeeming the South: Religious Cultures and Racial Identities among Southern Baptists, 1865–1925* (Chapel Hill: University of North Carolina Press, 1997); Sally G. McMillen, *To Raise Up the South: Sunday Schools in Black and White Churches, 1865–1915* (Baton Rouge: Louisiana State University Press, 2001); and Daniel W. Stowell, *Rebuilding Zion: The Religious Reconstruction of the South, 1863–1877* (New York: Oxford University Press, 1998). For examples of the works that the new historians are calling into question, see Kenneth Bailey, *Southern White Protestantism in the Twentieth Century* (New York: Harper and Row, 1964); and Samuel S. Hill Jr., *Southern Churches in Crisis* (New York: Holt, Rinehart, and Winston, 1966).

44. Although he relies more on film and television, Jack Temple Kirby has also addressed this issue. See Jack Temple Kirby, *Media-Made Dixie: The South in the American Imagination*, rev. ed. (Athens: University of Georgia Press, 1986).

45. The phrase "custodians of culture" belongs to Henry May. See May, *End of American Innocence*, 30–51.
46. Other historians have noticed the importance of the thematic approach to this time period. See, for example, Warren Susman, *Culture as History: The Transformation of American Society in the Twentieth Century* (New York: Pantheon, 1984).
47. Critics believed that black southern Christians had little if any morality at all. The presence, however, of the condemnations of white southern morality lend support to Samuel S. Hill's thesis in *Southern Churches in Crisis*.
48. Anti-Catholic nativism expressed a similar fear. Nativists often accused the Roman Catholic Church of planning to replace American democracy with allegiance to a temporally powerful pope. For examples of such anti-Catholic rhetoric, see Ray Allen Billington, *The Protestant Crusade* (New York: Macmillan, 1938).
49. I am not the first historian to use a mirror analogy when discussing the South. Although he does not make the connection to a funhouse mirror, David Goldfield does call the South "a national mirror" in *Still Fighting the Civil War: The American South and Southern History* (Baton Rouge: Louisiana State University Press, 2002), 7.
50. The use of the South to describe and criticize cultural differences stands in interesting counterpoint to R. Laurence Moore's thesis that American Protestant groups have defined themselves as Americans precisely by labeling themselves as different from the "mainstream." In this case, cultural elites pointed to southerners as examples of what went wrong when Americans strayed from the culturally orthodox view. See Moore, *Religious Outsiders and the Making of Americans* (New York: Oxford University Press, 1986).

Chapter 1

1. "Chicago 'Indicts' the South," *Literary Digest*, 2 October 1915, 698–99.
2. For an overview of the South's history of violence, see Edward L. Ayers, *Vengeance and Justice: Crime and Punishment in the 19th Century American South* (New York: Oxford University Press, 1983).
3. See David W. Blight, *Race and Reunion: The Civil War in American Memory* (Cambridge: Belknap Press of Harvard University Press, 2001); Bertram Wyatt-Brown, *Honor and Violence in the Old South* (New York: Oxford University Press, 1986); and Ayers, *Vengeance and Justice*.
4. W. Fitzhugh Brundage, *Lynching in the New South: Georgia and Virginia, 1880–1930* (Urbana: University of Illinois Press, 1993), 7–8.
5. A survey of the literature on lynching reveals a variety of opinions on its cause. Joel Williamson holds that white southern culture and race relations in general underwent a marked change as the entire country shifted toward an industrial and modern society. See Joel Williamson, *The Crucible of Race: Black-White Relations in the American South since Emancipation* (New York: Oxford University Press, 1984), 511. Sociologists Stewart E. Tolnay and E. M. Beck credit economic distress as the trigger for increased lynchings. See Tolnay and Beck, *A Festival of Violence: An Analysis of Southern Lynching, 1882–1930* (Urbana: University of Illinois Press, 1995). W. Fitzhugh Brundage sees regional variations in the causes of lynchings in the South (*Lynching in the New South*, 13–15).

6. Grace Elizabeth Hale, *Making Whiteness: The Culture of Segregation in the South, 1890–1940* (New York: Random House, 1998), 201.

7. Henry D. Shapiro chronicled the creation of the "idea of Appalachia," arguing that the image of the southern mountaineers as needy and different arose from a notion of Appalachian otherness. See Shapiro, *Appalachia on Our Mind: The Southern Mountains and Mountaineers in the American Consciousness, 1870–1920* (Chapel Hill: University of North Carolina Press, 1978). More recently, C. Brenden Martin has explored the commercialization of southern Appalachia in his essay "To Keep the Spirit of Mountain Culture Alive: Tourism and Historical Memory in the Southern Highlands," in *Where These Memories Grow: History and Southern Identity*, ed. W. Fitzhugh Brundage (Chapel Hill: University of North Carolina Press, 2000), 249–69. For more on Appalachia and the creation of southern distinctiveness, see chapter 2.

8. Grace Hale has pointed out that Smith's death was the first example of a phenomenon she calls "spectacle lynching" (*Making Whiteness*, 199–239).

9. B. O. Flowers, "The Burning of Negroes in the South: A Protest and A Warning," *Arena*, April 1893, 634–35.

10. "Was Tortured and Burned. Death at Stake of a Negro Assailant in Texas. His Victim a Mere Babe," *Washington Post*, 2 February 1893.

11. "Another Negro Burned. Henry Smith Dies at the Stake. Drawn Through the Streets on a Car—Tortured for Nearly an Hour with Hot Irons and Then Burned—Awful Vengeance of a Paris (Texas) Mob," *New York Times*, 2 February, 1893.

12. "Negro Dies at the Stake," *New York Times*, 24 April 1899; see also, "Put to Death by Fire," *Chicago Daily Tribune*, 24 April 1899.

13. "At the Stake: Negro Burned to Death in Newman [sic], Ga.," *Boston Globe*, 24 April 1899.

14. "Keeping the Facts in View," *Atlanta Constitution*, 24 April 1899. Apparently, the *Constitution* did not ascertain or see the need to include the gender of the child in question. Such a detail was irrelevant; only the sensational mattered here.

15. "Lynching and Its Fruits," *Boston Globe*, 25 April 1899. See also "Tortured and Burned: The Terrible Fate of a Negro Criminal in Georgia," *San Francisco Chronicle*, 24 April 1899.

16. *Southern Churchman*, 4 May 1899, 2.

17. Mary Church Terrell, "Lynching from a Negro's Point of View," *North American Review*, June 1904, 854. W. E. B. Du Bois often used the *Crisis* magazine as a means of inciting action against lynching. See, for example, "The Lynching Industry," in *Selections from "The Crisis,"* ed. Herbert Aptheker, Writings in Periodicals Edited by W. E. B. Du Bois (Millwood, N.Y.: Kraus-Thomson Organization, 1983), 1:88–89.

18. "Barbarism and Heroism in the South," *World's Work*, October 1901, 1250.

19. Herbert J. Seligmann, "Protecting Southern Womanhood," *Nation*, 14 June 1919, 939.

20. "Tortured and Burned: The Terrible Fate of a Negro Criminal in Georgia," *San Francisco Chronicle*, 24 April 1899.

21. "Sam Hose is Lynched. Georgia Mob Chain and Burn Negro at a Tree. Remains Cut Up As Souvenirs," *Washington Post*, 24 April 1899; "Negro Dies at the Stake," *New York Times*, 24 April 1899. For further examples of excruciating details, see "Georgia Mob Kills an Innocent Man?" *New York Times*, 25 April 1899; "Morbid Throngs View Body: Thousands File Past Casket After Police Give Way to Mob Threat," *New York Times*, 18 August 1915; "Negro Boy Burned by Mob of Texans,"

Atlanta Constitution, 16 May 1916; untitled editorial, *New Republic*, 2 June 1917, 120; and untitled editorial, *New Republic*, 9 July 1919, 296.

22. "A Lynch Court," *Outlook*, 5 December 1908, 758. The phrase "champion popularizer" of liberal Protestant thought comes from William R. Hutchison, *The Modernist Impulse in American Protestantism* (Durham, N.C.: Duke University Press, 1992), 116.

23. *Nation*, 30 July 1903, 86.

24. "An Appeal to Terror," *Outlook*, 27 August 1904, 972.

25. Quoted in "The Disgrace of Georgia and Alabama," *Current Literature*, October 1904, 294.

26. "State Police a Cure for Lynchings," *World's Work*, April 1918, 585. Events in Europe led the same publication to compare lynching to Bolshevism and to declare that "the essence of Bolshevism is lawlessness and anarchy. . . ." "The Fight in Texas Against Lynching," *World's Work*, April 1919, 615.

27. For additional charges of lawlessness in the South, see "The South Carolina War," *Nation*, 5 April 1894, 246–57; "The Killing of Ex-Senator Carmack," *Outlook*, 21 November 1908, 603–4; "The Judicial 'Recall' in Virginia," *Philadelphia Inquirer*, 16 March 1912; "A Georgian Investigation," *Harper's Weekly*, 2 October 1915, 335; and "Law and Lynching in Georgia," *Outlook*, 1 March 1916, 484.

28. "Ten Are Dead for Crimes on Atlanta Women," *Washington Evening Star*, 23 September 1906.

29. "Mob in Atlanta Wipes Out Blacks," *Chicago Daily Tribune*, 23 September 1906.

30. "Kill Ten in Race War in Atlanta. Forty Other Negroes Dragged from Cars and Seriously Beaten," *Boston Globe*, 24 September 1906.

31. *New York Times*, 24 September 1906.

32. "Bloody Race Riot in City of Atlanta," *San Francisco Chronicle*, 23 September 1906.

33. "A Kentucky Desperado. A Murderer and His Friends Holding a Town," *Philadelphia Inquirer*, 16 May 1885.

34. "A Bloody Battle in Kentucky. One Man Shot Dead and Five Probably Fatally Wounded," *New York Times*, 4 January 1893.

35. Untitled editorial, *Nation*, 8 February 1900, 102.

36. C. T. Revere, "Beyond the Gap: The Breeding Grounds of Feuds," *Outing*, February 1907, 615. *Outing* was published in New York, had a circulation of "a little over a hundred thousand in the five years 1905–1910," and was "a gentleman's outdoor magazine." Frank Luther Mott, *A History of American Magazines*, vol. 4, *1885–1905* (Cambridge: Belknap Press of Harvard University Press, 1957), 633, 638.

37. Leonidas Hubbard Jr., "The Moonshiner at Home," *Atlantic Monthly*, August 1902, 236. For additional examples of reports of violence as commonplace in the South, see "Why He Killed His Man. A Fatal Shooting Affray Explained by the Survivor Stating that His Victim Had Named a Dog After the Slayer's Sister," *Chicago Tribune*, 17 May 1885; "The State Dispensary War," *Harper's Weekly*, 14 April 1894, 346; and untitled editorial, *Nation*, 26 April 1894, 305.

38. "Outlaws Slay Judge in Court," *New York Times*, 15 March 1912. The account added that the village found itself "helpless and stripped of all power either of pursuit or punishment. . . . ."

39. "Court Wiped Out by Outlaw Band. Judge, Prosecutor, and Sheriff Shot at Hillsville, Va. Reward, Dead or Alive, for Slayers, Who Escape to Mountains," *Boston Globe*, 15 March 1912.

40. "Judge Slain on the Bench. State's Attorney and the Sheriff Killed, Too," *Boston Globe*, 14 March 1912.
41. "Five Shot Dead in Courtroom at Hillsville, VA," *Washington Evening Star*, 14 March 1912; "The Recall by Murder," *Washington Evening Star*, 15 March 1912.
42. "The Recall at Hillsville," *New York Times*, 15 March 1912.
43. William Brown Meloney, "The Man from Down Yonder: The Story of the Mountain Wolf-Pack at Hillsville and the Judge Who Braved Them," *Everybody's Magazine*, June 1912, 783.
44. For additional examples highlighting Appalachian violence, see John Gilmer Speed, "The Kentuckian," *Century*, April 1900, 946–52; Hartley Davis and Clifford Smyth, "The Land of Feuds," *Munsey's Magazine*, November 1903, 161–72; and Frederick W. Neve, "Virginia Mountain-Folk," *Outlook*, 11 December 1909, 825–29.
45. Frederick Douglass, "Lynch Law in the South," *North American Review*, July 1892, 23–24.
46. *Nation*, 28 June 1894, 478–79.
47. Atticus G. Haygood, "The Black Shadow in the South," *Forum*, October 1893, 171. Haygood did, however, object to the practice of burning people alive.
48. "Lynching and Illiteracy," *World's Work*, October 1915, 637.
49. "Prevention or Vengeance," *Christian Advocate*, 2 September 1915, 1177.
50. Mary Church Terrell, "Lynching from a Negro's Point of View," *North American Review*, June 1904, 866.
51. H. L. Mencken, *American Mercury*, November 1924, 291–92; "The 'Invisible Empire' in the Spotlight," *Current Opinion*, November 1921, 562.
52. "Leo Frank Lynched by Mob in Georgia. Taken 100 Miles from Prison and Hanged to a Tree. Near Mary Phagan's Home. Former Judge Prevents Crowd from Mutilating Body," *Washington Post*, 18 August 1915.
53. "Rope, Fire, Knife Down in Georgia," *Philadelphia Inquirer*, 25 April 1899; "Sam Hose is Captured and Burned; Lige Strickland Lynched Today: Hose Was Caught Near Marshallville Saturday Night, Carried to Newnan Yesterday and Slowly Roasted to Death, After Being Tortured with Knives—Other Negroes Implicated Are Now Being Chased by Infuriated Men," *Atlanta Journal*, 24 April 1899.
54. Mary Church Terrell, "Lynching from a Negro's Point of View," *North American Review*, June 1904, 859.
55. B. J. Ramage, "Homicide in the Southern States," *Sewanee Review* 4 (1895–96): 214.
56. W. E. B. Du Bois, "Georgia: Invisible Empire State," *Nation*, 21 January 1925, 66. For more evidence that white southern clergy were members of the Ku Klux Klan, see chapter 4. For additional coverage of how outside observers saw the Frank lynching as shameful, see "The Shame of Georgia," *Washington Post*, 18 August 1915; "Frank Lynched—Georgia's Shame," *Philadelphia Inquirer*, 18 August 1915; and "Georgia's Shame," *New York Times*, 18 August 1915. For coverage of lynchings between 1915 and 1917, see *Nation*, 27 January 1916, 91–92; "The Lynching 'Championship,'" *Literary Digest*, 5 February 1916, 274–75; *Nation*, 24 February 1916, 210; *Nation*, 4 May 1916, 470; and "Last Year's Lynchings," *Literary Digest*, 27 January 1917, 178. Almost all of these articles singled out Georgia as being particularly violent.
57. "Lynching," *Nation*, 14 December 1899, 440.

58. *Nation*, 21 August 1902, 141–42.

59. "Heathen or Christian," *Methodist Advocate Journal*, 10 March 1904, 4. See also Winthrop D. Sheldon, "Shall Lynching Be Suppressed, and How?" *Arena*, September 1906, 225–33.

60. Ray Stannard Baker, "What is Lynching? A Study of Mob Justice, North and South," *McClure's Magazine*, January 1905, 306.

61. Walter H. Page, "The Last Hold of the Southern Bully," *Forum*, November 1893, 305, 313.

62. Franklin H. Giddings, "Sociological Questions," *Forum*, October 1903, 251.

63. Ray Stannard Baker, "What is Lynching?" *McClure's Magazine*, January 1905, 301.

64. *Nation*, 1 March 1906, 168–69.

65. J. L. Kesler, letter to the editor of the *Nation*, 28 December 1916, 609.

66. See, for example, "No Christian Condonation of Lynching," *Literary Digest*, 9 September 1922, 35; and T. J. Woofter Jr., "Southern Backfires Against Lynch Law," *Survey*, 15 October 1923, 99–100.

67. "Our Own Barbarians," *San Francisco Chronicle*, 25 April 1899. The editor contrasted the public outcry over Turks killing Armenian Christians with the pulpit's silence about lynching.

68. W. P. Trent, "The Tendencies of Higher Life in the South," *Atlantic Monthly*, June 1897, 769.

69. Robert T. Handy, ed., *The Social Gospel in America, 1870–1920* (New York: Oxford University Press, 1966), 10.

70. Henry Stillwell Edwards, "The Negro and the South," *Century Magazine*, June 1906, 215.

71. John Carlisle Kilgo, D.D., *South Atlantic Quarterly* 1 (January 1902), 13. The *South Atlantic Quarterly* was published in Durham, North Carolina. Kilgo's article was the first to appear in the new publication.

72. "A Remedy for Lynching," letter to the editor, *Nation*, 12 December 1902, 478.

73. "The Race Question," *Methodist Protestant*, 3 May 1899, 1.

74. A Southern Lawyer, "Remedies for Lynch Law," *Sewanee Review* 8 (January 1900): 5–6.

75. "A Collegiate Move on Lynching," *Literary Digest*, 22 January 1916, 178.

76. "A Growing Social Effort in the South," *Survey*, 20 May 1916, 196. For a hagiographic biography of Weatherford, see Wilma Dykeman, *Prophet of Plenty: The First Ninety Years of W. D. Weatherford* (Knoxville: University of Tennessee Press, 1966).

77. For additional, generally sympathetic coverage of positivism in general, see "The Church of Humanity," *Current Literature*, April 1900, 75–76; Frederic Harrison, "Positivism: Its Position, Aims, and Ideals," *North American Review*, March 1901, 456–67; and "Nineteenth-Century Positivism and the Coming Idealistic Reaction," *Arena*, July 1904, 76–80.

78. "Lynching and Its Fruits," *Boston Globe*, 25 April 1899.

79. "The Horror in Georgia," *Washington Post*, 25 April 1899; "The Palmetto Lynchings," *Chicago Tribune*, 25 April 1899.

80. Cardinal Gibbons, "Lynch Law: Its Causes and Remedy," *North American Review*, October 1905, 503. Gibbons maintained a political distance from the bitter sectionalism that usually pervaded commentary about lynching in the South. Instead, he noted that lynchings had taken place in all but five states. Information on Gibbons

from James Hennesey, S.J., *American Catholics: A History of the Roman Catholic Community in the United States* (New York: Oxford University Press, 1981), 240.

81. Quoted in "Lynching a Family," *Literary Digest*, 30 January 1915, 178–79. The same article reported the *New York Evening Post* as holding that "vengeance on supposed enemies of society" could not got further "unless it takes to stringing up negro school children" (178).

82. Untitled editorial, *Nation*, 2 November 1893, 322–23.

83. "Lynching," *Nation*, 14 December 1899, 440; untitled editorial, *Nation*, 1 March 1917, 227. For additional examples, see "Horrible," *Atlanta Constitution*, 2 February 1893; "Law in the Mountains," *Chicago Daily Tribune*, 16 March 1912; untitled editorial, *Nation*, 5 November 1908, 428–29; editorial note, *Christian Observer*, 3 May 1899, 409; "A Reversion to Savagery," *Outlook*, 11 August 1915, 835–36; "Lynchings in General and Particular," *Washington Post*, 5 February 1893; "The Atlanta Mob," *Washington Evening Star*, 24 September 1906; "The Atlanta Massacre," *Independent*, 4 October 1906, 799–800; "A Double Lynching in Virginia," *Independent*, 29 March 1900, 783–84; "Leo Frank Hanged to Tree Near Home of Murdered Girl," *Philadelphia Inquirer*, 18 August 1915; and "The Virginia Tragedy," *San Francisco Chronicle*, 16 March 1912.

84. "Lynching and Illiteracy," *World's Work*, October 1915, 637.

85. "An Outlaw State," *Outlook*, 25 August 1915, 946.

86. "Mob Murder in Atlanta," *Chicago Daily Tribune*, 24 September 1906.

87. "Race Riots in Atlanta and Memphis," *Churchman*, 29 September 1906, 463. The *Churchman* was published in New York City.

88. "Troops Patrol Riot Stricken Atlanta Streets," *Philadelphia Inquirer*, 24 September 1906.

89. "The Virginia Frontier," *Washington Evening Star*, 18 March 1912.

90. "Their Point of View," *Boston Globe*, 16 March 1912.

91. They also indicate that, as David E. Whisnant has perceptively observed, there was a "cultural manipulation" at work in accounts both of Appalachia and of the white South in general. See Whisnant, *All That Is Native and Fine: The Politics of Culture in an American Region* (Chapel Hill: University of North Carolina Press, 1983).

92. Josiah Strong, *Our Country* (1885; Cambridge: Belknap Press of Harvard University Press, 1963), 201. Italics in original.

93. John P. Fort, "Is Lynching Ever Defensible?—The Mind of the Mob," *Forum*, December 1926, 818.

94. *Nation*, 28 September 1893, 222–23.

95. "Lynching," *Nation*, 14 December 1899, 440. Italics in original.

96. "The Shame of the South," *Washington Evening Star*, 24 April 1899.

97. B. O. Flowers, "The Burning of Negroes in the South: A Protest and A Warning," *Arena*, April 1893, 631. According to journalism historian Frank Luther Mott, Flowers had a religiously active background. He studied for one year at the Bible School of Transylvania University, and his father was a Disciples of Christ minister. See Mott, *History of American Magazines*, 4:401–2.

98. "The Will-to-Lynch," *New Republic*, 14 October 1916, 261; "Moving against Lynching," *Nation*, 3 August 1916, 101. In another article, Herbert L. Stewart wrote in the *Nation* that lynching was Georgia's version of the Roman "*panem et circenses* [bread and circuses]." "The Casuistry of Lynch Law," *Nation*, 24 August 1916, 173–74.

99. "A Thirty Years' Record in Lynching," *World's Work*, March 1920, 433–34.
100. L. E. Bleckley, "Negro Outrage No Excuse for Lynching," *Forum*, November 1893, 300.
101. Atticus G. Haygood, "The Black Shadow in the South," *Forum*, October 1893, 171.
102. Quoted in "Barbarism and Heroism in the South," *World's Work*, October 1901, 1250–51.
103. L. P. Chamberlayne, letter to the editor, *Nation*, 13 July 1916, 35.
104. George Elliott Howard, "The Social Cost of Southern Race Prejudice," *American Journal of Sociology* 22 (March 1917): 577–93.
105. Quoted in "What the Baptist Editors Say," *Christian Index*, 4 May 1899, 7.
106. Quoted in "Lynching," *Baptist Argus*, 11 October 1906, 12.
107. "The Atlanta Horror," *Southern Churchman*, 6 October 1906, 3. Although not a southern publication, the *Christian Advocate* worried that should lynching continue, "it will surely corrupt religion to its purpose." "The Great Problem," *Christian Advocate*, 8 November 1906, 1723–24.
108. William Hayne Levell, "On Lynching in the South," *Outlook*, 16 November 1901, 732.
109. *Nation*, 27 November 1902, 413.
110. Andrew Sledd, "The Negro: Another View," *Atlantic Monthly*, July 1902, 69–70. Although he did not state explicitly the role of the lower classes, former judge-advocate general of Virginia Marion L. Dawson hinted at it in "The South and the Negro," *North American Review*, February 1901, 279–84.
111. Hooper Alexander, "Race Riots and Lynch Law: The Cause and the Cure; I—A Southern Lawyer's View," *Outlook*, 2 February 1907, 259.
112. Thomas Gibson, "The Anti-Negro Riots in Atlanta," *Harper's Weekly*, 13 October 1906, 1458.
113. "Mob-Law in Georgia," *Literary Digest*, 28 August 1915, 392.
114. "Georgia's Shame," *Independent*, 30 August 1915, 280.
115. "The Will-to-Lynch," *New Republic*, 14 October 1916, 261.
116. Mary White Ovington, "Is Mob Violence the Texas Solution of the Race Problem?" *Independent*, 6 September 1919, 320.
117. For examples of writers referring to lynching as a "disease" that could spread, see Edward Leigh Pell, "The Prevention of Lynch-Law Epidemics," *American Monthly Review of Reviews*, March 1898, 321–25; and "The Lynching Evil," *New Republic*, 3 May 1919, 7–8.

Chapter 2

1. W. E. B. Du Bois, "The South and a Third Party," *New Republic*, 3 January 1923, 140.
2. For a more detailed discussion of the motives and results of the educational reformers, see William A. Link, who correctly argues in *The Paradox of Southern Progressivism, 1880–1930* (Chapel Hill: University of North Carolina Press, 1992) that "'social efficiency'" reformers, as he refers to them, believed that the "key ingredients of [regional] progress would be regional modernization through the extension of public education and public health" (124).

3. "The Conference for Southern Education," *Nation*, 11 May 1905, 369.
4. James D. Anderson, "Ex-Slaves and the Rise of the Universal Education in the New South, 1860–1880," in *Education and the Rise of the New South*, ed. Ronald K. Goodenow and Arthur O. White (Boston: G. K. Hall, 1981), 20.
5. Edward L. Ayers, *The Promise of the New South: Life after Reconstruction* (New York: Oxford University Press, 1992), 419.
6. For an overview of the progressive movement in American education, see Lawrence A. Cremin, *The Transformation of the School: Progressivism in American Education, 1876–1957* (New York: Alfred A. Knopf, 1969); and Cremin, *American Education: The Metropolitan Experience, 1876–1980* (New York: Harper and Row, 1988).
7. Quoted in Cremin, *Transformation of the School*, 100.
8. Edgar W. Knight, "Education in the Southern Mountains," *School and Society*, 29 July 1922, 126.
9. Lawrence Cremin describes the interest in the social sciences in *Transformation of the School*, viii–ix.
10. "The Real Southern Question Again," *World's Work*, May 1902, 2066, 2067. Italics in original.
11. "Education in Virginia," *Outlook*, 7 May 1904, 7.
12. David Y. Thomas, "The Cotton Tax and Southern Education," *North American Review*, November 1909, 691–92.
13. William H. Hand, *The Need for Compulsory Education in the South*, U.S. Bureau of Education Bulletin no. 2 (1914), 99.
14. Norman Frost, A *Statistical Study of the Public Schools of the Southern Appalachian Mountains*, U.S. Bureau of Education Bulletin no. 11 (1915), 10.
15. Walter A. Dyer, "A Whole-Hearted Half-Time School," *World's Work*, August 1914, 452–53. Here Dyer used the same source as William Hand did. Winthrop Talbot used the same source in his article in the *North American Review* to extol the South's progress in education. See note 109 in this chapter.
16. Littell McClung, "An Educational Revival in Alabama," *Outlook*, 28 February 1917, 351.
17. "Backward North Carolina," *School and Society*, 8 January 1921, 49.
18. Beulah Amidon Ratliff, "These United States—III: Mississippi: Heart of Dixie," *Nation*, 17 May 1922, 589. The next year, the same magazine published a profile of North Carolina in which it quoted former North Carolina governor Charles Brantley Aycock as having said, "'Thank God for South Carolina! She keeps North Carolina from the foot of the column of illiteracy.'" Robert Watson Winston, "These United States—XXIII: North Carolina: A Militant Mediocrity," *Nation*, 21 February 1923, 209.
19. "Industrial Weakness and Poor Schools," *World's Work*, August 1925, 356.
20. Historian Ferenc Morton Szasz has convincingly argued that the nascent fundamentalist movement was in part a reaction to the rise of the educational elite. See Szasz, *The Divided Mind of Protestant America, 1880–1930* (Tuscaloosa: University of Alabama Press), 132.
21. See, for example, Charles H. Levermore, "Impressions of a Yankee Visitor in the South," *New England Magazine*, November 1890, 311–19; "The War in South Carolina," *Harper's Weekly*, 14 April 1894, 339; W. P. Trent, "Dominant Forces in Southern Life," *Atlantic Monthly*, January 1897, 42–53; "Life of a Georgia Cracker," *New York Sun*, quoted in *Current Literature*, January 1900, 30–31; "Backwaters of Human-

ity," *World's Work*, June 1913, 149; and Clement Wood, "Alabama: A Study in Ultra-Violet," *Nation*, January 10, 1923, 33–35.

22. The Reverend A. D. Mayo, A.M., "The Third Estate of the South," *New England Magazine*, November 1890, 306.

23. Andrew Sledd, "Illiteracy in the South," *Independent*, 17 October 1901, 2471–74. Italics in original.

24. Ayers, *Promise of the New South*, 424–25.

25. Cheesman A. Herrick, "Reclaiming a Commonwealth," *Outlook*, 20 June 1903, 455.

26. "The Conference for Southern Education," *Nation*, 11 May 1905, 369.

27. Agnes Valentine Kelley, M.D., "Popular Education in Rural District the Supreme Educational Need of the South," *Arena*, September 1905, 282. According to Frank Luther Mott, historian of American publishing, the *Arena's* editor, B. O. Flower, the son of a Disciples of Christ minister, used the magazine to promote social reform. See Mott, *A History of American Magazines*, vol. 4, *1885–1905* (Cambridge: Belknap Press of Harvard University Press, 1957), 401–3.

28. Frank T. Carlton, "The South During the Last Decade," *Sewanee Review* 12 (April 1904): 179–80. Information on the publication of the *Sewanee Review* from Mott, *History of American Magazines*, 4:733–40.

29. "Education in the South and the Aristocracy," *Independent*, 3 August 1905, 276. American journalism historian Frank Luther Mott notes that the *Independent*, like the *Outlook*, was once a denominational publication, and, in Mott's words, the two publications "did not forget their Congregational upbringing" (*History of American Magazines*, 4:292).

30. For examples of writers who believed disease and unsanitary conditions hampered education in the South, see William H. Glasson, "Working for the Common Good: Rural and City Improvements in the South," *South Atlantic Quarterly* 8 (July 1909), 201–6; Constance D. Leupp, "Removing the Blinding Curse of the Mountains," *World's Work*, August 1914, 426–30; "The Campaign Against Pellagra," *World's Work*, April 1916, 597–98; and Thomas J. LeBlanc, "Malaria," *American Mercury*, November 1924, 366–71. For examples of educational deficits being blamed on poverty, see "The Problems of the Author in the South," *South Atlantic Review* 1 (July 1902), 201–8; and Martha Hensley Bruere and Robert W. Bruere, "The Church of the Lean Land," *Outlook*, 28 April 1915, 987–95. For citations of rural conditions as a barrier to education, see "The Bottom of the Matter," *South Atlantic Quarterly* 1 (April 1902), 99–106; and Frank T. Carlton, "The South During the Last Decade," *Sewanee Review* 12 (April 1904), 174–81. For examples of writers who believed that economic conditions helped suppress educational advancement, see Mary Applewhite Bacon, "The Problem of the Southern Cotton Mill," *Atlantic Monthly*, February 1907, 224–31; and "Renters and 'Croppers' in the South," *World's Work*, May 1923, 21–23. For a more creative theory about the deficiencies of southern schooling, see Roland M. Harper's article on how geology and soil may have shaped white southern society. Harper, Geological Survey of Alabama, "Some Relations Between Soil, Climate, and Civilization in the Southern Red Hills of Alabama," *South Atlantic Quarterly* 19, July 1920, 201–15.

31. Examples of scholars who agree with my contention that Appalachian "distinctiveness" was not real but created include Henry D. Shapiro, *Appalachia on Our Mind: The Southern Mountains and Mountaineers in the American Consciousness, 1870–1920*

(Chapel Hill: University of North Carolina Press, 1978); and Allen W. Batteau, *The Invention of Appalachia* (Tucson: University of Arizona Press, 1990). There are a few historians who do believe that Appalachia is somehow different from the rest of the South and the rest of the country, but they admit that the stereotypes attached to Appalachia have been largely manufactured. See, for example, Altina L. Waller, who holds that feuding in Appalachia "gripped the popular imagination and fastened upon the people of Southern Appalachia a cultural stereotype of violent irrationality that is still potent today." Waller, "Feuding in Appalachia: Evolution of a Cultural Stereotype," in *Appalachia in the Making: The Mountain South in the Nineteenth Century*, ed. Mary Beth Pudup, Dwight B. Billings, and Altina L. Waller (Chapel Hill: University of North Carolina Press, 1995), 347–48. For an example of a recent work that contends that Appalachia "represents a significant and distinct region within the larger American society," see Richard B. Drake, *A History of Appalachia* (Lexington: University Press of Kentucky, 2001), ix. And for a history of how non-Appalachian reformers used Appalachia as their laboratory, see David E. Whisnant, *All That Is Native and Fine: The Politics of Culture in an American Region* (Chapel Hill: University of North Carolina Press, 1983).

32. "In the Tennessee Mountains," *Good Work*, September 1907, 77. The *Good Work* was published by the American Baptist Publication Society in Philadelphia.

33. John L. Mathews, "The Sunday Lady of 'Possum Trot,'" *Everybody's Magazine*, December 1908, 723.

34. Martha Berry, "The Evolution of a Sunday School," *Charities and the Commons*, 3 November 1906, 195.

35. Norman Frost, *A Statistical Study of the Public Schools of the Southern Appalachian Mountains*, U.S. Bureau of Education Bulletin no. 11 (1915), 10.

36. Elizabeth Wysor Klingberg, "Glimpses of Life in the Appalachian Highlands," *South Atlantic Quarterly* 14 October 1915, 375.

37. "A People Who 'Hanker Fer Larnin,'" *Literary Digest*, 10 February 1923, 35. Note that the title includes a phrase in Appalachian dialect, further proof of the ignorance of the Appalachian mountaineers—they could not even speak proper English.

38. Information on the *Literary Digest's* circulation from Mott, *History of American Magazines*, 4:569–75. According to Mott, the *Digest* was published in New York City and was founded by Isaac Kauffman Funk, "a Lutheran clergyman, a publisher of books and periodicals, and a leader in the Prohibition party" (4:569). For further examples of articles disparaging the region, see J. Cleveland Cady, "In the Mountains," *Outlook*, 5 October 1901, 320–25; John Gilmer Speed, "The Kentuckian," *Century*, April 1900, 946–52; Hartley Davis and Clifford Smith, "The Land of Feuds," *Munsey's Magazine*, November 1903, 161–72; and Frederick W. Neve, "Virginia Mountain-Folk," *Outlook*, 11 December 1909, 825–29.

39. George E. Vincent, "A Retarded Frontier," *American Journal of Sociology* 4 (July 1898): 1–20.

40. S. S. MacClintock, "The Kentucky Mountains and Their Feuds. I. The People and Their Country," *American Journal of Sociology* 7 (July 1901): 1–28; MacClintock, "The Kentucky Mountains and Their Feuds. II. The Causes of Feuds," *American Journal of Sociology* 7 (September 1901): 171–87.

41. Anthropologist Allen Batteau credits the work of these sociologists with "firmly establish[ing] on the American cultural landscape an image of and an identity for Appalachia" (*Invention of Appalachia*, 81).

42. Fred H. Matthews, *Quest for an American Sociology: Robert E. Parks and the Chicago School* (Montreal: McGill-Queen's University Press, 1977), 93.

43. Ibid.

44. The Right Reverend Junius M. Horner, "Educational Work in the Mountains of North Carolina," *Outlook*, 12 March 1910, 589.

45. "Civilizing the Mountaineers," *New York Times*, 21 March 1912.

46. William Goodell Frost, "Our Contemporary Ancestors in the Southern Mountains," *Atlantic Monthly*, March 1899, 311.

47. Frost served as Berea's president during its transition from an interracial school to a school that enrolled primarily white Appalachian residents. For biographical material on Frost, see his obituary in the *New York Times*, "Dr. William Frost, Educator, is Dead," 13 September 1938. For more on the transition he presided over, see Richard Sears, *A Utopian Experiment in Kentucky: Integration and Social Equality at Berea, 1866–1904* (Westport, Conn.: Greenwood, 1996).

48. "Lighting Up the Southern Mountains," *Literary Digest*, 4 March 1922, 32.

49. Allen W. Batteau has an extensive analysis of scientific racism and its role in the "invention" of Appalachia. He sees the debate over racial traits as linking "the white populations of the South to the discussions of racial classification that were current in their time" (*Invention of Appalachia*, 61).

50. Edward Alsworth Ross, "Pocketed Americans," part 1, *New Republic*, 9 January 1924, 170–71.

51. Lillian Walker Williams, "In the Kentucky Mountains: Colonial Customs That Are Still Existing in That Famous Section of the Country," *New England Magazine*, March 1904, 40.

52. Thomas R. Dawley, "Our Southern Mountaineers," *World's Work*, March 1910, 12704–14.

53. Quoted in John H. Ashworth, "The Virginia Mountaineers," *South Atlantic Quarterly* 12 (July 1913), 193.

54. Ibid.

55. Walter A. Dyer, "Training New Leaders for the Industrial South," *World's Work*, July 1914, 287.

56. Frank Waldo, "Among the Southern Appalachians," *New England Magazine*, May 1901, 239.

57. The Right Reverend Junius M. Horner, "Educational Work in the Mountains of North Carolina," *Outlook*, 12 March 1910, 589–90.

58. *Ladies' Home Journal* article quoted in "A Memorial to Mrs. Wilson," *Literary Digest*, 3 July 1915, 22. For additional evidence of the trend to exalt "Anglo-Saxon stock," see John Gilmer Speed, "The Kentuckian," *Century*, 946; Thomas Nelson Page, "The Southern People During Reconstruction," *Atlantic Monthly*, September 1901, 289–304; "The Spectator," *Outlook*, 14 December 1901, 969; Hartley Davis and Clifford Smyth, "The Land of Feuds," *Munsey's Magazine*, November 1903, 172; and Arthur W. Page, "The Cotton Mills and the People," *World's Work*, June 1907, 8996–97.

59. Batteau, *Invention of Appalachia*, 62.

60. John L. Mathews, "The Sunday Lady of 'Possum Trot,'" *Everybody's Magazine*, December 1908, 723.

61. I am not the first scholar to notice this trend. See James C. Klotter, "The Black South and White Appalachia," *Journal of American History* 66 (March 1980): 832–49, for a more in-depth analysis.

62. Hartley Davis and Clifford Smyth, "The Land of Feuds," *Munsey's Magazine*, November 1903, 172.

63. Edward Alsworth Ross, "Pocketed Americans," part 1, *New Republic*, 9 January 1924, 171.

64. Thomas R. Dawley Jr., "Our Southern Mountaineers," *World's Work*, March 1910, 12704. Reports of poor breeding were not confined to Appalachia. In 1902, S. A. Hamilton of Roaring Spring, Pennsylvania, wrote in the *Arena* that Georgia "crackers" "degenerated from the beginning into a besotted, ignorant, and vicious class," that was "multiplying with the usual fecundity of the poverty-stricken. . . ." Hamilton, "The New Race Question in the South," *Arena*, April 1902, 352.

65. Batteau, *Invention of Appalachia*, 72.

66. John Fox, *The Little Shepherd of Kingdom Come* (New York: C. Scribner's Sons, 1903).

67. Warren I. Titus, *John Fox, Jr.* (New York: Twayne, 1971), 70.

68. Ibid., 70, 141.

69. For a slightly different interpretation of *The Little Shepherd of Kingdom Come*, see Nina Silber, *The Romance of Reunion: Northerners and the South, 1865–1900* (Chapel Hill: University of North Carolina Press, 1993), 143–56.

70. "The Conference for Southern Education," *Nation*, 11 May 1905, 368.

71. S. C. Mitchell, "The Task of the College in the South," *South Atlantic Quarterly* 6 (July 1907): 260–61.

72. Fronde Kennedy, "Fighting Adult Illiteracy in North Carolina," *South Atlantic Quarterly* 19 (July 1920): 189.

73. John H. Ashworth, "The Virginia Mountaineers," *South Atlantic Quarterly* 12 (July 1913), 193.

74. Edgar W. Knight, "Public Education in the South. Some Inherited Ills and Some Needed Reforms," *School and Society*, 10 January 1920, 34–35.

75. Edgar W. Knight, "Education in the Southern Mountains," *School and Society*, 29 July 1922, 127.

76. The Reverend A. D. Mayo, A.M., "The Third Estate of the South," *New England Magazine*, November 1890, 310.

77. Lyman Abbott, "The South and Education: A Record of Progress," *Outlook*, 27 July 1907, 637.

78. "Evangelist Jones for Governor," *New York Times*, 20 February 1898.

79. Frederick Morgan Davenport, "The Religious Revival and the New Evangelicalism," *Outlook*, 8 April 1905, 897.

80. "The Causes of Feuds and Moonshining," *Literary Digest*, 22 April 1922, 35.

81. Tyler Dennett, "The Interchurch World Movement," *World's Work*, April 1920, 574.

82. William Goodell Frost, "In the Land of the Saddle-Bags: The Protestant People of Appalachia," *Missionary Review of the World*, January 1901, 23. According to Frank Luther Mott, the *Missionary Review of the World* was an "interdenominational" magazine, "despite its Presbyterian leanings" (*History of American Magazines*, 4:305).

83. William Goodell Frost, "The Southern Mountaineer: Our Kindred of the Boone and Lincoln Type," *Review of Reviews*, March 1900, 306.

84. Paul Neff Garber, *John Carlisle Kilgo, President of Trinity College, 1894–1910* (Durham, N.C.: Duke University Press, 1937), 35. Garber quotes Kilgo as writing, "'Universal history bears testimony to the primacy of religious faith among the forces of civilization. . . . The revival of religious faith has always been a revival of all the

other forces of civilization. Learning has its taproot in the moral sentiments and forces, not in the political and industrial sentiments'" (*John Carlisle Kilgo*, 35).

85. John Carlisle Kilgo, "Some Phases of Southern Education," *South Atlantic Quarterly* 2 (April 1903): 137–51.
86. The Reverend B. M. Beckham, "Social Service and the Country Church," in *Education in the South: Abstracts of Papers Read at the Sixteenth Conference for Education in the South, Held at Richmond, Virginia, April 15 to 18, 1913*, U.S. Bureau of Education Bulletin no. 30 (1913), 32–33.
87. Ennion Williams, M.D., "The Rural Church and Public Health," in *Education in the South*, U.S. Bureau of Education Bulletin no. 30 (1913), 33. Several magazines ran articles about the diseases often prevalent in the South. See, for example, John A. Ferrell, "The North Carolina Campaign Against Hookworm Disease," *South Atlantic Quarterly* 11 (April 1912), 128–35; Constance D. Leupp, "Removing the Blinding Curse of the Mountains," *World's Work*, August 1914, 426–30; Burton J. Hendrick, "The Mastery of Pellagra," *World's Work*, April 1916, 633–39; and "The Hookworm Story of One County," *World's Work*, August 1922, 354–55.
88. "The Southern Methodists," *Outlook*, 2 June 1906, 258.
89. Theodore T. Munger, "The Church: Some Immediate Questions," *Atlantic Monthly*, December 1903, 721. Frank S. Mead and Samuel S. Hill document the history of this obscure denomination in *Handbook of Denominations in the United States*, 8th ed. (Nashville: Abingdon, 1985), 57–58.
90. Walter Hines Page, "The Rebuilding of the Old Commonwealth," *Atlantic Monthly*, May 1902, 651.
91. William E. Barton, D.D., "The Church Militant in the Feud Belt," *Outlook*, 10 October 1903, 351. The five points of Calvinism include total depravity (everyone is completely unworthy of salvation), unconditional election (God saves people not by any merit of their own but through infinite mercy), limited atonement (Christ died only for the elect), irresistible grace (if you are elect, you cannot refuse grace), and perseverance of the saints (once saved, always saved). Clifton Johnston also mentioned the Hardshell Baptists, or as he said they preferred to be called, "'the Old Primitive Baptist Church,'" in "Among the Georgia Crackers," *Outing*, February 1904, 522.
92. C. T. Revere, "Beyond the Gap: The Breeding Ground of Feuds," *Outing*, February 1907, 620. According to Revere, the three groups got into a dispute over who would first use their newly constructed joint church, and a gun battle erupted on Easter morning, with "three 'Feet Washers' and two 'Muddy Heads' killed and about a dozen wounded altogether" ("Beyond the Gap," 621).
93. A. T. Hanes, "That Article on Arkansas," *Nation*, 13 June 1923, 696.
94. S. S. MacClintock, "The Kentucky Mountains and Their Feuds. I. The People and Their Country," *American Journal of Sociology* 7 (July 1901): 20.
95. William Goodell Frost, "Our Contemporary Ancestors in the Southern Mountains," *Atlantic Monthly*, March 1899, 316–17. See also Frost, "In the Land of the Saddle-Bags: The Protestant People of Appalachian America," *Missionary Review of the World*, January 1901, 21–31.
96. William Preston Few, "Southern Public Opinion," *South Atlantic Quarterly* 4 (January 1905): 6–7.
97. Clarence Hamilton Poe, "The Rebound of the Upland South," *World's Work*, June 1907, 8978. Greenough White of the University of the South also called his readers'

attention to the prevalence of "Puritanism" in the South. See White, "The South, Past and Present," *School Review* 7 (March 1899), 149.

98. Edwin A. Alderman, "The Growing South: A Comprehensive Statement of the Status and Forces of this Emerging Era," *World's Work*, June 1908, 10380–81. Alderman went on to declare that "it seems to me a godsend that a good section of [the South] is not yet quite 'up to date'" (10381).

99. For more on the perceived Puritan influences on fundamentalism and religion in the South, see chapter 4.

100. Historian Karen Coffing chronicles the pains Harris's husband, Lundy Harris, caused her in her article "Corra Harris and the *Saturday Evening Post*: Southern Domesticity Conveyed to a National Audience, 1900–1930," *Georgia Historical Quarterly* 69, no. 2 (Summer 1995): 367–93. According to Coffing, Lundy suffered from debilitating mental illness and committed suicide after a long disappearance from his wife and daughter.

101. Corra Harris, *A Circuit Rider's Wife* (Philadelphia: Henry Altemus, 1910), 334. I am grateful to Don Mathews for drawing my attention to this novel.

102. Harris, *A Circuit Rider's Wife*, 335–36.

103. Thomas Dixon Jr., *The Leopard's Spots: A Romance of the White Man's Burden, 1865–1900* (New York: A. Wessels, 1908), 337.

104. "The Peabody Fund," *Nation*, 2 February 1905, 85.

105. Mott, *History of American Magazines*, 4:268. Mott adds that the journal paid particular attention to "what it called the 'philosophy of education.'"

106. Caroline Matthews, "The South," *Educational Review* 34 (December 1907), 459.

107. Leonora Beck Ellis, "Georgia's Educational Center," *Review of Reviews*, May 1902, 571–74.

108. "Meetings of Progress," *The World's Work*, June 1909, 11642.

109. Winthrop Talbot, "Illiteracy and Democracy," *North American Review*, December 1915, 875. Talbot here employed the same statistics that Walter Dyer used in the *World's Work* in 1914 to smear the South. See note 15 in this chapter.

110. For examples of Abbott's articles, see "For the Schools of the South," *Outlook*, 24 October 1908, 363–64; and "The Conference for Education in the South," *Outlook*, 1 May 1909, 8–9. Ira V. Brown discusses the criticism Abbott received in his biography, *Lyman Abbott, Christian Evolutionist: A Study in Religious Liberalism* (Westport, Conn.: Greenwood, 1970), 204–5.

111. Margaret Hancock, "The Unique Governor of Arkansas," *New Republic*, 16 November 1921, 351.

112. William H. Hand, *Need of Compulsory Education in the South*, U.S. Bureau of Education Bulletin no. 2 (1914), 104.

113. Carl Holliday, "One Phase of Literary Conditions in the South," *Sewanee Review* 11 (October 1903): 466.

114. George Edward Woodberry, "The South in American Letters," *Harper's Monthly Magazine*, October 1903, 735–41.

115. "Freedom of Opinion in the South," *Nation*, 4 January 1906, 6.

Chapter 3

1. Henry W. Grady, "The New South," *New England Magazine*, March 1891, 86. The preacher's comment about being "fearfully and wonderfully made" is an allusion to Psalm 139:14.
2. "In Kentucky's Mountains," *New York Times*, 12 December 1898.
3. In covering the South, these critics rarely counted black southerners as southerners; instead they referred to them as "Negroes," and ignored the fact that white and black southerners constantly interacted with and influenced each other. Instead, the writers and editors concerned themselves largely with whites and ignored blacks, much as white southerners would have liked to do.
4. The Reverend I. T. Tichenor, "The South and Its Future," *Christian Index*, 21 May 1885, 11
5. Clarence Hamilton Poe, "The South: Backward and Sectional or Progressive and National?" *Outlook*, 11 October 1916, 330.
6. Mrs. L. H. Harris [Corra Harris], "The Southern White Woman," *Independent*, 15 February 1900, 431; Mrs. L. H. Harris, "The Confederate Veteran," *Independent*, 3 October 1901, 2357; and Mrs. L. H. Harris, "The Cheerful Life in the South," *Independent*, 20 July 1905, 137. Information on the *Independent* from Frank Luther Mott, *A History of American Magazines* vol. 4, *1885–1905* (Cambridge: Belknap Press of Harvard University Press, 1957), 292. For more on Corra Harris's take on white southern religion, see chapter 2.
7. For additional examples of southerners affirming the "religious" nature of their region, see "A Southern Visitor," "Northern Men and Women," *Independent*, 12 March 1903, 600–603; Mrs. L. H. Harris [Corra Harris], "The Willipus-Wallipus in Tennessee Politics," *Independent*, 25 March 1909, 622–26; and Roy L. Garis, professor of economics at Vanderbilt University, "Misconceptions About the South," *North American Review*, December 1925–February 1926, 246.
8. J. Cleveland Cady, "In the Mountains," *Outlook*, 5 October 1901, 324.
9. Ernest Hamlin Abbott, "Religious Life in America: V.—New Tendencies in the Old South," *Outlook*, 11 January 1902, 131.
10. Walter A. Dyer, "Training New Leaders for the Industrial South," *World's Work*, July 1914, 287.
11. John Temple Graves, "The Fight Against Alcohol: Third Article—Georgia Pioneers the Prohibition Crusade," *Cosmopolitan*, June 1908, 86–87.
12. Edward Alsworth Ross, "Pocketed Americans," part 2, *New Republic*, 23 January 1924, 224.
13. "Epidemic of Church Building in the South," *Literary Digest*, 24 June 1922, 30–31.
14. Nicholas Worth [Walter Hines Page], "The Autobiography of a Southerner Since the Civil War," *Atlantic Monthly*, July 1906, 171.
15. Greenough White, "The South, Past and Present," *School Review* 7 (March 1899): 149.
16. Holland Thompson, "Life in a Southern Mill Town," *Political Science Quarterly* 15 (March 1900): 7–8.
17. "The Causes of Feuds and Moonshining," *Literary Digest*, 22 April 1922, 35.
18. Gerald W. Johnson, "The South Takes the Offensive," *American Mercury*, May 1924, 72.

19. George F. Milton, "Can We Save the Democratic Party? As One Democratic Editor Sees It," *Century Magazine*, May 1925, 95.

20. "The Spectator," editorial column, *Outlook*, 14 December 1901, 969.

21. Quoted in "Lighting Up the Southern Mountains," *Literary Digest*, 4 March 1922, 32.

22. Quoted in "A People Who 'Hanker Fer Larnin,'" *Literary Digest*, 10 February 1923, 35.

23. W. P. Trent, "The Tendencies of Higher Life in the South," *Atlantic Monthly*, June 1897, 769. Later in the same article, Trent acknowledged that the white southern clergy were becoming more tolerant but asserted that they had to "contend against . . . easy-going indifference" among church members (777).

24. Edward Alsworth Ross, "Pocketed Americans," part 1, *New Republic*, 9 January 1924, 172.

25. A Southerner, "The Sociology of the South: The Influence of Old Habits and Prejudices," *New York Times*, 10 May 1885.

26. William Garrot Brown, "The South and the Saloon," *Century Magazine*, July 1908, 464–65.

27. Flannery O'Connor, "The Grotesque in Southern Fiction," in *Mystery and Manners: Occasional Prose*, ed. Sally Fitzgerald and Robert Fitzgerald (New York: Farrar, Straus, and Giroux, 1969), 44.

28. Rollin Lynde Hartt, "In Fairness to the South," *Outlook*, 3 January 1923, 22. Hartt would have been concerned by Sam Jones's pronouncement in 1892 that Grover Cleveland would win the presidential election. The *New York Times* ran the election prediction story under the headline "Sam Jones Writes Politics," 3 April 1892.

29. "The Southern Baptists Question of Divorce Under Discussion—Wavering in Opinion," *Philadelphia Inquirer*, 11 May 1885.

30. T. W. Bacot, "Divorce Not Allowed in South Carolina," *Churchman*, 23 May 1903, 13. Italics in original.

31. William L. O'Neill, *Divorce in the Progressive Era* (New Haven: Yale University Press, 1967), 36. According to O'Neill, many other states were experimenting with legislation "which had the effect of making divorces harder to get than they had been at any time since the Civil War," but only South Carolina had completely banned it. Other states found it difficult to close the door on divorce, as the public had come to expect some sort of legal end to failed marriages (*Divorce in the Progressive Era*, 26–27).

32. "Sunday Bathing to be Permitted. Park Board Holds that Cleanliness is Next to Godliness," *Atlanta Constitution*, 2 August 1911. The next year, the *Sunday School Times*, prompted by a question from a reader in Texas, devoted its attention to whether "'dancing [was] sinful?'" "What of Dancing?" *Sunday School Times*, 21 December 1912, 810.

33. "Bichloride of Mercury," *Time*, 31 December 1923, 22. Italics in original.

34. "Our Sunday and Anti-Sunday Laws," *Literary Digest*, 12 September 1925, 33.

35. Thomas Nelson Page, "An Old Virginia Sunday," *Scribner's Magazine*, December 1901, 728. According to journalism historian Frank Luther Mott, *Scribner's* was near its peak circulation during the period when Page wrote his acclamation of the South. Mott reports that the magazine had a circulation of 165,000 at "the end of the century," a number that rose steadily over the next decade (*History of American Magazines*, 4:723).

36. John Carlisle Kilgo, "The Silent South," *South Atlantic Quarterly* 6 (April 1907): 206.

37. Ernest Hamlin Abbott, "Religious Life in America: V.—New Tendencies in the Old South," *Outlook*, 11 January 1902, 131.

38. Quoted in "The Causes of Feuds and Moonshining," *Literary Digest*, 22 April 1922, 35.
39. The Reverend John E. White, D.D., "The True and False in Southern Life," *South Atlantic Quarterly* 5 (April 1906), 111–12.
40. William E. Dodd, "Freedom of Speech in the South," letter to the editor, *Nation*, 25 April 1907, 383.
41. John Kilgo, D.D., "Some Phases of Southern Education," *South Atlantic Quarterly* 2 (April 1903): 148–49.
42. Edward L. Ayers, *The Promise of the New South: Life after Reconstruction* (New York: Oxford University Press, 1992), 173.
43. For a more complete biography of Jones, see Kathleen Minnix, *Laughter in the Amen Corner: The Life of Evangelist Sam Jones* (Athens: University of Georgia Press, 1993).
44. For an overview of Dwight L. Moody's life and his popularity, see James F. Findlay Jr., *Dwight L. Moody: An American Evangelist, 1837–1899* (Chicago: University of Chicago Press, 1969).
45. *Atlanta Constitution*, 11 May 1885. The *Constitution* kindly provided its readers with the complete text of the pamphlet the next day. *Atlanta Constitution*, 12 May 1885.
46. "A Southern Revivalist. Some of Sam Jones's Sayings in His Public Addresses," *New York Times*, 10 May 1885.
47. "Sam Jones's Prophecy," *New York Times*, 9 January 1890.
48. Quoted in the *Atlanta Constitution*, 15 May 1885.
49. "Sam Jones the Revivalist," *New York Times*, 31 May 1885.
50. "Sam Jones's Success: Number and Character of the Southern Revivalist's Converts," *New York Times*, 17 July 1885.
51. "Unregenerate St. Louis: Evangelist Sam Jones Fails to Redeem the Wicked City," *New York Times*, 24 December 1885.
52. "Sam Jones Talks to Empty Benches," *New York Times*, 4 July 1887.
53. For information on the *Critic*, see Frank Luther Mott, *A History of American Magazines*, vol. 3, *1865–1885* (Cambridge: Harvard University Press, 1938), 548–51. According to Mott, the journal's circulation was low, "in the neighborhood of 5,000 during most of its life" (*History of American Magazines*, 3:551).
54. Calvin Dill Wilson, "The Phenomenon of Sam Jones," *Critic*, April 1902, 356–57. While Wilson did not include specific slurs in his analysis of Jones, historian William G. McLoughlin Jr. noted that Jones would often point to a particular audience member and cry, "'You, old feller!' and every eye would turn to see who had been singled out as the erring sinner." See McLoughlin, *Modern Revivalism: Charles Grandison Finney to Billy Graham* (New York: Ronald, 1959), 288.
55. "Sam Did Not Advise Murder," *New York Times*, 3 March 1886.
56. "Sam Jones Assaulted," *New York Times*, 4 February 1891.
57. "Clergymen Out For Blood," *New York Times*, 24 March 1893.
58. "Struck the Rev. Sam Jones," *New York Times*, 15 September 1903.
59. McLoughlin, *Modern Revivalism*, 303.
60. Like so many other public figures, Jones needed help with his relatives as well. His daughter eloped with someone Jones objected to, and his nephew was arrested for the murder of a mill manager near Atlanta in 1894. See "Sam Jones's Daughter," *New York Times*, 10 March 1888; and "A Mill Manager Murdered," *New York Times*, 20 September 1894.
61. "Sam P. Jones Dies Suddenly on a Train," *New York Times*, 16 October 1906.
62. "Rev. 'Sam' Jones Drops Dead," *Boston Globe*, 15 October 1906.

63. "Sam Jones Is Dead," *Washington Evening Star*, 15 October 1906.
64. "The Passing of Rev. Sam Jones," *Atlanta Constitution*, 16 October 1906. It should be noted that the *Constitution's* hometown rival, the *Journal*, was always effusive in its praise for Jones, and its coverage of his death was no exception. See "Rev. Sam P. Jones, World Famous Evangelist, Dies on Sleeping Car Near Little Rock, Ark.," *Atlanta Journal*, 15 October 1906.
65. *World's Work*, December 1906, 8262–63. Here Page refers to "Captain Tom Ryman," a "notorious riverboat man," who, after hearing Jones, built Union Gospel Tabernacle, which later became known as Ryman Auditorium and was the first home of the Grand Ole Opry. See Charles K. Wolfe, *A Good-Natured Riot: The Birth of the Grand Ole Opry* (Nashville: Country Music Foundation Press and Vanderbilt University Press, 1999), 28.
66. *Methodist Protestant*, 24 October 1906, 6. Interestingly, the New York–based *Christian Advocate*, another northern Methodist publication, buried the news of Jones's death on the 38th page of the October 25, 1906, issue. The note read in its entirety: "The Rev. Sam P. Jones dies of heart failure on Rock Island train, near Little Rock, Ark.; born 1847." *Christian Advocate*, 25 October 1906, 1678. This author could find no subsequent article. Likewise, the *Methodist Advocate Journal* paid only a brief paragraph's attention to his passing. *Methodist Advocate Journal*, 25 October 1906, 6.
67. John Temple Graves, "The Fight Against Alcohol: Third Article—Georgia Pioneers the Prohibition Crusade," *Cosmopolitan*, June 1908, 83. According to Frank Luther Mott, *Cosmopolitan's* circulation was over 300,000 at the turn of the century (*History of American Magazines*, 4:484–85).
68. There are, however, many theories about the causes of prohibition sentiment. In Richard Hofstadter's view, prohibition was not really a reform movement but an exercise in hypocrisy. "Prohibition," Hofstadter wrote, "was a pseudo-reform, a pinched, parochial substitute for reform which had a widespread appeal to a certain type of crusading mind." Hofstadter, *The Age of Reform* (New York: Vintage 1955), 287. Providing an important corrective to Hofstadter's one-dimensional analysis, Norman H. Clark distinguishes among three phases—"temperance, Prohibition, and repeal"—and argues that the reform effort really belonged to a larger movement that emphasized the "developing consciousness of individual, rather than community, dignity." Clark, *Deliver Us from Evil: An Interpretation of American Prohibition* (New York: W. W. Norton, 1976), 5, 12. Sociologist Jack S. Blocker Jr., on the other hand, saw the prohibition movement as a part of the social upheaval that accompanied the rise of industrialization, an effort by those in power to look as if they were in charge by enacting "reform which changes nothing, but satisfies the middle way's need for the appearance of change while retaining power in the same hands." Blocker, *Retreat from Reform: The Prohibition Movement in the United States 1890–1913* (Westport, Conn.: Greenwood, 1976), 4. Blocker holds that there was not a "popular majority" for prohibition after 1913 (*Retreat from Reform*, 239). More recently, Austin Kerr studied the Anti-Saloon League as a "distinct part of the organizational revolution that swept through American society during its lifetime." Unlike past historians, Kerr gives attention to the South's own battle for temperance, arguing that the statewide prohibition victories were "not so much due to league organization as to the zeal of the churches abetted by league propaganda." Kerr, *Organized for Prohibition: A New History of the Anti-Saloon League* (New Haven: Yale University Press, 1985), 7, 125. Finally, Thomas Pegram advances the notion that prohibition was the result of both

"real rather than imagined problems" and a cultural struggle between the established mores concerning alcohol and those of a new generation of immigrants. Pegram's analysis moves away from the simple view that prohibition represented a rural-urban split, with rural areas supporting prohibition and urban areas opposing it. Pegram also correctly observes that the temperance movement in the South was both an effort to exert white control over blacks and an effort to improve the South in general in order to make it more hospitable to business development. Pegram, *Battling Demon Rum: The Struggle for a Dry America* (Chicago: Ivan R. Dee, 1998), xii–xiii, 127.

69. *Temperance* and *prohibition* have two distinct meanings. *Temperance* is the appeal to the individual to restrict consumption of or even refrain from consuming alcoholic beverages, while *prohibition* refers to a general or partial ban on the sale and consumption of alcohol. The South experimented with both.

70. Appleton Morgan, "Recent Legislation Against the Drink Evil," *Popular Science Monthly*, August 1899, 438–50.

71. "The Dispensary in North Carolina," *Outlook*, 22 September 1900, 193–94. A dispensary is a state-run institution that "dispenses" alcohol to customers.

72. "Tennessee Almost Saloon-Free," *Outlook*, 2 May 1903, 11.

73. Frank Foxcroft, "The Drift Away from Prohibition," *Atlantic Monthly*, March 1905, 302–8.

74. Edward Lissner, "Dry Days in the South," *Harper's Weekly*, July 1907, 1057.

75. For additional coverage in newspapers and magazines of prohibition advances in the South, see, "The Anti-Saloon Victories," *New York Times*, 20 November 1907; "Women Rout Rum in Alabama War," *Chicago Tribune*, 20 November 1907; "Senate Votes Alabama Dry," *San Francisco Chronicle*, 20 November 1907; "War on the Liquor Traffic: Progress of the Prohibition Movement in the Southern States," *San Francisco Chronicle*, 21 November 1907; "Georgia's Example to the Nation," *Independent*, 6 January 1908, 162–63; A. J. McKelway, "Local Option and State Prohibition in the South," *Charities and the Commons*, 25 January 1908, 1452–53; Booker T. Washington, "Prohibition and the Negro," *Outlook*, 14 March 1908, 587–89; "State Prohibition in North Carolina," *Outlook*, 6 June 1908, 271–72; Samuel Dickie, "Is Prohibition the Remedy for the Liquor Evil? When and Where Prohibition Has Succeeded," *Ladies' Home Journal*, 1 February 1911, 21, 62–63; "Virginia Votes Dry," *Washington Post*, 23 September 1914; "Virginia Goes Dry. Only Three Counties of the State Vote Against Prohibition," *New York Times*, 23 September 1914; James Cannon Jr., "How Virginia Broke Loose," *Sunday School Times*, 24 October 1914, 643; and "Alabama Dry Again," *Literary Digest*, 30 January 1915, 180–81.

76. "Amidst Cheers, Alabama Steps in 'Dry' Column," *Atlanta Constitution*, 20 November 1907.

77. Rev. A. J. McKelway, "The Dispensary in North Carolina," *Outlook*, 8 April 1899, 820–22. Eight years later in the same publication, McKelway reported on the singing of the Long Meter Doxology as Georgia passed the statewide prohibition measure. He also stated that "the enactment of the new law was not due to Puritan fanaticism." McKelway, "State Prohibition in Georgia and the South," *Outlook*, 31 August 1907, 947–49.

78. S. Mays Ball, "Prohibition in Georgia: Its Failure to Prevent Drinking in Atlanta and Other Cities," *Putnam's Magazine*, March 1909, 700.

79. John Koren, "Drink Reform in the United States," *Atlantic Monthly*, November 1915, 590.

80. "Prohibition for Georgia. House Passes Bill to Make the State Dry," *New York Times*, 31 July 1907.
81. "Georgia's Liquor Interests. Trade Disturbance Caused by Victory of 'Drys.' Breweries and Distilleries Will Be Removed to Florida and Alabama. Speculating on Loss and Gain," *Washington Evening Star*, 1 August 1907.
82. "Prohibition in the South," *Christian Advocate*, 29 August 1907, 1373.
83. "The Narrowing Bounds of the Saloon," *Christian Century*, 1 November 1907, 979. Information on the Chicago-based publication from Mott, *History of American Magazines*, 4:295.
84. "Progress of Prohibition," *Churchman*, 23 November 1907, 770.
85. *Methodist Protestant*, 27 November 1907, 3.
86. Frank Foxcroft, "Prohibition in the South," *Atlantic Monthly*, May 1908, 632.
87. "Negro Riots in Atlanta," *The Baptist Argus*, 17. Joan L. Silverman has convincingly argued that the film *The Birth of a Nation* promoted prohibition. See Silverman, "*The Birth of a Nation*: Prohibition Propaganda," in *The South and Film*, ed. Warren French (Jackson: University Press of Mississippi, 1981), 23–30.
88. Rev. John E. White, "Prohibition: The New Task and Opportunity of the South," *South Atlantic Quarterly* 7 (April 1908): 141.
89. P. H. Whaley, "Some Aspects of Prohibition in the South," *Collier's*, 31 May 1913, 32.
90. W. G. Chafee, "The South Carolina Liquor Law," *North American Review*, September 1893, 379. Here Chafee demonstrated that white males in South Carolina were largely split along class lines in their support for Tillman. Chafee was most likely a member of the state's more affluent class, a group that saw Tillman and his supporters as dangerous and uneducated. For more about Tillman, see Ayers, *Promise of the New South*, 286–89. Historian Frank Luther Mott called the *North American Review* "lively and successful" (*History of American Magazines*, 4:51).
91. Greenough White, "The South, Past and Present," *School Review* 7 (March 1899): 149.
92. William Garrott Brown, "The South and the Saloon," *Century Magazine*, July 1908, 463.
93. S. Mays Ball, "Prohibition in Georgia," *Putnam's Magazine*, March 1909, 699.
94. R. W. Simpson Jr., "Near-prohibition in the South," *Harper's Weekly*, 10 July 1909, 15.
95. R. E. Pritchard, "The Failure of Prohibition in the South," *Harper's Weekly*, 18 March 1911, 12.
96. Quoted in "Keeping Tennessee Dry," *Literary Digest*, 1 November 1913, 803.
97. Lurana Sheldon Ferris, letter to the editor, *New York Times*, 1 May 1919.
98. "Prohibition in Virginia," *New York Times*, 20 May 1919.
99. Quoted in "Two Years of Prohibition," *Literary Digest*, 4 February 1922, 15.
100. John J. Fleming, "What About Prohibition?" *World's Work*, August 1924, 424.
101. Edgar Lee Masters, "Demos the Despot," *New Republic*, 25 January 1919, 374–75. Masters's allusion to Ham was a reference to the white southern clergy's preaching, before the Civil War, that African Americans were descendants of Ham, Noah's son, whom Noah had cursed for seeing him naked. The effect of that curse, reasoned the white ministers, was slavery.
102. H. L. Mencken, untitled editorial, *American Mercury*, December 1924, 420; "Ins and Outs of Prohibition," *Independent*, 22 December 1923, 300.
103. Rollin Lynde Hartt, "The Church in Politics," *World's Work*, July 1925, 301.

Chapter 4

1. "A Welcome Conservative Publication," *Outlook*, 23 April 1910, 870–71. For more information on the publication of *The Fundamentals*, see George Marsden, *Fundamentalism and American Culture: The Shaping of Twentieth-Century Evangelicalism, 1870–1925* (New York: Oxford University Press, 1980), 118–23. In his memoir, Abbott continued to discount fundamentalism. See Lyman Abbott, *Reminiscences* (Boston: Houghton Mifflin, 1915).
2. H. L. Mencken, editorial, *American Mercury*, October 1925, 160.
3. For an excellent overview of how evangelicals dealt with the issues of evolution and education, see Charles A. Israel, *Before Scopes: Evangelicals, Education, and Evolution in Tennessee, 1870–1925* (Athens: University of Georgia Press, 2004).
4. For an example of a historian who sees the South as inclined toward both fundamentalism and creationism, see Ferenc Morton Szasz, *The Divided Mind of Protestant America, 1880–1930* (Tuscaloosa: University of Alabama Press, 1982).
5. For a more thorough discussion of fundamentalist beliefs, see the introduction to the present volume. William R. Glass describes the formal spread of fundamentalism through the South in *Strangers in Zion: Fundamentalists in the South, 1900–1950* (Macon, Ga.: Mercer University Press, 2001). According to Glass, the fundamentalists encountered resistance to dispensational premillennialism among white southern Protestants who saw themselves as orthodox, many of whom also rejected the fundamentalist calls to separate from their own denominations (*Strangers in Zion*, xvii, 34).
6. For an overview of the changing cultural and political landscape of this period, see Ann Douglas, *Terrible Honesty: Mongrel Manhattan in the 1920s* (New York: Farrar, Straus, and Giroux, 1995); John Higham, *Send These to Me: Immigrants in Urban America* (Baltimore: Johns Hopkins University Press, 1975); William R. Hutchison, *The Modernist Impulse in American Protestantism* (Durham, N.C.: Duke University Press, 1992); T. J. Jackson Lears, *No Place of Grace: Antimodernism and the Transformation of American Culture, 1880–1920* (Chicago: University of Chicago Press, 1981); and Henry F. May, *The End of American Innocence: A Study of the First Years of Our Own Time* (New York: Alfred A. Knopf, 1959).
7. For a comprehensive overview of the antievolutionists (or creationists), see Ronald L. Numbers's excellent work *The Creationists* (New York: Alfred A. Knopf, 1992).
8. Herbert Spencer, not Charles Darwin, coined the term, "survival of the fittest." See Szasz, *Divided Mind of Protestant America*, 4.
9. "Ideas of Today Not Like Bible Teaching. Distinction Brought Out at Opening Session on Fundamentals of Christianity. Survival of the Fittest Versus Helping Weak and Unfortunate, Speaker Asserts," *Philadelphia Inquirer*, 27 May 1919.
10. See "Seminarians Use Profanity; Charge. 200 Girls Found Addicted, Speaker Tells Bible Conference Delegates. Those Present Urged to Battle with Powers Undermining Christian Faith," *Philadelphia Inquirer*, 28 May 1919; and "Return of Christ Discussed at Congress. Belief in Future Punishment Also Topic at Christian Fundamentals Session," *Philadelphia Inquirer*, 1 June 1919. The second article began, "Before an audience that filled the main auditorium of the Academy of Music and overflowed into the lobby, two of the most important factors of the Christian belief were analytically discussed at yesterday afternoon's session of the World Conference on Christian Fundamentals."

11. "Who Can Be Saved?" *Time*, 12 May 1923, 18. Magazine historian Frank Luther Mott describes the New York–based publication as quickly expanding during its initial years of publication, with 175,000 subscribers in 1927. See Mott, *A History of American Magazines*, vol. 5, *Sketches of 21 Magazines, 1905–1930* (Cambridge: Belknap Press of Harvard University Press, 1968), 298.
12. "Who is Fundamental?" *Time*, 19 May 1923, 20.
13. "The Orthodoxy of Democracy," *Nation*, 6 June 1923, 645.
14. "The Case of the Fundamentalists," *Nation*, 26 December 1923, 729.
15. "The Parsons' Battle," *New Republic*, 9 January 1924, 162.
16. "Modernists Will Fight," *New York Times*, 17 December 1923.
17. Charles William Eliot, "The Great Religious Revival," *Atlantic Monthly*, March 1924, 379–85.
18. "Does Fundamentalism Obstruct Social Progress?" *Survey*, 1 July 1924, 389–92.
19. There were, of course, exceptions to the initial response to fundamentalism. In one example, the literary critic of the *New York Tribune*, Heywood Broun, satirized the Reverend John Roach Straton's opposition to playing baseball on the Sabbath. In "A Bolt from the Blue," Broun has Straton die and request God to "'Let New York be destroyed'" for allowing the Yankees to play ball. When the Almighty refuses, Straton then asks for "'a good husky tidal wave.'" Broun, "A Bolt from the Blue," *Nation*, 31 July 1920, 128.
20. Quoted in "The Coming Doctrinal Storm," *Literary Digest*, 13 May 1922, 34.
21. "Presbyterians," *Time*, 10 June 1924, 19–20.
22. Glenn Frank, "An American Looks at His World: Fashions in Bigotry," *Century*, May 1923, 158.
23. Marsden, *Fundamentalism and American Culture*, 125.
24. Rollin Lynde Hartt, "The War in the Churches," *World's Work*, September 1923, 469.
25. "The Coming Doctrinal Storm," *Literary Digest*,13 May 1922, 34. Frank Luther Mott reports that the *Digest* had a circulation of "nine hundred thousand" by the end of World War I and "it went on . . . to a million and a half by 1927." Mott, *A History of American Magazines*, vol. 4, *1885–1905* (Cambridge: Belknap Press of Harvard University Press, 1957), 574.
26. "The Catastrophe of a Church War," *Literary Digest*, 10 November 1923, 32.
27. J. D. M. Buckner, "How I Lost My Job as a Preacher: The Dispute Between the 'Fundamentalists' and the 'New School' in the Protestant Churches, Brought to an Issue in Nebraska," *World's Work*, January 1923, 303–10.
28. "Evangelist Predicts Destruction of City," *New York Times*, 17 August 1925.
29. Charles William Eliot, "The Great Religious Revival," 382.
30. Some fundamentalists went beyond rejection of the notion of progress to an outright belief that progress was the work of Satan. I. M. Haldeman was a premillennialist who opposed progress as Satan's doing. See Marsden, *Fundamentalism and American Culture*, 125. For an extensive and well-written overview of premillennialism, see Timothy P. Weber, *Living in the Shadow of the Second Coming: American Premillennialism, 1875–1925* (New York: Oxford University Press, 1979). Weber provides information on different types of premillennialism and nicely outlines the conflicts fundamentalists faced when dealing with progress and the possibility of the future.
31. Heywood Broun, "A Bolt from the Blue," *Nation*, 31 July 1920, 128.
32. "Insists Bible is Right," *New York Times*, 3 December 1923.

33. Rollin Lynde Hartt, "Deep Conflict Divides Protestantism," *New York Times*, 16 December 1923.
34. For a more complete account of the battle between Fosdick and Presbyterian fundamentalists, see Robert Moats Miller, *Harry Emerson Fosdick: Preacher, Pastor, Prophet* (New York: Oxford University Press, 1985), 112–49.
35. "Law and Order in the Church," *New Republic*, 29 October 1924, 215.
36. Kirsopp Lake, "The Real Divisions in Modern Christianity," *Atlantic Monthly*, June 1925, 757.
37. "Methodism vs. Intellectual Honesty," *New Republic*, 1 November 1922, 239.
38. "Presbyterians," *Time*, 10 June 1924, 19–20.
39. John Dewey, "Fundamentals," *New Republic*, 6 February 1924, 276. For additional information on Dewey's thought, see Bruce Kuklick, *Churchmen and Philosophers: From Jonathan Edwards to John Dewey* (New Haven: Yale University Press, 1985).
40. For additional information on the influences on Croly, see David W. Levy, *Herbert Croly of "The New Republic"* (Princeton: Princeton University Press, 1985).
41. "Huxley Shocked by Fundamentalism: Grandson of Famous Scientist Scores Intolerance," *Current Opinion*, March 1925, 339. Huxley was living in England at the time of the article, and the concern the editors of *Current Opinion* showed over his opinion on fundamentalism reflected an interest on the part of American liberals with all things British. If Huxley had been Italian or Japanese, his comments would have been of less importance to the cultural elite of this country.
42. Henshaw Ward, "Uncle Jasper and Mr. Bryan: Fundamentalism and Absurdity," *Independent*, 2 May 1925, 494.
43. "Mind in the Making," *Time*, 16 July 1923, 17.
44. "In Tennessee," *Time*, 30 July 1923, 19.
45. For additional information on Mathews, see William R. Hutchison, *The Modernist Impulse in American Protestantism* (Durham, N.C.: Duke University Press, 1995), 275–82.
46. Rollin Lynde Hartt, "Down With Evolution!" *World's Work*, October 1923, 606.
47. Dr. T. V. Smith, "Bases of Bryanism," *Scientific Monthly*, May 1923, 505–7.
48. Chester T. Crowell, "I'm for the Fundamentalists," *New Republic*, 18 March 1925, 95.
49. A. Wakefield Slaten, "Academic Freedom, Fundamentalism, and the Dotted Line," *Educational Review* 65 (February 1923), 74–77.
50. Glenn Frank, "An American Looks at His World: Fashions in Bigotry," 158.
51. Henry S. Pritchett, "Copernicus and the Fundamentalists," *Scribner's Magazine*, January 1924, 28.
52. Rollin Lynde Hartt, *The Man Himself: The Nazarene* (London: George G. Harrap, 1924), 283.
53. Howard Chandler Robbins, "'Fundamentalism' and 'Modernism': Two Misnomers," *Forum*, May 1924, 652.
54. "Abolishing Freedom and War—By Resolution," *Outlook*, 4 June 1924, 180. Information on the *Outlook* from Mott, *A History of American Magazines*, vol. 3, *1850–1865* (Cambridge: Harvard University Press, 1938), 422.
55. Quoted in "The Coming Doctrinal Storm," *Literary Digest*, 13 May 1922, 34.
56. George M. Gibson Jr., "An Inquisition in the South," *Churchman*, 11 July 1925, 13.
57. John F. Scott, "Alice in Literal-Land: An Allegory of the War in the Churches," *Century*, May 1924, 58.

58. Nancy MacLean, *Behind the Mask of Chivalry: The Making of the Second Ku Klux Klan* (New York: Oxford University Press, 1994), 5–22.

59. Charles P. Sweeney, "Bigotry in the South," *Nation*, 24 November 1920, 585–86.

60. Albert De Silver, "The Ku Klux Klan—'Soul of Chivalry,'" *Nation*, 14 September 1921, 285–86. For a sampling of other general articles on the Klan, see "Quaint Customs and Methods of the Ku Klux Klan," *Literary Digest*, 5 August 1922, 44; "The Ku Klux Klan Victory in Texas," *Literary Digest*, 5 August 1922, 14; Hubert C. Herring, "The Ku Klux to the Rescue," *New Republic*, 23 May 1923, 341–42; and "Why They Join the Klan," *New Republic*, 21 November 1923, 321–22.

61. Leroy Percy, "The Modern Ku Klux Klan," *Atlantic Monthly*, July 1922, 127.

62. *Ladies' Home Journal*, January 1924, 24.

63. W. E. B. Du Bois, "Georgia: Invisible Empire State," *Nation*, 21 January 1925, 63–67. For additional examples of coverage of religion and the Klan, see "The Ku Klux Klan and the Church," *Literary Digest*, 8 April 1922, 38; Charles P. Sweeney, "Great Bigotry Merger," *Nation*, 5 July 1922, 8–10; Frank Tannenbaum, "The Ku Klux Klan: Its Social Origin in the South," *Century Magazine*, April 1923, 873–82; Mark Sullivan, "Behind the Convention Scenes," *World's Work*, September 1923, 533–39; Max Bentley, "A Texan Challenges the Klan," *Collier's*, 3 November 1923, 12; Stanley Frost, "When the Klan Rules: Invoking the Whirlwind," *Outlook*, 16 January 1924, 100–103; William Robinson Pattangall, "Is the Ku Klux Un-American?" *Forum*, September 1925, 321–32; and Stanley Frost, "The Masked Politics of the Klan," *World's Work*, February 1928, 399–407. Not all coverage of the Klan and religion was derogatory. The *Literary Digest* published an article in 1921 detailing the religious newspapers' condemnation of the KKK. See "Ku Klux Condemned by the Religious Press," *Literary Digest*, 1 October 1921, 30–31.

64. Leroy Percy, "The Modern Ku Klux Klan,"127.

65. Leonard Lanson Cline, "In Darkest Louisiana," *Nation*, 14 March 1923, 292–93.

66. *Time*, 10 March 1923, 5.

67. See "The Ku Klux Klan and the Church," *Literary Digest*, 8 April 1922, 38; Max Bentley, "A Texan Challenges the Klan," *Collier's*, 3 November 1923, 12; "The Ku Klux Victory in Texas," *Literary Digest*, 5 August 1922, 14; "Klan Victories in Oregon and Texas," *Literary Digest*, 25 November 1922, 12; "The Klan and The Bottle," *Nation*, 21 November 1923, 570; and Rollin Lynde Hartt, "Prohibition As It Is: III. St. Louis—The Dry South—Washington," *World's Work*, March 1925, 507–13. One recent historian has alleged clergy involvement in the Klan, while another has described the method by which the Klan would approach Protestant churches for support. See Wyn Craig Wade, *The Fiery Cross: The Ku Klux Klan in America* (New York: Simon and Schuster, 1987), 171; and Kathleen Blee, *Women of the Klan: Racism and Gender in the 1920s* (Berkeley: University of California Press, 1991), 21.

68. Robert L. Duffus, "How The Ku Klux Klan Sells Hate," *World's Work*, June 1923, 178–81. See also Robert L. Duffus, "Salesmen of Hate: The Ku Klux Klan," *World's Work*, May 1923, 31–38.

69. H. L. Mencken was always delighted to link the southern clergy to the Ku Klux Klan, but so were other writers. See Mencken, *The Gist of Mencken: Quotations from America's Critic*, ed. Mayo DuBasky (Metuchen, N. J.: Scarecrow, 1990), 41; editorial, *American Mercury*, November 1925, 286–88; William G. Shepherd, "The Whip Hand," *Collier's*, 7 January 1928, 8–9; Shepherd, "The Whip Hand Wins," *Collier's*,

14 January 1928, 10–11; and James D. Bernard, "The Methodists," *American Mercury*, April 1926, 411–32.

70. Historian W. Fitzhugh Brundage documents the increase in racial violence in the South in his book *Lynching in the New South: Georgia and Virginia, 1880–1930* (Urbana: University of Illinois Press, 1993), 227–28. Sociologists Stewart E. Tolnay and E. M. Beck provide statistical evidence of this trend in their work *A Festival of Violence: An Analysis of Southern Lynchings, 1882–1930* (Urbana: University of Illinois Press, 1995), 271–72.

71. Untitled editorial, *Nation*, 25 January 1919, 108.

72. "Negro Churches Burned: Georgians Seek Arrest of Supposed Revivers of Kuklux Klan," *New York Times*, 29 May 1919.

73. "The Shame of America: How the Officials of an American City Connived at a Mob's Crimes—Why there Must be Federal Action to Suppress Lynching," *Nation*, 19 July 1919, 89.

74. "Southern Protests Against Lynching," *Outlook*, 30 July 1919, 493.

75. William Pickens, "The American Congo—Burning of Henry Lowry," *Nation*, 23 March 1921, 426–27.

76. "Mob Burns Negro After 100-Mile Trip," *New York Times*, 27 January 1921; and "They Fed Before They Killed," *New York Times*, 28 January 1921.

77. "The Most Disreputable Act," *Washington Evening Star*, 28 January 1921.

78. For a complete narration of this awful crime, see Gregory A. Freeman, *Lay This Body Down: The 1921 Murders of Eleven Plantation Slaves* (Chicago: Lawrence Hill Books, 1999).

79. See "Eleven Negroes Slain; White Farmer Accused," *New York Times*, 25 March 1921; "Farmer Charged with Murder of Eleven Negroes," *Chicago Daily Tribune*, 25 March 1921; "Find Nine Bodies in Georgia Peonage Inquiry," *New York Times*, 27 March 1921; "Slain Peons Dug Their Graves as Killer Watched," *New York Times*, 28 March 1921; "Made to Dig Graves Before Being Slain," *Boston Globe*, 28 March 1921; "Armed Men Rush to Peonage Murder Farm at Rumor of Intended Negro Uprising," *New York Times*, 29 March 1921; "Georgia Governor Asks Early Trial of Planter and Negro for Peonage Murders," *New York Times*, 30 March, 1921; "Admitted A Killing on His Farm," *New York Times*, 3 April 1921; "Jury is Completed for Peonage Trial," *New York Times*, 6 April 1921; "Chained Negroes Thrown Off Bridge," *New York Times*, 7 April 1921; "Williams Denies He Killed Negroes," *New York Times*, 8 April 1921; "Convict Williams of Peonage Murder," *New York Times*, 10 April 1921; "Georgia's Death Farm," *Literary Digest*, 16 April 1921, 13–14; and "Georgia Declares War on Peonage," *Literary Digest*, 14 May 1921, 17–18. Writers had warned of the peonage system's dangers decades before, but their protests had gone unheeded. See W. E. B. Du Bois, "The Spawn of Slavery: The Convict-Lease System in the South," *Missionary Review of the World*, October 1901, 737–45; and "A Georgia Negro Peon," "The New Slavery in the South—An Autobiography," *Independent*, 25 February 1904, 409–14.

80. "The Williams Peonage Case," *New York Times*, 11 April 1921.

81. "The Fruits of Peonage," *New Republic*, 20 April 1921, 223–24. In 1923, the *Literary Digest* carried an account of a white man from North Dakota who was arrested for riding a train without a ticket and leased to a lumber company for convict labor. See "A Victim of Convict 'Slavery,'" *Literary Digest*, 21 April 1923, 40–46. The *Nation*

later commented on the incident, saying the "ghost of Martin Talbert of North Dakota, killed in a convict camp in Florida, has not yet found peace, and where it walks society is troubled." "After Florida, Alabama," *Nation*, 11 July 1923, 31.

82. Herbert Seligmann, "Slavery in Georgia, A.D. 1921," *Nation*, 20 April 1921, 591.
83. Walter F. White, "Election by Terror in Florida," *New Republic*, 12 January 1921, 197.
84. "Applied Violence," *New Republic*, 31 August 1921, 5–6.
85. "Three Burned by Texas Mob for Murder of Girl," *Chicago Tribune*, 7 May 1922; and "Mob Burns Three Negroes at Stake," *New York Times*, 7 May 1922. For additional accounts, see "Fourth Lynching In Texas," *New York Times*, 9 May 1922; "Fear Texas Race War Result of Lynchings," *Washington Post*, 9 May 1922; "Race Riot in Texas After 4 Lynchings," *Washington Post*, 3 June 1922; and "Race Riot Prevented," *New York Times*, 4 June 1922, 22. For a complete account of the murders and the national press attention they garnered, see Monte Akers, *Flames after Midnight: Murder, Vengeance, and the Desolation of a Texas Community* (Austin: University of Texas Press, 1999). Tying additional unrest in the South to the Kirvin deaths, *New York Times* told of lynchings in Texas in "Two Negroes Lynched for Attacks on Girls," 21 May 1922.
86. See "Kill Six in Florida; Burn Negro Houses," *New York Times*, 6 January 1923; "Florida Race War Costs Seven Lives," *Washington Post*, 6 January 1923; "Florida Race Riot Has Seventh Victim," *New York Times*, 7 January 1923; "Last Negro Homes Razed in Rosewood," *New York Times*, 8 January 1923; and "Rest of Negro Houses in Rosewood Burned," *Washington Post*, 8 January 1923.
87. "Saturday Night," *Time*, 5 May 1923, 6.
88. Quoted in "Mer Rouge Murders Unpunished," *Literary Digest*, 31 March 1923, 10.
89. There are many books that give more detailed accounts of the events and debates leading up to the Scopes Trial. Two of the more helpful ones are Paul R. Conkin, *When All the Gods Trembled: Darwinism, Scopes, and American Intellectuals* (Lanham, Md.: Rowman and Littlefield, 1998); and Edward J. Larson, *Summer for the Gods: The Scopes Trial and America's Continuing Debate over Science and Religion* (New York: Basic, 1997). For a compelling analysis of notions about race at work in the debate, see Jeffrey P. Moran, "Reading Race into the Scopes Trial: African American Elites, Science, and Fundamentalism," *Journal of American History* 90, no. 3, (December 2003): 891–911.
90. "The Battle of Tennessee," *Nation*, 27 May 1925, 590.
91. "Freedom in the Mountains," *Outlook*, 27 May 1925, 132.
92. "The Menace of Fundamentalism," *Independent*, 30 May 1925, 602.
93. "Tennessee vs. Truth," *Nation*, 8 July 1925, 58.
94. William G. Shepherd, "Monkey Business in Tennessee," *Collier's*, 18 July 1925, 8.
95. "Fundamentalist Prototypes," *Christian Century*, 16 July 1925, 913.
96. "The Fanatics Also Serve," *Collier's*, 1 August 1925, 24.
97. The editors of *Time* saw a close parallel between the Scopes Trial and the trial and execution of Socrates. See "Dixit," *Time*, 10 August 1925, 18–19.
98. Forrest Davis, "Some Impressions from Dayton," *Churchman*, 25 July 1925, 13.
99. Edward L. Rice, "Darwin and Bryan—A Study in Method," *Science*, 6 March 1925, 243.
100. Szasz, *Divided Mind of Protestant America*, 107–16.
101. "Freedom in the Mountains," *Outlook*, 27 May 1925, 132.
102. "The Cure for Fundamentalism," *New Republic*, 10 June 1925, 58–59.

103. "The Established Church of Tennessee," *Christian Century*, 11 June 1925, 756–67.
104. Quoted in "Larger Aspects of Dayton," *Literary Digest*, 1 August 1925, 10.
105. Dixon Merritt, "Smoldering Fires: Editorial Correspondence from Dayton, Tennessee," *Outlook*, 22 July 1925, 422.
106. "A Fundamentalized America," *Churchman*, 1 August 1925, 8.
107. George E. G. Catlin, "Daytonism and the Church of England: The Significance of the Prayer Book Defeat," *Harper's Monthly Magazine*, April 1928, 598.
108. "Tennessee vs. Civilization," *New Republic*, 22 July 1925, 220.
109. The Reverend James Sheerin, "Evolution and Evil Notions," *Southern Churchman*, 25 July 1925, 7.
110. Forrest Davis, "Some Impressions from Dayton," *Churchman*, 25 July 1925, 12.
111. "Booming Medievalism in Tennessee," *Christian Century*, 23 July 1925, 943; "Tennessee Plans to Sweep Back the Tides," *Christian Century*, 28 May 1925, 688.
112. Royce Jordan, "Tennessee Goes Fundamentalist," *New Republic*, 29 April 1925, 258.
113. Untitled editorial, *New Republic*, 24 June 1925, 111.
114. Frank R. Kent, "On the Dayton Firing Line," *New Republic*, 29 July 1925, 259. For information on Kent, see Frank Luther Mott, *American Journalism: A History, 1690–1960*, 3rd ed. (New York: Macmillan, 1962), 691.
115. H. L. Mencken, "In Tennessee," *Nation*, 1 July 1925, 21.
116. "As to Evolution," *Los Angeles Times*, 21 July 1925. The day before, the paper had referred to the Tennessee enthusiasts of William Jennings Bryan as "rustics." "Bryan Again Vehement," *Los Angeles Times*, 20 July 1925.
117. *Christian Century*, 16 July 1925, 913.
118. George F. Milton, "Can Minds Be Closed By Statute? An Article on the Background of Tennessee's Evolution Trial," *World's Work*, July 1925, 324.
119. Joseph Wood Krutch, "Tennessee's Dilemma," *Nation*, 22 July 1925, 110.
120. Quoted in *Science*, 17 July 1925, 52.
121. Rollin Lynde Hartt, "The Disruption of Protestantism," *Forum*, November 1925, 679–87.
122. "Evolution, the Court, and the Church," *Scientific Monthly*, December 1925, 670.
123. W. E. B. Du Bois saw the trial as a referendum not just on the South but on the country. "Dayton, Tennessee," he wrote, "is America: a great, ignorant simple-minded land, curiously compounded of brutality, bigotry, religious faith, and demagoguery, and capable not simply of mistakes but of persecution, lynching, murder and idiotic blundering, as well as charity, missions, love and hope." Du Bois, *Selections from "The Crisis,"* ed. Herbert Aptheker, Writings in Periodicals Edited by W. E. B. Du Bois (Millwood, N.Y.: Kraus Thomson Organization, 1983), 2:427.
124. John Porter Fort, "Behind the Scenes in Tennessee," *Forum*, August 1925, 259.
125. *New Republic*, 10 June 1925, 71.
126. "Tennessee vs. Truth," *Nation*, 8 July 1925, 58.
127. Rollin Lynde Hartt, "What Lies Beyond Dayton," *Nation*, 22 July 1925, 111.
128. "In Virginia," *Time*, 24 August 1925, 15–16.

Chapter 5

1. *Methodist Protestant*, 28 July 1926, 9.
2. See "Slayer Preaches to Packed Church. Rev. J. F. Norris, Charged with Murder, Embraced by Many After Sermon on Faith. He is Invited to New York. 'Texas Tornado' Says He Will Preach at First Baptist Church Here Aug. 1," *New York Times*, 19 July 1926, 1; "Norris Fills Pulpit on Day After Slaying. No Allusion by Texas Pastor to Tragedy," *Chicago Tribune*, 19 July 1926, 1; and "Pastor Fills Pulpit After Slaying Man. Fort Worth Baptist Church Throng Shakes Hand of Dr. Norris At Close of Service," *Boston Globe*, 19 July 1926, 1.
3. William R. Glass argues that fundamentalists in this period were just beginning to realize the potential for converts in the South during the 1920s. See Glass, *Strangers in Zion: Fundamentalists in the South, 1900–1950* (Macon, Ga.: Mercer University Press, 2001), 79.
4. Robert A. Slayton agrees with my contention about the ugly nature of the 1928 presidential election and the role religion played in it. See Slayton, *Empire Statesman: The Rise and Redemption of Al Smith* (New York: Free Press, 2001).
5. See George Marsden, *Fundamentalism and American Culture: The Shaping of Twentieth Century Evangelicalism, 1870–1925* (New York: Oxford University Press, 1980); and Joel Carpenter, *Revive Us Again: The Reawakening of American Fundamentalism* (New York: Oxford University Press, 1997).
6. Herbert Croly, "Christians, Beware!" *New Republic*, 25 November 1925, 13.
7. "Fancies," letters to the editor, *Forum*, April 1926, 630.
8. "Klansmen Attack Eucharist Meeting and Gov. Al Smith," *Washington Post*, 14 September 1926.
9. William B. Munro, "The Worst Fundamentalism," *Atlantic Monthly*, October 1926, 451–59. Interestingly, the *New York Times* compared conservative Muslims to Christian fundamentalists in an article entitled "Islam Fundamentalists Fight Modernist Trend," 20 September 1925.
10. See "Smith and M'Doo May Wage Decisive Battle in Senate," *New York Times*, 12 July 1925, 14; and "State Rights Issue Basis of Campaign for Smith in East," *Washington Post*, 10 July 1925, 3.
11. "What is a Fundamentalist?" *Forum*, December 1926, 861–2.
12. Albert C. Dieffenbach, "Religious Liberty—the Great Illusion. The Eclipse of Protestantism," *Independent*, 8 January 1927, 36–38. See also Dieffenbach, "Religious Liberty—the Great Illusion. The Fundamentalists Possess the Land," *Independent*, 15 January 1927, 64–66; and Dieffenbach, "Religious Liberty—the Great Illusion. Will Freedom Triumph Over Intolerance?" *Independent*, 29 January 1927, 120–22.
13. "Unitarian Dismay at Fundamentalist Triumph," *Literary Digest*, 26 November 1927, 26.
14. "The Last Laugh," *Churchman*, 29 January 1927, 8.
15. "A State Church in America," *Independent*, 11 September 1926, 285.
16. Maynard Shipley, "Fundamentalism Summed Up," *New York Times*, 26 July 1931, BR 9.
17. Glass, *Strangers in Zion*, 79. For a detailed look at the resistance they found there, see Glass, 33–81. Interestingly, the South's religion also made it a new battleground for atheists. See Homer Croy, "Atheism Beckons to Our Youth: How Unbelief is Being Spread in Schools and Colleges," *World's Work*, May 1927, 18–26.

18. "Urges Church to Cling to Old-Time Religion," *Washington Post*, 24 March 1926.
19. "The 'Flying' and Fighting Fundamentalists," *Literary Digest*, 28 May 1927, 30–31.
20. Miriam Allen de Ford, "After Dayton: A Fundamentalist Survey," *Nation*, 2 June 1926, 604–5.
21. "Anti-Evolution Act Faces Court Fight," *New York Times*, 25 November 1928, quoted in "Banishing Evolution in the South," *Literary Digest*, 3 April 1926, 30. The article also pointed out that the Baptist General Conference of McComb, Mississippi, met at the same time the Mississippi legislature did. The attention to the conference's resolutions and their timing hinted at the involvement of church officials in writing state legislation.
22. Untitled editorial, *Nation*, 31 October 1928, 438.
23. Clay Fulks, "Arkansas," *American Mercury*, July 1926, 294.
24. "Lauds Bryan as Reformer," *New York Times*, 18 March 1929.
25. "Tennessee Clings to Anti-Evolution Law; House Defeats Repeal by 58 Votes to 14," *New York Times*, 11 June 1931.
26. Sara Haardt, "Alabama," *American Mercury*, September 1925, 90.
27. Nell Battle Lewis, "North Carolina," *American Mercury*, May 1926, 37–38.
28. Owen P. White, "Reminiscences of Texas Divines," *American Mercury*, September 1926, 95–97.
29. Edgar W. Knight, "Monkey or Mud in North Carolina?" *Independent*, 14 May 1927, 515–16.
30. E. DeForest Leach, "The Old Churches in the New South," *Christian Century*, 16 October 1929, 1277–78.
31. John Beauchamp Thompson, "Southern Prayers," *Christian Century*, 3 September 1930, 1061.
32. Gerald W. Johnson, "A Tar Heel Looks at Virginia," *North American Review*, August 1929, 238.
33. French Strother, "Tennessee Strides Forward: What a 'Backward' State is Doing," *World's Work*, August 1926, 390–91.
34. Edwin Mims, "Why the South is Anti-Evolution," *World's Work*, September 1925, 548–52.
35. Lillian Perrine Davis, "A Word for the Tennesseans," *Sewanee Review* 34 (July–September 1926), 307–8. Frank Luther Mott called the *Sewanee Review*, published in Sewanee, Tennessee, in affiliation with the University of the South, a "fairly conservative literary quarterly with a circulation of less than 500" during its first half century (from 1892 to 1945). Mott, *A History of American Magazines*, vol. 4, *1885–1905* (Cambridge: Belknap Press of Harvard University Press, 1957), 733, 738.
36. Historian Edward L. Ayers has called the "New South . . . a notoriously violent place. Homicide rates among both blacks and whites were the highest in the country, among the highest in the world. Lethal weapons seemed everywhere. Guns as well as life were cheap. . . ." Ayers, *The Promise of the New South: Life after Reconstruction* (New York: Oxford University Press, 1992), 155. Ayers also provided evidence for the lower educational standards in the South: "The region lagged far behind the rest of the country in literacy and school attendance, for both races" (*Promise of the New South*, 418).
37. George Marsden includes among this number William B. Riley, A. C. Dixon, Curtis Lee Laws, John Roach Straton, J. C. Massee, J. Gresham Machen (who may or may not have considered himself a fundamentalist), and J. Frank Norris. See Marsden,

Fundamentalism and American Culture, 258. Joel Carpenter notes that William Bell Riley was born in Kentucky. See Carpenter, *Revive Us Again*, 36.

38. See "Should Christians Play on Sunday?" *Literary Digest*, 30 January 1926, 27–28; "The Storm Over 'Elmer Gantry,'" *Literary Digest*, 6 April 1927, 28–29; "Dr. Straton Deplores Tendencies of Press," *New York Times*, 18 February 1929; "Straton Defends Healing Services," *New York Times*, 24 June 1927; "Dr. Straton Very Ill at Clifton Springs," *New York Times*, 23 October 1929; and "Dr. Straton Dies, Modernism Foe," *Minneapolis Journal*, 29 October 1929.

39. Haywood Broun, "A Bolt from the Blue," *Nation*, 31 July 1920, 128.

40. Stanley Walker, "The Fundamentalist Pope," *American Mercury*, July 1926, 263.

41. Samuel Taylor Moore, "Strange Bedfellows in the Supreme Kingdom: Dr. John Roach Straton, Militant Fundamentalist Minister, Helps to Promote a Georgia Corporation," *Independent*, 12 March 1927, 282. Even though Moore investigated Straton's business dealings in the South, he did not mention the preacher's roots there.

42. See Bruce Tarrant, "Minnesota: Modern or Medieval?" *Independent*, 1 January 1927, 8; "The 'Flying' and Fighting Fundamentalists," *Literary Digest*, 28 May 1927, 30; W. B. Riley, "The Faith of the Fundamentalists," *Current History*, June 1927, 434; and "Anti-Evolutionists Still Fighting," *Literary Digest*, 10 December 1927, 29. For an excellent investigation into Riley and his Northwestern Bible and Missionary Training School, see William Vance Trollinger, *God's Empire: William Bell Riley and Midwestern Fundamentalism* (Madison: University of Wisconsin Press, 1990).

43. See Tarrant, "Minnesota: Modern or Medieval?" *Independent*, 1 January 1927, 8; "Campaigning for Genesis," *Literary Digest*, 19 February 1927, 33; W. B. Riley, "The Faith of the Fundamentalists," *Current History*, June 1927, 434–40; and Riley, "A Square Deal for Genesis," *Independent*, 12 November 1927, 470–72. Only a few of the obituaries for John Roach Straton mentioned his southern roots. For an example of one that did, see "John Roach Straton Dies in Sanitarium," *New York Times*, 30 October 1929. More common was the omission of such regional ties. See "Died," *Time*, 11 November 1929, 53; and untitled editorial, *New Republic*, 13 November 1929, 335. Because it fell very close to the stock market crash of 1929, his death did not receive a great deal of press attention.

44. Barry Hankins, *God's Rascal: J. Frank Norris and the Beginnings of Southern Fundamentalism* (Lexington: University Press of Kentucky, 1996), 5–6. Hankins also credits Norris with "help[ing] to shift the center of gravity of the [fundamentalist] movement from the North to the South" (*God's Rascal*, 176). William Glass takes exception to this claim, arguing instead that the "itinerant fundamentalists" who traveled the region in the 1920s were the ones who made the South more hospitable to fundamentalism. See Glass, *Strangers in Zion*, 77–80.

45. Hankins, *God's Rascal*, 9–10.

46. Ibid., 9, 16–17.

47. Rollin Lynde Hartt, "Fighting for Infallibility," *World's Work*, November 1923, 53.

48. "No Surrender for Baptist Fundamentalists," *Literary Digest*, 8 August 1925, 26; "Should Christians Play on Sunday?" *Literary Digest*, 30 January 1926, 57.

49. "Pledged to Heat Up Straton's Pulpit," *New York Times*, 26 March 1922, section 2, p. 1. Calvary Baptist Church was home to the Reverend John Roach Straton, a prominent fundamentalist. In 1926, the *Literary Digest* repeated the nickname "'Texas Tornado'" in covering Norris and his role in the doctrinal disputes of the

Northern Baptist Convention. It added that he had urged the convention to "deal the Modernists a 'knock-out' blow." "Baptists in the Middle of the Road," *Literary Digest*, 19 June 1926, 26–27.

50. "Insists Bible Is Right," *New York Times*, 3 December 1923.
51. Hankins, *God's Rascal*, 118–19.
52. "Slayer Preaches to Packed Church," *New York Times*, 19 July 1926.
53. "Pastor Kills Man in Church," *Minneapolis Morning Tribune*, 18 July 1926; "Texas Pastor Kills Enemy in Church," *Minneapolis Journal*, 18 July 1926.
54. "Slayer Preaches to Packed Church," *New York Times*, 19 July 1926. One day earlier the headline read, "Texas Minister Kills Man in Church: The Rev. J. Frank Norris, Fundamentalist, Shoots Fort Worth Lumberman," *New York Times*, 18 July 1926.
55. "Slayer Preaches to Packed Church," *New York Times*, 19 July 1926.
56. "Norris Fills Pulpit on Day After Slaying, No Allusion by Texas Pastor to Tragedy," *Chicago Tribune*, 19 July 1926. See also "Noted Baptist Pastor Slays Man in Church, Shot in Self-Defense, Plea of Evangelist," *Chicago Sunday Tribune*, 18 July 1926.
57. "Pastor Ignores Murder Accusation in Sermon," *Los Angeles Times*, 19 July 1926.
58. "Pastor Fills Pulpit After Slaying Man, Fort Worth Baptist Church Throng Shakes Hand of Dr. Norris At Close of Service," *Boston Globe*, 19 July 1926.
59. Owen P. White, "Reminiscences of Texas Divines," *American Mercury*, September 1926, 97.
60. "Baptist," *Time*, 26 July 1926, 18.
61. Ibid. The account went on to describe how "his minions have gathered about their shepherd in mesmerized faith" and to say that after the service, many were "touching his robes, admiring the prophet" (19).
62. Nels Anderson, "The Shooting Parson of Texas," *New Republic*, 1 September 1926, 36.
63. See "Norris Wins Acquittal in Texas Church Killing," *Washington Post*, 26 January 1927; "Norris Acquitted by Jury of Murder Charge," *Atlanta Constitution*, 26 January 1927; and "Jubilee," *Time*, 15 November 1926, 26.
64. "Norris Jury Picked, Seat Ex-Klansman," *New York Times*, 14 January 1927; and "Klan Backs Norris, Says Texas Dragon," *New York Times*, 24 July 1926.
65. Hankins, *God's Rascal*, 165.
66. Bruce Bliven, "Sister Aimee: Mrs. McPherson (Saint or Sinner?) and Her Flock," *New Republic*, 3 November 1926, 291.
67. Edgar W. Knight, "Monkey or Mud in North Carolina?" 14 May 1927, 516.
68. *Churchman*, 29 January 1927, 7.
69. "Expects 20,000 Baptists," *New York Times*, 2 May 1927.
70. "Fire Razes Church of J. Frank Norris," *New York Times*, 13 January 1929; "Norris Church Fire Yields Slim Clues," *New York Times*, 14 January 1929; and "New Fire Razes Dr. Norris's School," *New York Times*, 17 August 1929.
71. "Milestones" column, *Time*, 1 September 1952, 73.
72. The Al Smith/Herbert Hoover campaign has had some attention from historians, but it could use a fresh perspective. See Michael Williams, *The Shadow of the Pope* (New York: McGraw-Hill, 1932); Edmund A. Moore, *A Catholic Runs for President: The Campaign of 1928* (New York: Ronald, 1956); Ruth Caridad Silva, *Rum, Religion, and Votes: 1928 Re-examined* (University Park: Pennsylvania State University Press, 1962); and Allan J. Lichtman, *Prejudice and the Old Politics: The Presidential Election of 1928* (Chapel Hill: University of North Carolina Press, 1979). Two recent

biographies of Al Smith have attempted to shed new light on the candidate, and both hold that the "religion issue" was important. See Slayton, *Empire Statesman;* and Christopher M. Finan, *Alfred E. Smith: The Happy Warrior* (New York: Hill and Wang, 2002).

73. George Washington Hays, "The Solid South and Al Smith in 1928," *Forum,* November 1926, 700.
74. George W. Hays, "The Solid South Backs 'Al' Smith," *Nation,* 2 February 1927, 117.
75. Ruby A. Black, "'Al' Smith in Texas," *Nation,* 6 July 1927, 14, 15.
76. "'Law or Liquor,'" *Time,* 9 July 1923, 3.
77. George F. Milton Jr., "The South—and 1924,"*Outlook,* 2 January 1924, 29–30. For additional examples of negative coverage long before 1928, see Finan, *Alfred E. Smith,* 167; and Slayton, *Empire Statesman,* 204.
78. "The Religious Issue in the Democratic Party," *World's Work,* January 1925, 235.
79. "Governor Smith's Victory," *Nation,* 18 November 1925, 562.
80. "A Catholic President?" *New Republic,* 23 March 1927, 128–29.
81. Judge Pierre Crabites, "Is It Time for a Catholic President?" *Outlook,* 17 August 1927, 506.
82. Ibid.
83. Ibid., 507.
84. Louis M. Jiggitts, "Al's Chances in Dixie," *Independent,* 15 October 1927, 377.
85. "A Catholic President?" *New Republic,* 23 March 1927, 130.
86. William H. Crawford, "What Will the South Do to Al Smith?" *Outlook,* 2 November 1927, 275.
87. Dixon Merritt, "What Mississippi and Alabama Think of Al Smith," *Outlook,* 9 November 1927, 306–7.
88. "Dixie's Dilemma," *Independent,* 10 March 1928, 221.
89. "Rum, Romanism, and Rebellion: A Democratic Catholic Presents Pertinent Views on Al Smith and the South," *Forum,* June 1928, 951.
90. Untitled editorial, *Nation,* 4 July 1928, 2.
91. Lewis S. Gannett, "The Big Show at Houston," *Nation,* 11 July 1928, 35.
92. "Governor Smith the Nominee," *Nation,* 11 July 1928, 30.
93. Lewis S. Gannett, "It's All Al Smith," *Nation,* 4 July 1928, 8.
94. "All But 7 States in Smith Parade," *New York Times,* 28 June 1928.
95. "Fist Fights and Oratory Mark Houston Sessions," *Los Angeles Times,* 6 June 1928.
96. "All But 7 States in Smith Parade," *New York Times,* 28 June 1928.
97. "Mississippi Tied Up on Swing to Smith," *New York Times,* 28 June 1928.
98. "Calls Drys in South to Bolt on Smith," *New York Times,* 29 June 1928.
99. For a sampling of articles on Cannon's financial scandals, see "Dallas and Washington Investigate Bishops," *Christian Century,* 21 May 1930, 643; "Methodists Exonerate Bishop Cannon," *Christian Century,* 28 May 1930, 675; "Figure of a Bishop," *Commonweal,* 28 May 1930, 89–90; Paul Y. Anderson, "The Bishop's Challenge," *Nation,* 18 June 1930, 701–2; and "The Lost Leader," *Christian Century,* 25 June 1930, 806–8.
100. For two very different views of Cannon, see Virginius Dabney, *Dry Messiah: The Life of Bishop Cannon* (New York: Alfred A. Knopf, 1949); and Robert A. Hohner, *Prohibition and Politics: The Life of Bishop James Cannon, Jr.* (Columbia: University of South Carolina Press, 1999).

101. "Holds Dry Issue May Split the Solid South," *Washington Post*, 16 May 1924.

102. James Cannon Jr., "We're Going to Stay Dry," *Collier's*, 31 July 1926, 8.

103. See "Prohibition is Issue in Coming Election, Says Bishop Cannon," *Washington Post*, 13 November 1927; and "South Will Knife Wet, Bishop Says," *New York Times*, 18 January 1927.

104. James Cannon Jr., "Al Smith—Catholic, Tammany, Wet," *Nation*, 4 July 1928, 9–10.

105. "The Progress of the World" editorial column, *Review of Reviews*, March 1928, 238.

106. "Churches Mixing in the Political Fray," *Literary Digest*, 15 September 1928, 8–9.

107. Dixon Merritt, "James Cannon, Jr.: Leader of the Dry Revolt in the Democratic Party," *Outlook*, 12 September 1928, 765–76.

108. Ibid., 765, 797.

109. "Views of Southern Leaders on Prohibition," *Review of Reviews*, March 1928, 261.

110. George W. Hinman Jr., "Protestantism in Politics," *Outlook*, 29 August 1928, 683–85.

111. "Smith Threats Laid Largely to Clergy," *New York Times*, 15 July 1928.

112. "Clash at Institute Religious Issue: Minister's Declaration Against a Catholic for President Stirs Demonstration," *New York Times*, 17 August 1928.

113. Quoted in "Churches Mixing in the Political Fray," *Literary Digest*, 15 September 1928, 9.

114. Owen P. White, "Workers in the Vineyard," *Collier's*, 6 October 1928, 8.

115. Ibid.

116. Ibid., 9.

117. Ibid.

118. Ibid., 36.

119. "Governor Smith's Religion," *Literary Digest*, 20 October 1928, 32.

120. Richard V. Oulahan, "Fight in Virginia Laid to 'Religion,'" *New York Times*, 18 September 1928.

121. Richard V. Oulahan, "Anti-Smith Sheets Deluge Virginia," *New York Times*, 19 September 1928.

122. "Challenges Straton to Debate on Smith," *New York Times*, 19 August 1928. The title of the article refers to John Roach Straton, who had called Smith "'the deadliest foe in America today of the forces of moral progress and true political wisdom.'" The challenge to debate came from Benjamin E. Greenspan of the Bronx.

123. Quoted in "Methodist Denounces Smith Pulpit Critics," *New York Times*, 7 September 1928.

124. Quoted in "The Job of Mending the 'Cracked' Solid South," *Literary Digest*, 24 November 1928, 8.

125. Ibid.

126. "By-Products," *New York Times*, 11 November 1928.

127. "The Election," *Christian Advocate*, 15 November 1928, 1387.

128. Julian Harris, "Hold Thanksgiving for Smith's Defeat," *New York Times*, 25 November 1928; "Why the South Voted," *New York Times*, 7 November 1928.

129. J. A. MacCallum, "Babbitt Mounts the Pulpit," *North American Review*, March 1929, 271.

130. Virginius Dabney, "Bishop Cannon Wins an Award," *Nation*, 17 April 1929, 452.

131. H. L. Mencken, untitled editorial, *American Mercury*, November 1929, 278.

132. James Cannon Jr., "The Modern Prophet," *Forum*, May 1930, 268.
133. Heywood Broun, "God's Proxies," *Forum*, May 1920, 270.
134. Grover C. Hall, "We Southerners," *Scribner's Magazine*, January 1928, 88.
135. James M. Cain, "The Solid South," *The Bookman: A Review of Books and Life*, November 1928, 264.
136. Donald Davidson, "First Fruits of Dayton," *Forum*, June 1928, 896.
137. Sam H. Reading, "Corra Harris, Humorist," *Forum*, April 1928, 636–37.
138. "Moody Compares Texas and Chicago," *New York Times*, 26 November 1930.
139. Willie Snow Ethridge, "Liberalism Stirs Southern Churches," *Christian Century*, 9 March 1932, 317. Ethridge, a resident of Macon, Georgia, argued a bit too optimistically that southern churches had "flung off completely that old blanket of obligation to preach 'only the gospel'" (317).

Conclusion

1. John Higham, *Strangers in the Land: Patterns of American Nativism, 1869–1925* (New York: Atheneum, 1963), 27.
2. Henry May, *The End of American Innocence: A Study of the First Years of Our Own Time* (New York: Alfred A. Knopf, 1959), 30–51.
3. See R. Laurence Moore, *Religious Outsiders and the Making of Americans* (New York: Oxford University Press, 1986); and Robert Wuthnow, *The Restructuring of American Religion: Society and Faith since World War II* (Princeton: Princeton University Press, 1988).
4. See George M. Marsden, *Fundamentalism and American Culture: The Shaping of Twentieth-Century Evangelicalism, 1870–1925* (New York: Oxford University Press, 1980); and William R. Glass, *Strangers in Zion: Fundamentalists in the South, 1900– 1950* (Macon, Ga.: Mercer University Press, 2001), for a discussion of the northern origins of fundamentalism.
5. See Peter S. Onuf, "Federalism, Republicanism, and the Origins of American Sectionalism," in *All Over the Map: Rethinking American Regions*, ed. Edward L. Ayers, Patricia Nelson Limerick, Stephen Nissenbaum, and Peter S. Onuf (Baltimore: Johns Hopkins University Press, 1996), 11–37.
6. For documentation of these efforts, see Edward L. Ayers, *The Promise of the New South: Life after Reconstruction* (New York: Oxford University Press, 1992); and Douglas Flamming, *Creating the New South: Millhands and Managers in Dalton, Georgia, 1884–1984* (Chapel Hill: University of North Carolina Press, 1992).
7. Robert Preston Brooks, "Georgia Goes Marching On," *Forum*, November 1926, 749–50.

BIBLIOGRAPHY

Primary Sources

Newspapers and Magazines

American Mercury

American Monthly Review of Reviews

Atlanta Constitution

Atlanta Journal

Atlantic Monthly

Arena

Bookman

Boston Globe

Century Magazine

Charities and the Commons

Chicago [Daily] Tribune

Collier's

Cosmopolitan

Critic

Current Literature

Current Opinion

Educational Review

Everybody's Magazine

Forum

Harper's [New] Monthly Magazine

Harper's Weekly

Independent

Ladies' Home Journal

Literary Digest

Los Angeles Times

McClure's Magazine

Minneapolis Journal

Minneapolis Morning Tribune

Munsey's Magazine

Nation

National Geographic Magazine

New England Magazine

New Republic

New York Times

North American Review

Outing

Outlook

Philadelphia Inquirer

Popular Science Monthly

Putnam's Magazine

San Francisco Chronicle

Saturday Evening Post

School and Society

School Review

Science

Scientific American

Scientific Monthly

Scribner's Magazine

Survey

Time

Washington Evening Star

Washington Post

World's Work

Scholarly Journals, Denominational Publications, and U.S. Government Publications

American Journal of Sociology	Methodist Advocate Journal
Baptist Argus	Methodist Protestant
Catholic World	Missionary Review of the World
Christian Advocate	Political Science Quarterly
Christian Century	Sewanee Review
Christian Index	South Atlantic Quarterly
Churchman	Southern Churchman
Commonweal	Sunday School Times
Good Work	U.S. Bureau of Education Bulletin

Books

Abbott, Lyman. *Reminiscences*. Boston: Houghton Mifflin, 1915.

Dixon, Thomas. *The Leopard's Spots: A Romance of the White Man's Burden, 1865–1900*. New York: A. Wessels, 1906.

Du Bois, W. E. B. *Selections from "The Crisis."* 2 vols. Ed. Herbert Aptheker. Writings in Periodicals Edited by W. E. B. Du Bois. Millwood, N.Y.: Kraus-Thomson Organization, 1983.

Durkheim, Emile. *On Morality and Society: Selected Essays*. Ed. Robert N. Bellah. Chicago: University of Chicago Press, 1973.

———. *The Elementary Forms of Religious Life*. Trans. Karen E. Fields. New York: Free Press, 1995.

Fox, John. *The Little Shepherd of Kingdom Come*. New York: C. Scribner's Sons, 1903.

Harris, Corra. *A Circuit Rider's Wife*. Philadelphia: Henry Altemus, 1910.

Hartt, Rollin Lynde. *The Man Himself: The Nazarene*. London: George G. Harrap, 1924.

Mencken, H. L. *Prejudices: Second Series*. New York: Alfred A. Knopf, 1920.

———. *The Gist of Mencken: Quotations from America's Critic*. Ed. Mayo DuBasky. Metuchen, N.J.: Scarecrow, 1990.

Strong, Josiah. *Our Country*. 1885. Cambridge: Belknap Press of Harvard University Press, 1963.

Secondary Sources

Akers, Monte. *Flames after Midnight: Murder, Vengeance, and the Desolation of a Texas Community*. Austin: University of Texas Press, 1999.

Aldridge, Marion D., and Kevin Lewis, eds. *The Changing Shape of Protestantism in the South*. Macon, Georgia: Mercer University Press, 1996.

Allen, Frederick Lewis. *Only Yesterday: An Informal History of the 1920s*. New York: Harper and Brothers, 1931.

Ammerman, Nancy T. "North American Protestant Fundamentalism." In *Fundamentalisms Observed*, ed. Martin E. Marty and R. Scott Appleby. Chicago: University of Chicago Press, 1991.

Anderson, James D. "Ex-Slaves and the Rise of Universal Education in the New South." In *Education and the Rise of the New South*, ed. Ronald K. Goodenow and Arthur O. White. Boston: G. K. Hall, 1981.

Applebome, Peter. *Dixie Rising: How the South Is Shaping American Values, Politics, and Culture*. New York: Times Books, 1998.

Ayers, Edward L. *Vengeance and Justice: Crime and Punishment in the 19th Century South*. New York: Oxford University Press, 1984.

———. *The Promise of the New South: Life after Reconstruction*. New York: Oxford University Press, 1992.

Ayers, Edward L., Patricia Limerick, Stephen Nissenbaum, and Peter S. Onuf, eds. *All Over the Map: Rethinking American Regions*. Baltimore: Johns Hopkins University Press, 1996.

Bailey, Kenneth. *Southern White Protestantism in the Twentieth Century*. New York: Harper and Row, 1964.

Batteau, Allen W. *The Invention of Appalachia*. Tucson: University of Arizona Press, 1990.

Billington, Ray Allen. *The Protestant Crusade*. New York: Macmillan, 1938.

Blee, Kathleen. *Women of the Klan: Racism and Gender in the 1920s*. Berkeley: University of California Press, 1991.

Blight, David W. *Race and Reunion: The Civil War in American Memory*. Cambridge: Belknap Press of Harvard University Press, 2001.

Blocker, Jack S., Jr. *Retreat from Reform: The Prohibition Movement in the United States*, Westport, Conn.: Greenwood, 1976.

Boles, John B. *The Great Revival, 1785–1805: The Origins of the Southern Evangelical Mind*. Lexington: University Press of Kentucky, 1972.

———. *The Irony of Southern Religion*. New York: P. Lang, 1994.

Brereton, Virginia. *Training God's Army: The American Bible School, 1880–1940*. Bloomington: Indiana University Press, 1990.

Brown, Ira V. *Lyman Abbott, Christian Evolutionist: A Study in Religious Liberalism*. 1953. Westport, Conn.: Greenwood Press, 1970.

Brundage W. Fitzhugh. *Lynching in the New South: Georgia and Virginia, 1880–1920*. Urbana: University of Illinois Press, 1993.

———, ed. *Where These Memories Grow: History, Memory, and Southern Identity*. Chapel Hill: University of North Carolina Press, 2000.

Calhoun, Robert. *Evangelicals and Conservatives in the Early South, 1740–1861*. Columbia: University of South Carolina Press, 1988.

Carpenter, Joel A. *Revive Us Again: The Reawakening of American Fundamentalism*. New York: Oxford University Press, 1997.

Cash, W. J. *The Mind of the South*. 1954. New York: Vintage, 1991.

Clark, Norman. *Deliver Us from Evil: An Interpretation of American Prohibition.* New York: W. W. Norton, 1976.

Coffing, Karen. "Corra Harris and the *Saturday Evening Post*: Southern Domesticity Conveyed to a National Audience." *Georgia Historical Quarterly* 79, no. 2 (Summer 1995): 367–93.

Conkin, Paul Keith. *When All the Gods Trembled: Darwinism, Scopes, and American Intellectuals.* Lanham, Md.: Rowman and Littlefield, 1998.

Cook, Raymond A. *Thomas Dixon.* New York: Twayne, 1974.

Cooper, John Milton, Jr. *Walter Hines Page: The Southerner as American, 1855–1918.* Chapel Hill: University of North Carolina Press, 1977.

Cremin, Lawrence A. *The Transformation of the School: Progressivism in American Education, 1876–1957.* New York: Alfred A. Knopf, 1969.

———. *American Education: The Metropolitan Experience, 1876–1980.* New York: Harper and Row, 1988.

Dabney, Virginius. *Dry Messiah: The Life of Bishop Cannon.* New York: Alfred A. Knopf, 1949.

Diner, Steven J. *A Very Different Age: Americans of the Progressive Era.* New York: Hill and Wang, 1998.

Douglas, Ann. *Terrible Honesty: Mongrel Manhattan in the 1920s.* New York: Farrar, Straus, and Giroux, 1995.

Drake, Richard B. *A History of Appalachia.* Lexington: University Press of Kentucky, 2001.

Dykeman, Wilma. *Prophet of Plenty: The First Ninety Years of W. D. Weatherford.* Knoxville: University of Tennessee Press, 1966.

Eagles, Charles W., ed. *"The Mind of the South": Fifty Years Later.* Jackson, Miss.: University Press of Mississippi, 1992.

Ellis, William E. *"A Man of Books and A Man of the People": E. Y. Mullins and the Crisis of Moderate Southern Baptist Leadership.* Macon, Ga.: Mercer University Press, 1985.

Finan, Christopher M. *Alfred E. Smith: The Happy Warrior.* New York: Hill and Wang, 2002.

Findlay, James F., Jr. *Dwight L. Moody: An American Evangelist, 1837–1899.* Chicago: University of Chicago Press, 1969.

Flamming, Douglas. *Creating the New South: Millhands and Managers in Dalton, Georgia, 1884–1984.* Chapel Hill: University of North Carolina Press, 1992.

Forcey, Charles. *The Crossroads of Liberalism: Croly, Weyl, Lippmann, and the Progressive Era, 1900–1925.* New York: Oxford University Press, 1967.

Freeman, Gregory A. *Lay This Body Down: The 1921 Murders of Eleven Plantation Slaves.* Chicago: Chicago Review Press, 1999.

Garber, Paul Neff. *John Carlisle Kilgo, President of Trinity College, 1894–1910.* Durham, N.C.: Duke University Press, 1937.

Gaston, Paul. *The New South Creed: A Study in Modern Mythmaking.* New York: Alfred A. Knopf, 1970.

Glass, William Robert. *Strangers in Zion: Fundamentalists in the South, 1900–1950*. Macon, Ga.: Mercer University Press, 2001.

Goldfield, David. *Still Fighting the Civil War: The American South and Southern History*. Baton Rouge: Louisiana State University Press, 2002.

Grantham, Dewey. *Southern Progressivism: The Reconciliation of Progress and Tradition*. Knoxville: University of Tennessee Press, 1983.

Hale, Grace Elizabeth. *Making Whiteness: The Culture of Segregation in the South, 1890–1940*. New York: Pantheon, 1998.

Handy, Robert T., ed. *The Social Gospel in America, 1870–1920*. New York: Oxford University Press, 1966.

Hankins, Barry. *"God's Rascal": J. Frank Norris and the Beginnings of Southern Fundamentalism*. Lexington: University Press of Kentucky, 1996.

Harp, Gillis J. *Positivist Republic: Auguste Comte and the Reconstruction of American Liberalism, 1865–1920*. University Park: Pennsylvania State University Press, 1995.

Harper, Keith. *The Quality of Mercy: Southern Baptists and Social Christianity, 1890*. Tuscaloosa: University of Alabama Press, 1996.

Hartell, David E., Jr., ed. *The Varieties of Southern Evangelicalism*. Macon, Ga.: Mercer University Press, 1981.

Harvey, Paul. *Redeeming the South: Religious Cultures and Racial Identities among Southern Baptists, 1865–1925*. Chapel Hill: University of North Carolina Press, 1997.

Hennesey, James, S.J. *American Catholics: A History of the Roman Catholic Community in the United States*. New York: Oxford University Press, 1981.

Heyrman, Christine. *Southern Cross: The Beginnings of the Bible Belt*. New York: Alfred A. Knopf, 1997.

Higham, John. *Strangers in the Land: Patterns of American Nativism, 1869–1925*. New York: Atheneum, 1963.

————. *Send These to Me: Immigrants in Urban America*. Baltimore: Johns Hopkins University Press, 1975.

Hill, Samuel S., Jr. *Southern Churches in Crisis*. New York: Holt, Rinehart, and Winston, 1966.

————, ed. *Religion and the Solid South*. Nashville: Abingdon Press, 1972.

————. *The South and the North in American Religion*. Athens: University of Georgia Press, 1980.

————. *One Name But Several Faces: Variety in the Popular Christian Denominations in Southern History*. Athens: University of Georgia Press, 1996.

————. "Fundamentalism in Recent Southern Culture: Has It Done What the Civil Rights Movement Couldn't Do?" *Journal of Southern Religion* 1 (1998): http://jsr.lib.virginia.edu/essay.htm.

Hobson, Fred C. *Serpent in Eden: H. L. Mencken and the South*. Chapel Hill: University of North Carolina Press, 1974.

————. *Tell about the South: The Southern Rage to Explain*. Baton Rouge: Louisiana State University Press, 1983.

Hofstadter, Richard. *The Age of Reform*. New York: Vintage, 1955.

Hohner, Robert A. *Prohibition and Politics: The Life of Bishop James Cannon, Jr.* Columbia: University of South Carolina Press, 1999.

Holifield, E. Brooks. *The Gentlemen Theologians: American Theology in Southern Culture, 1795–1860*. Durham, N.C.: Duke University Press, 1978.

Horwitz, Tony. *Confederates in the Attic: Dispatches from the Unfinished Civil War*. New York: Vintage, 1998.

Hutchison, William R. *The Modernist Impulse in American Protestantism*. Durham, N.C.: Duke University Press, 1992.

Israel, Charles A. *Before Scopes: Evangelicals, Education, and Evolution in Tennessee, 1870–1925*. Athens: University of Georgia Press, 2004.

John, Arthur. *The Best Years of the Century: Richard Watson Gilder, Scribner's Monthly, and the* Century *Magazine, 1870–1909*. Urbana: University of Illinois Press, 1981.

Karl, Barry D. *The Uneasy State: The United States from 1915 to 1945*. Chicago: University of Chicago Press, 1983.

Kerr, K. Austin. *Organized for Prohibition: A New History of the Anti-Saloon League*. New Haven: Yale University Press, 1985.

Kirby, Jack Temple. *Media-Made Dixie: The South in the American Imagination*. Rev. ed. Athens: University of Georgia Press, 1986.

Klotter, James C. "The Black South and White Appalachia." *Journal of American History* 66, no. 4 (1980): 832–49.

Kuklick, Bruce. *Churchmen and Philosophers: From Jonathan Edwards to John Dewey*. New Haven: Yale University Press, 1985.

Larson, Edward J. *Summer for the Gods: The Scopes Trial and America's Continuing Debate over Science and Religion*. New York: Basic, 1997.

Leach, William. *Land of Desire: Merchants, Power, and the Rise of a New American Culture*. New York: Vintage, 1993.

Lears, T. J. Jackson. *No Place of Grace: Antimodernism and the Transformation of American Culture, 1880–1920*. Chicago: University of Chicago Press, 1981.

Leonard, Bill J., ed. *Christianity in Appalachia: Profiles in Regional Pluralism*. Knoxville: University of Tennessee Press, 1999.

Levine, Lawrence. *Defender of the Faith: William Jennings Bryan; the Last Decade, 1915–1925*. New York: Oxford University Press, 1965.

———. *Highbrow/Lowbrow: The Emergence of Cultural Hierarchy in America*. Cambridge: Harvard University Press, 1988.

Levy, David W. *Herbert Croly of "The New Republic": The Life and Thought of an American Progressive*. Princeton: Princeton University Press, 1985.

Lichtman, Allan J. *Prejudice and the Old Politics: The Presidential Election of 1928*. Chapel Hill: University of North Carolina Press, 1979.

Link, William A. *The Paradox of Southern Progressivism, 1880–1930*. Chapel Hill: University of North Carolina Press, 1992.

Luker, Ralph E. *The Social Gospel in Black and White: American Racial Reform, 1885–1912.* Chapel Hill: University of North Carolina Press, 1991.

MacLean, Nancy. *Behind the Mask of Chivalry: The Making of the Second Ku Klux Klan.* New York: Oxford University Press, 1994.

Marsden, George M. *Fundamentalism and American Culture: The Shaping of Twentieth-Century Evangelicalism, 1870–1925.* New York: Oxford University Press, 1980.

————. *Understanding Fundamentalism and Evangelicalism.* Grand Rapids, Mich.: William B. Eerdmans, 1991.

Martin, C. Brenden. "To Keep the Spirit of Mountain Culture Alive." In *Where These Memories Grow: History, Memory, and Southern Identity,* ed. W. Fitzhugh Brundage. Chapel Hill: University of North Carolina Press, 2000.

Marty, Martin E., and R. Scott Appleby, eds. *Fundamentalisms Observed.* Chicago: University of Chicago Press, 1991.

Mathews, Donald G. *Religion in the Old South.* Chicago: University of Chicago Press, 1977.

Matthews, Fred H. *Quest for an American Sociology: Robert E. Parks and the Chicago School.* Montreal: McGill-Queen's University Press, 1977.

May, Henry F. *The End of American Innocence: A Study of the First Years of Our Own Time.* New York: Alfred A. Knopf, 1959.

McCauley, Deborah V. *Appalachian Mountain Religion: A History.* Urbana: University of Illinois Press, 1995.

McDowell, John Patrick. *The Social Gospel in the South: The Woman's Home Mission Movement in the Methodist Episcopal Church, South, 1886–1939.* Baton Rouge: Louisiana State University Press, 1982.

McLoughlin, William G. *Modern Revivalism: Charles Grandison Finney to Billy Graham.* New York: Ronald Press Co., 1959.

McMillen, Sally G. *To Raise Up the South: Sunday Schools in Black and White Churches, 1865–1915.* Baton Rouge: Louisiana State University Press, 2001.

Mead, Frank S., and Samuel S. Hill. *Handbook of Denominations in the United States.* 8th ed. Nashville: Abingdon, 1985.

Meyer, D. H. "American Intellectuals and the Victorian Crisis of Faith." In *Victorian America,* ed. Daniel Walker Howe. Philadelphia: University of Pennsylvania Press, 1976.

Miller, Robert Moats. *Harry Emerson Fosdick: Preacher, Pastor, Prophet.* New York: Oxford University Press, 1985.

Minnix, Kathleen. *Laughter in the Amen Corner: The Life of Evangelist Sam Jones.* Athens: University of Georgia Press, 1993.

Moore, Edmund A. *A Catholic Runs for President: The Campaign of 1928.* New York: Ronald, 1956.

Moore, Howard Edgar. "The Emergence of Moderate Fundamentalism: John R. Rice and 'The Sword of the Lord.'" Ph.D. diss., George Washington University, 1990.

Moore, R. Laurence. *Religious Outsiders and the Making of Americans.* New York: Oxford University Press, 1986.

Moran, Jeffrey P. "Reading Race into the Scopes Trial: African American Elites, Science, and Fundamentalism." *Journal of American History* 90, no. 3 (December 2003): 891–911.

Mott, Frank Luther. *A History of American Magazines.* Vol. 3, *1850–1865.* Cambridge: Harvard University Press, 1938.

———. *A History of American Magazines.* Vol. 4, *1885–1905.* Cambridge: Belknap Press of Harvard University Press, 1957.

———. *American Journalism: A History, 1690–1960.* 3rd ed. New York: Macmillan, 1962.

———. *A History of American Magazines.* Vol. 5, *Sketches of 21 Magazines, 1905–1930.* Cambridge: Belknap Press of Harvard University Press, 1968.

Murphy, Cullen. "Protestantism and the Evangelicals." *Wilson Quarterly* 5, no. 4 (1981): 105–19.

Naipaul, V. S. *A Turn in the South.* New York: Vintage, 1989.

Nardini, Robert Francis. "H. L. Mencken and the 'Cult of Smartness.'" M.A. thesis, University of Virginia, 1981.

Niebuhr, H. Richard. *Christ and Culture.* 1951. Expanded ed., New York: Harper Collins, 2001.

Nord, David Paul. "Reading the Newspaper: Strategies and Politics of Reader Response, Chicago, 1912–1917," *Journal of Communication* 45, no. 3 (1995): 67–88.

Numbers, Ronald L. *The Creationists.* New York: Alfred A. Knopf, 1992.

O'Connor, Flannery. *Mystery and Manners: Occasional Prose.* Ed. Sally Fitzgerald and Robert Fitzgerald. New York: Farrar, Strauss, and Giroux, 1969.

O'Neill, William. *Divorce in the Progressive Era.* New Haven: Yale University Press, 1967.

Oney, Steve. *And the Dead Shall Rise: The Murder of Mary Phagan and the Lynching of Leo Frank.* New York: Pantheon, 2003.

Ownby, Ted. *Subduing Satan: Religion, Recreation, and Manhood in the Rural South,* Chapel Hill: University of North Carolina Press, 1990.

Painter, Nell Irvin. *Standing at Armageddon: The United States, 1877–1919.* New York: W. W. Norton, 1987.

Pals, Daniel L. *Seven Theories of Religion.* New York: Oxford University Press, 1996.

Pegram, Thomas R. *Battling Demon Rum: The Struggle for a Dry America, 1800–1933.* Chicago: Ivan R. Dee, 1998.

Peterson, Theodore. *Magazines in the Twentieth Century.* Urbana: University of Illinois Press, 1956.

Pope, Liston. *Millhands and Preachers.* New Haven: Yale University Press, 1993.

Ross, Dorothy. *The Origins of American Social Science.* Cambridge: Cambridge University Press, 1991.

Rusnak, Robert J. *Walter Hines Page and "The World's Work," 1900–1913.* Washington, D.C.: University Press of America, 1982.

Russell, C. Allyn. *Voices of American Fundamentalism: Seven Biographical Studies.* Philadelphia: Westminster, 1976.

Sandeen, Ernest. *The Roots of Fundamentalism: British and American Millenarianism*. Chicago: University of Chicago Press, 1970.

Schneirov, Matthew. *The Dream of a New Social Order: Popular Magazines in America*. New York: Columbia University Press, 1994.

Schweiger, Beth Barton. *The Gospel Working Up: Progress and the Pulpit in Nineteenth-Century Virginia*. New York: Oxford University Press, 2000.

Sears, Richard. *A Utopian Experiment in Kentucky: Integration and Social Equality at Berea, 1866–1904*. Westport, Conn.: Greenwood, 1996.

Shapiro, Henry D. *Appalachia on Our Mind: The Southern Mountains and Mountaineers in the American Consciousness, 1870–1920*. Chapel Hill: University of North Carolina Press, 1978.

Silber, Nina. *The Romance of Reunion: Northerners and the South, 1865–1900*. Chapel Hill: University of North Carolina Press, 1993.

Silva, Ruth Caridad. *Rum, Religion, and Votes: 1928 Re-examined*. University Park: Pennsylvania State University Press, 1962.

Silverman, Joan L. "*The Birth of a Nation*: Prohibition Propaganda." In *The South and Film*, ed. Warren French. Jackson: University Press of Mississippi, 1981.

Singal, Daniel Joseph. *The War Within: From Victorian to Modernist Thought in the South, 1919–1945*. Chapel Hill: University of North Carolina Press, 1982.

Slayton, Robert A. *Empire Statesman: The Rise and Redemption of Al Smith*. New York: Free Press, 2001.

Spring, Joel. *The American School: 1642–1996*. 4th ed. New York: MacGraw-Hill, 1997.

Stowell, Daniel W. *Rebuilding Zion: The Religious Reconstruction of the South, 1863–1877*. New York: Oxford University Press, 1998.

Susman, Warren. *Culture as History: The Transformation of American Society in the Twentieth Century*. New York: Pantheon, 1984.

Sutton, Matthew A. "'Between the Refrigerator and the Wildfire': Aimee Semple McPherson, Pentecostalism, and the Fundamentalist-Modernist Controversy." *Church History* 72, no. 1 (March 2003): 159–88.

Szasz, Ferenc Morton. *The Divided Mind of Protestant America, 1880–1930*. Tuscaloosa: University of Alabama Press, 1982.

Thompson, James J., Jr. *Tried as by Fire: Southern Baptists and the Religious Controversies of the 1920s*. Macon, Ga.: Mercer University Press, 1982.

Tindall, George B. "The Benighted South: Origins of a Modern Image," *Virginia Quarterly Review* 40 (Spring 1964): 281–94.

———. *The Emergence of the New South, 1913–1945*. Baton Rouge: Louisiana State University Press, 1967.

Titus, Warren I. *John Fox, Jr*. New York: Twayne, 1971.

Tolnay, Stewart E., and E. M. Beck. *A Festival of Violence: An Analysis of Southern Lynchings, 1882–1930*. Urbana: University of Illinois Press, 1995.

Trachtenberg, Alan. *The Incorporation of America: Culture and Society in the Gilded Age*. New York: Hill and Wang, 1982.

Trollinger, William Vance. *God's Empire: William Bell Riley and Midwestern Fundamentalism*. Madison: University of Wisconsin Press, 1990.

Tullock, Samuel K. "The Transformation of American Fundamentalism: The Life and Career of John Franklyn Norris." Ph.D. diss., University of Texas at Dallas, 1997.

Turley, Briane K. *A Wheel within a Wheel: Southern Methodism and the Georgia Holiness Association*. Macon, Ga.: Mercer University Press, 1999.

Turner, James. *Without God, Without Creed: The Origins of Unbelief in America*. Baltimore: Johns Hopkins University Press, 1985.

Wade, Wyn Craig. *The Fiery Cross: The Ku Klux Klan in America*. New York: Simon and Schuster, 1987.

Waller, Altina L. "Feuding in Appalachia: Evolution of a Cultural Stereotype." In *Appalachia in the Making: The Mountain South in the Nineteenth Century*, ed. Mary Beth Pudup, Dwight Billings, and Altina L. Waller. Chapel Hill: University of North Carolina Press, 1995.

Weaver, Richard M. *The Southern Tradition at Bay: A History of Postbellum Thought*. Ed. George Core and M. E. Bradford. New Rochelle, N.Y.: Arlington House, 1968.

Weber, Timothy P. *Living in the Shadow of the Second Coming: American Premillennialism, 1875–1925*. New York: Oxford University Press, 1979.

Wetherington, Mark V. *The New South Comes to Wiregrass Georgia, 1860–1910*. Knoxville: University of Tennessee Press, 1994.

Whisnant, David E. *All That Is Native and Fine: The Politics of Culture in an American Region*. Chapel Hill: University of North Carolina Press, 1983.

Williams, Michael. *The Shadow of the Pope*. New York: McGraw-Hill, 1932.

Williamson, Joel. *The Crucible of Race: Black-White Relations in the American South since Emancipation*. New York: Oxford University Press, 1984.

Wilson, Charles Reagan. *Baptized in Blood: The Religion of the Lost Cause, 1865–1920*. Athens: University of Georgia Press, 1980.

———, ed. *Religion in the South*. Jackson: University Press of Mississippi, 1985.

———. *Judgment and Grace in Dixie: Southern Faiths from Faulkner to Elvis*. Athens: University of Georgia Press, 1995.

Woodward, C. Vann. *Origins of the New South, 1877–1913*. Baton Rouge: Louisiana State University Press, 1951.

Wolfe, Charles K. *A Good-Natured Riot: The Birth of the Grand Ole Opry*. Nashville: Country Music Foundation Press and Vanderbilt University Press, 1999.

Wuthnow, Robert. *The Restructuring of American Religion: Society and Faith since World War II*. Princeton: Princeton University Press, 1988.

Wyatt-Brown, Bertram. *Honor and Violence in the Old South*. New York: Oxford University Press, 1986.

INDEX

Abbott, Ernest Hamlin, 53–54, 77, 85–86

Abbott, Lyman, 7, 16, 26, 37, 38, 39, 44, 51, 60, 67, 77

African Americans, xv, xx, xxii, 89, 106; ignored by the press, xv, 11–12, 24–25, 50; speak out against the South, 5, 9, 10, 23, 79–80; as victims of southern violence, 2–8, 79–80

Alabama: delegation to the 1928 Democratic National Convention, 106, education and, 28; educational statistics of, 26, 27; Sam Jones and, 55; Ku Klux Klan in, 105; opposition to lynching in, 12–13; prohibition in, xxiv, 60, 61; religion in, 96; Sabbath observance in, 53; Al Smith and, 103, 109; violence in, 11, 79

Alderman, Edwin A., 41

American: Anglo-Saxons as, 33–34; definition of, 16, 114; and immigration, 114; southern exclusion from definition of, 16, 112, 114, 116

American Journal of Sociology, 18, 31, 40

American Mercury: circulation figures for, 119; on fundamentalism, 96; on J. Frank Norris, 101; on southern clergy, 95; on southern religion, 96; on southern Sabbath observance, 53; on John Roach Straton, 98

American Monthly Review of Reviews: on James Cannon, 107; on Al Smith, 108

Anglo-Saxons, 43; Appalachian residents as "pure," 33–34, 113

antievolution movement, 68, 72, 84–85, 89, 97, 111; and fundamentalism, 69, 75, 92, 95, 115; as medieval, 84–85; as uneducated, xv, 75–76, 87–88

Anti-Saloon League, 36, 103, 106

Appalachia, xxiii, 2, 25–27, 37, 40, 42, 48, 49, 51, 88, 113; accounts of, 29–35; intermarriage in, 34; residents as "pure" Anglo-Saxons, xxiii, 33–34, 113; as scene of lawlessness, 8–9

Arena: on lynching in the South, 3, 17; on southern education, 28

Arkansas: antievolution efforts in 95; education in 44; religion in, 40; Sabbath observance in, 53; Al Smith and, 103; violence in, 81–82

Atlanta Constitution: on Sam Jones, 55, 58; on J. Frank Norris, 101; on southern prohibition efforts, 60; on southern Sabbath observance, 52; on southern violence, 4

Atlanta Journal: on southern mob violence, 10

Atlanta Race Riots, 7–8, 16, 18–19, 61, 62

Atlantic Monthly: on Appalachia, 32; circulation figures for, 120; on fundamentalism, 71, 74, 93; on Ku Klux Klan in the South, 79, 80; on southern clergy, 13, 40, 51, 80; on southern prohibition efforts, 60, 61, 62; on southern religion, 39, 40, 61; on southern violence, 8, 13, 19, 28, 62

Baptist Argus, 62

Baptists: as a dominant force in the South, 12, 40, 50, 95, 111; and fundamentalists, 94; lack of educated clergy, 52; opposition to Al Smith in the South, 109

Berry, Martha, 30

Jasper, John, 75
Johnson, Gerald W., 51, 97
Jones, Bob, 108
Jones, Sam, 37, 48–49, 55–59, 99; tributes
to, 58–59

Kentucky: in John Fox's fiction, 34–35;
religion in, 40, 80; residents of as "pure"
Anglo-Saxons, 33; William Bell Riley's
roots in, 98; Al Smith and, 103; violence in, 8, 11, 17, 31
Kilgo, John Carlisle, 13–14, 38, 53, 55
Knight, Edgar W., 25, 36, 102
Krutch, Joseph Wood, 87
Ku Klux Klan, xi, xv, 10, 68, 83, 105, 110;
domination of the South, 88; opposition
to Al Smith, 103–4, 105; re-emergence
of, 78–81; southern clergy's involvement
in, 80–81; tied to fundamentalism,
80–81, 88, 93, 94–95, 96; ties to J. Frank
Norris, 101

Ladies Home Journal: on Appalachian
residents as "pure" Anglo-Saxons, 34;
on the Ku Klux Klan in the South, 79
Lake, Kirsopp, 93
The Leopard's Spots. See Dixon, Thomas
Literary Digest: on Appalachia, 31, 32, 37;
circulation figures for, 119; on fundamentalism, 72–73; 94, 95; on lynching,
14, 20; on Al Smith, 107, 108, 109; on
southern antievolution efforts, 95; on
southern clergy, 37, 107, 108; on southern education, 31; on southern religion,
50, 51, 95; and southern roots of fundamentalist leaders, 98; on southern
Sabbath observation, 53
The Little Shepherd of Kingdom Come. See
Fox, John
Los Angeles Times: on the Democratic
Convention of 1928, 106; on J. Frank
Norris, 100, on Tennessee, 87

Louisiana: education and, 28; educational
statistics of, 26; Ku Klux Klan and, 80;
Al Smith and, 103; temperance efforts
in, 60; violence in, 83
lynching: descriptions of, 2–6; 81, 105; of
Henry Lowry, 81–82; of Henry Smith,
3–4; of Jesse Washington, 20; of Leo
Frank, 1, 10, 20; participants in, 19–20;
of Sam Hose, 4–5

MacClintock, S. S., 31, 40
Masters, Edgar Lee, 64
Mathews, Shailer, 75
May, Henry, 114
Mayo, A. D., 28, 36
McClure's Magazine, 11; circulation figures
for, 119
McKelway, Alexander J., 60
Mencken, H. L., xiii, 10, 64, 67–68, 87,
110
Methodist Protestant, 14, 59, 61, 91; circula-
tion figures for, 121
Merritt, Dixon, 105, 107
Methodists: as a dominant force in the
South, 12, 50, 64, 111; need for
Southern to become more modern, 39
Mims, Edwin, 97
Minneapolis Journal, 100
Minneapolis Tribune, 7, 100
Missionary Review of the World: circulation
figures for, 119; religion in Appalachia,
37, 40, 51
Mississippi: antievolution efforts in 95;
delegation from Democratic Conven-
tion of 1928, 106; educational statistics
of, 26, 27; Ku Klux Klan power in, 105;
prohibition in, 61; Sabbath observance
in, 53; Al Smith and 103, 104–5; sup-
port for lynching in, 9; violence in,
5–6, 19
Mitchell, S.C., 36
Montgomery (Alabama) Advertiser, xi, 111
Munsey's Magazine, 34

Page, Thomas Nelson, 53
Page, Walter Hines, 11, 25–26, 39–40, 43, 50
Peonage, 81–83
Philadelphia Inquirer: on fundamentalism, 69–70; on Southern Baptists, 52; on southern violence, 8, 10, 16
Popular Science Monthly, 60
Presbyterians, 12, 40, 55, 68, 70
Prohibition, 103, 106–7; lack of effective enforcement in the South, 63–64; negative views of the South's role in enacting, 62–64. *See also* Temperance
Putnam's, 60, 63

Religion, southern, 65, 114; as conservative, 41–42, 50–51, 53, 96–97; definition of, 50; as "fundamentalist," 80, 83, 89, 92; as homogeneous, xxi, 50, 104, 114; as too focused on the "other world," 45, 48, 53
Review of Reviews. See American Monthly Review of Reviews
Riley, William Bell, 98, 100
Ross, Edward A. 33, 51

Sabbath observance, 52–53
San Francisco Chronicle: on southern religion, 13; on southern violence, 4, 6, 7–8, 13
Saturday Evening Post, xvi, 42
School Review, 63; circulation figures for, 120
School and Society: circulation figures for, 120; on southern education, 27, 36
Science, 85; circulation figures for, 120
Scientific Monthly, 76, 88; circulation figures for, 120
scientific racism, 33, 41, 43
Scopes Trial, 83–88, 92
Scribner's Magazine, 53, 77; circulation figures for, 120
separation of church and state, 12, 85–86

Sewanee Review, 14, 28, 44, 97; circulation figures for, 121
Sledd, Andrew, 19, 28
Smith, Al, 92, 102–3; Catholicism as a political liability in the South, 103–5, 108–10; and Democratic Convention of 1928, 105–6; Ku Klux Klan's opposition to, 103–4, 105. *See also* Cannon, James
Smith, John 54
Social Gospel, xix, 13, 39, 48
South, the: as anti-Catholic, 107–11; biblical interpretation in, 47–48, 53–54; as fundamentalist, 83–84, 88–89, 92 95–97, 102, 110, 115; as "ignorant," 1, 25; as "lawless," 6–9; as "medieval," 17–18, 84–86; as new ground for fundamentalism, 95–96; as "Puritan," 41; as religious, 11–12, 49–50; as religiously intolerant, 109 111; southerners' attacks on, 4–5, 18, 27–28, 40–41, 51; southerners' defense of, 41, 44, 49, 54–55, 111; as supportive of temperance and prohibition, 60–64; as a theocracy, 85–86; as "uncivilized," 15–19, 44, 86–88; as "violent," xv, 1–2, 88, 92, 96, 105–6, 113, 114, 115
South Atlantic Quarterly: on Appalachian residents, 30–31, 33; circulation figures for, 121; on southern clergy, 38, 54; on southern education, 14, 36, 38; on southern prohibition efforts, 62; on southern religion, 40–41, 53
South Carolina: divorce legislation in, 52; education and, 43; educational statistics of, 26; Ku Klux Klan and, 79; religion in, 50–51; Sabbath observance in, 53; Al Smith and, 103; temperance efforts in, 60, 62–63; violence in, 79
Southern Churchman, 4–5, 19, 86–87; circulation figures for, 121
Straton, John Roach, 70, 73, 93, 98, 117
Survey, 14–15, 71; circulation figures for, 120

Rethinking Zion was designed and typeset on a Macintosh computer system using QuarkXPress software. The body text is set in 10/13.5 Goudy and display type is set in Futura Book and Bold. This book was designed and typeset by Barbara Karwhite and manufactured by Thomson-Shore, Inc.